Rock Your Code: Coding Standards for Microsoft .NET

Copyright © 2005 - 2021 by David McCarter

All rights reserved. This book or any part thereof may not be reproduced or used in any manner whatsoever without the *express* written permission of the publisher except for the use of brief quotations in a book review or scholarly journal.

Rock Your Code™ is trademarked by David McCarter

All other trademarks are the property of their respective owners.

Seventh Edition: January 2021

ISBN: 9798589711707

Contents

INTRODUCTION ... 1
Overview ... 1
About the Author ... 2
Contact Information ... 3
Thanks for the Help! ... 3
Rock Your Code: Live ... 3
Rock Your Code: Videos On-Demand ... 4
Acknowledgments ... 5
Special Offer ... 5
CodeRush from DevExpress ... 5
Companion Books ... 6
Rock Your Code: Code Performance for Microsoft.NET ... 6
How to Use This Book ... 7

PROJECT SETUP ... 9
Application Information ... 9
Application Information ... 9
.NET Package Information ... 10
Build Settings ... 11
Signing Settings ... 12
Analyzing Code for Issues ... 13
Visual Studio Analyze ... 13
Step 1: Analyze Setup ... 14
Step 2: Install EditorConfig Language Service Extension ... 14
Step 3: Create .editorConfig File ... 15
Step 4: Running Code Analysis ... 15
Running During Build ... 15
Running Using Analyze ... 16
.editorConfig File ... 16
Pain Is Good ... 17
Build Process ... 17
Release Build ... 17
Build Events ... 17
Source File Naming ... 18
Folder Structure ... 18

ASSEMBLY LAYOUT ... 21
General Tips to Get You Started ... 21
.NET Framework Assemblies ... 21
Element Order ... 21
Namespaces ... 23

NAMING STANDARDS ... 25
General Guidelines ... 25
Capitalization ... 25
Case Sensitivity ... 26
Classes ... 26
Generic Classes ... 26
Inheriting Classes ... 27
Abstract Classes ... 28
Partial Classes ... 28
Static Classes ... 29
Structures ... 29
Interfaces ... 30

Contents

    Checking Type for an Interface *31*
    Interfaces with Implementation *31*
  Constants 32
  Access Modifiers 32
  Private Variables 32
    Read-Only Fields *33*
    Public Instance Fields *34*
    Declaration Keyword Order *34*
    Underscores *34*
  Nullable Value Type Variables 35
  Constructors 35
    Finalizers (Destructors) *36*
    Events *37*
  Enumerations 38
  Properties 39
  Methods 41
    Method Overloading *42*
    Named Parameters *43*
    Methods with Variable Numbers of Arguments *43*
  Resources 44

CODING STYLE **45**

  Element Name Case 45
  Variables 45
    Constants *46*
    Local Variables *46*
  Accessing Class Members 46
  Objects 47
    Creating Objects Safely *48*
    Checking an Object for an Interface *49*
    Casting *49*
  Strings 49
    Using StringBuilder to Reduce Memory *49*
    Comparing Strings *52*
      string.Compare() 53
      Performance 54
  Arrays 55
    Using Array.ForEach() *55*
  Parenthesis Placement 55
  Bracket Placement 56
  Parameters 57
    Passing Parameter Values *58*
      Passing Parameters 59
      Parameter Arrays 59
  Blank Lines 59
  Indentation 60
  Control Flow 60
  Tuples 61
  LINQ 62
    Formatting *63*
    Formatting Lambda Expressions *63*
  Object Initializers 64
  Exceptions 64
    Trapping Exceptions *66*
    Exceptions in Reusable Assemblies *66*

Contents

    Exceptions in Applications 69
    Throwing Exceptions 69
    Documenting Exceptions Thrown in a Method or Property 71
    Custom Exceptions 72
    Logging Exceptions 72
  XML COMMENTING 74
    Section Tags 75
    Inline Tags 77
    Markup Tags 77
  HUNGARIAN NAMING 78

CLASS DESIGN **79**

  OBJECT-ORIENTED PROGRAMMING 79
    Encapsulation – The First Pillar of OOP 80
    Poor Class Design 81
    Data Hiding 82
    Validating the Data 82
    Encapsulating Business Logic in Class Properties 84
        Implementing New Business Rules 84
            Encapsulating Properties 85
            Fixing the EventDate Property 85
            Fixing the BillingStartDate Property 87
  CONSTRUCTORS 88
  IMPLEMENT ICOMPARABLE & ICOMPARABLE<T> INTERFACES 89
    Performance Increase 90
  OVERLOADING GETHASHCODE() 91
  MAKING CLASSES EASIER TO DEBUG 91
  OVERRIDE TOSTRING() 92
  SERIALIZATION 93
    Serializing to JSON 93
        Fixing JSON Formatting 94
    Serializing to XML 95
        Houston, We Have A Problem 97
    Summary 99
  ABSTRACT CLASSES 99
  RECORD CLASSES 102
  ENCAPSULATING LOGIC 103
  DO YOUR PROJECTS PROPERLY IMPLEMENT OOP? 105

DEFENSIVE PROGRAMMING **107**

    The Cost of Fixing Bugs 108
  INTRODUCTION 110
  STOP EXCEPTIONS BEFORE THEY HAPPEN 111
    Rule #1 – Code that Can Cause Exceptions 111
        Performance 112
    Rule #2 - Parameters 112
        Parameter Validation Rules 113
    Rule #3 - Enumerations 114
    Rule #4 – Casting Types 114
    Rule #5 – Let Type Checking Work for You 114
    Rule #6 – Check Resources 117
    Rule #7 – Users 118
    Rule #7.1 – Validate User Input 118
    Make Validation Easier 119
  DEALING WITH EXCEPTIONS 120

Contents

  Rule #1 – The Application Layer 120
  Rule #2 – Trap Exceptions Globally 120
  Rule #3 – The DLL Layer 121
 LOGGING EXCEPTIONS 122
  The More Information the Better 123
  How to Catch All Exceptions 125
  Logging in .NET 5 125
 MORE INFORMATION ON DEFENSIVE PROGRAMMING 126

APPLICATION DESIGN 127

 N-TIER ARCHITECTURE 128
  Data Layer 129
  Business Layer 130
   Business Entities 130
   Business Components 131
   Business Workflow 131
  Communications Layer 131
  User Experience (UX) 132
   Presentation Layer 133
   Client-Side Caching 134
  Identity 136
 N-TIER ARCHITECTURE & CODE REUSE 136
  Do Not Listen to Your Boss! 137
  Practice What You Preach Dave! 138
  Windows App Example 138
  Cloud App Example 139
  The Benefits of Reuse 141
   Unit Testable 141
   Easier to Maintain 141
   Easier to Share 142
   Easier to Update 142

WORD CHOICE 143

 Keywords 143
  Contextual Keywords 144

CAPITALIZATION SUMMARY 145

SOURCE CONTROL 147

 COMMITTING CODE TO SOURCE CONTROL WORKFLOW 147
  #1 - Document Classes and Methods 147
  #2 - Run StyleCop 147
  #3 - Run Analyze in Visual Studio 147
  #4 - Run Unit Tests 148
  #5 - Commit Code 148
 RULES FOR COMMITTING CODE 148
  #1 Code in Source Control Is Golden 149
  #2 Do Not Commit Binaries That Can Be Built 149
  #3 Do Not Commit User, Temp, or Other Files Not Used for the Build 150
  #4 Backup, Backup and Backup Some More 150
  #5 After You Commit Major Code Changes 151

DATABASE NAMING STANDARD 153

 STORED PROCEDURE NAMING STANDARD 153
  Predominant Actions: 153
  Project, Application, or Logical Segment 154

Contents

DEVELOPMENT WITH VISUAL STUDIO ... 155
Fixing NuGet Hell Issues ... 155
PowerShell Script ... 155

CODE QUALITY IS A FEATURE, NOT AN AFTERTHOUGHT ... 157
Management Does Not Care, So You Have To ... 158
Learning Code Quality ... 158
Books ... 159
Community Events ... 159
Online Training ... 159
Websites ... 160
Tools Help Find Issues & Help You Learn ... 160

WHAT CAN BE DONE TO MAKE CODE QUALITY BETTER? ... 161
1. Unit Test Integration ... 161
2. Training & Team Meetings ... 162
3. Code Review ... 162
4. Code Analytics ... 163
5. Develop a Culture of Quality ... 163
6. Caring About Our Craft ... 163
7. Keep Learning & Evolving ... 164
8. No One Is Perfect ... 164
9. Teach Students Standards & Architecture ... 165
10. Coding Standards = Secure, Robust & Maintainable Code ... 166

DEFINITIONS ... 167
Capitalization Styles Defined ... 167
Pascal case ... 167
Camel case ... 167
Uppercase ... 167
Hungarian Type Notation Defined ... 167

APPENDIX A - CODING STANDARDS SURVEY ... 169
#1: How Many Developers Are in Your Team? ... 169
#2: Does Your Team Use Documented Coding Standards? ... 169
#3: How Are Coding Standards Administered? ... 170
#4: What Does Your Team Use as Coding Standards Documentation? ... 171
#5: Where Did You Learn Coding Standards? ... 171
#6: Does Your Team Practice Object-Oriented Programming ... 172
#7: Does Your Company Provide Any Applications to Make It Easier to Abide by The Coding Standards? ... 173
#8: If You Took Over Someone's Code, How Painful Was That Experience? ... 173
#9: Do You Believe Coding Standards Are Important to Produce Stable Code? ... 174
Other Comments ... 175

APPENDIX B - DOTNETTIPS.UTILITY ... 177
Spargine ... 177
Download Source ... 177
NuGet ... 177
Bulletproof Disposable Types ... 178
Making Dispose Easier ... 179
Disposing Local Variables ... 179
Disposing Fields ... 179
Disposing Collections ... 180
Making Sure There Are Not Any Virtual Memory Leaks ... 180

Contents

Calculating Total Size of Files in a Directory 180
Checking that the User is an Administrator 180
Checking to See if the Current Process is Already Running 181
Checking to See if a Process is Running 181
Copying a File Asynchronously 181
Custom App Settings for .NET 182
    Introducing Config.cs 183
    Usage 185
DateTime & DateTimeOffset Extensions 186
    Looking for The Previous Day of the Week 186
    Looking for The Next Day of the Week 186
    Looking for a Date that Intersects a Date Range 186
    Looking for a Date in a Date Range 187
    Converting a Date using Time Zone Offset 187
    Looking for the Max Date 187
    Looking the Day After a Weekday 187
    Creating a Friendly Date String 188
Downloading File from Web Asynchronously 188
Ensuring a Host is Available 188
String Extensions 189
Retrieving Application Executing Folder 189
Retrieving Application Information 189
Retrieving & Changing Culture 190
Retrieving Computer Information 190
Retrieving Environment Variables 191
Retrieving the .NET Framework Description 192
Using Common Control Characters 192
Temporary File Manager 193
    Creating a Temporary File 193
    Creating Multiple Temporary Files 193
    Other Useful Methods 194
Deleting Files with Events 194
    Processor Class 194
Progressive Retry for Network Calls 196
IAsyncEnumerable Interface in .NET 197
    Performance 199
Making Encapsulation Easy 199
    Introducing the dotNetTips.Utility.OOP Namespace 200
String Builder Extensions 201
    Appending Bytes 201
    Appending Values 202
    Appending Values using an Action 202
Testing Assembly 202
    Person Types 203
    Coordinate Types 204
    Random Data Methods 204
    Usage Examples 207

APPENDIX C - DOTNETTIPS.COM APPS 209

dotNetTips.Utility Dev App 209
    Clean Visual Studio & SQL Server Temp and Cached Files 209
    Features 210
    Quickly Backup Source Code 210

APPENDIX D - THIRD PARTY PRODUCTS 211

Contents

GHOSTDOC 211
    Key Features *211*
CODERUSH 212
    Code Refactoring *213*
    Other Features *214*
    .NET Memory Profiler *214*
        Allocate the Time for Analysis 216
    My Favorite Visual Studio Extensions *216*

APPENDIX E - THE COMPLETE PERSON TYPE **219**

APPENDIX F – PROGRAMMING ACRONYMS & TERMS **233**

INDEX **321**

Introduction

This book is a compilation of the common Microsoft .NET coding standards in use today. In the past, for languages like Visual Basic, Microsoft published coding standards in a single document that developers could follow or use as a basis to build their standards. Microsoft has not provided this with .NET. They have provided some standards on their document web site, but you would have to dig through many web pages, and there is little or no examples provided.

Therefore, the purpose of this book is to consolidate the standards on the site, enhance them with additional standards (listed in the Acknowledgements section) and take guidance from Microsoft code checking programs like Visual Studio Analyze and StyleCop.

This book covers an evolving set of standards. As new versions of .NET are released, and better ways of coding are developed, this book will be updated. So be sure to check back for updates on Amazon.com.

If you have any comments or suggestions for this book, please contact David McCarter via email at dotnetdave@live.com.

Overview

I do not know how many times I have stood in front of attendees at user groups or conferences and stressed how important it is for programmers and their team to follow common .NET coding standards… any standard! This book is designed to get your team jump-started in creating and following common coding standards for Microsoft .NET.

I also realize that coding standards are a very personal thing, almost religious, usually stemming from the individual programmer's background. You might not agree with everything that is in the book… that is okay. If this book gets you thinking and helps you devise and implement a standard for your company, then this book has succeeded. Once the standard is created, welcome it with open arms. You might have to change your ways a little, but that is a good thing. It is good for the company and that, in turn, is good for you.

Introduction

This edition of the book is written for Microsoft .NET 5 and Visual Studio 2019 Profession and Enterprise versions. If you have an older version or a newer one, most of the code and ideas should still apply. As newer versions of .NET and Visual Studio are released, this book will be updated.

About the Author

David McCarter has been a software engineer for over 28 years. He is a Microsoft MVP (Most Valuable Professional), C# Corner MVP, solutions architect, speaker, consultant, patented inventor, professional code reviewer, and interviewer in San Diego, California USA. He is the editor-in-chief of dotNetTips.com; a website dedicated to helping software engineers in all aspects of programming since 1994.

David has written for programming magazines and has published many books including "Rock Your Code: Code and App Performance for Microsoft .NET", "Rock Your Code: Defensive Programming for Microsoft .NET" available at http://amazon.com/author/dotnetdave. David is a featured writer on the C# Corner website, among others.

David gives lectures on programming and technical interviewing at user groups, colleges, high schools, and conferences such as C# Corner Conference (India), NDC, Code Camp, SQL Saturday, DevConnections, VSLive, and more. He taught at the University of California San Diego for close to 18 years. He also runs his software & consulting company called McCarter Consulting. You can find upcoming speaking engagements by going to http://bit.ly/dotnetdaverocks.

He is one of the founders and directors of the San Diego .NET Developers Group for its 20-year run. In 2008 David won the INETA Community Excellence Award for his involvement in the .NET community. David is also an inventor of a software printing system that was approved by the US Patient Office in May 2008.

Introduction

If that's not enough, David is also an award-winning photographer and works for bands such as Queensryche, Buckcherry, Geoff Tate, Eric Johnson, Lit, Gary Hoey, P.O.D., Steel Panther, and too many other bands in the United States to list. David is also a guitarist and has had the honor to play with the Wayward Sons from Los Angeles, Carl Franklin from the .NET Rocks podcast, and one of the lead guitarists from Lynyrd Skynyrd.

His Microsoft MVP profile is found at http://bit.ly/davidmvp

Contact Information

Do you have a burning question about .NET? Do you have comments or suggestions for this book? Then *please* contact me at dotnetdave@live.com.

Thanks for the Help!

I would like to thank the technical reviewers for this book who provided a lot of help. They are **Jonathan Bachelor, Full Stack Software Engineer at Hunter Industries, and Kristine Khanh Tran, Software Engineer II at Verizon**.

Do you want to help review the next edition of this book? If so, please email me at dotnetdave@live.com.

Rock Your Code: Live

Attend a live version of this topic and more at a conference near you. Each year I travel the world to help you to learn to program for Microsoft .NET! For more information please go to http://bit.ly/dotnetdaverocks

Introduction

Rock Your Code: Videos On-Demand

To watch live recordings of my conference sessions, including this topic, please go to http://bit.ly/CodeQuality

Introduction

Acknowledgments

I would like to thank Woody Pewitt who wrote the original core of this standard from the internal Microsoft program StyleCop (before it was publicly released).

Other standards presented in this document came from the following sources: .NET Framework General Reference Naming Guidelines, C# Coding Style Guide by Mike Krüger, Design Guidelines for Class Library Developers, IDesign C# Coding Standard, Philips Coding Standard: C#.

Special Offer

For this edition of this book, I have worked out special deals for my readers from third-party companies. I use these products every day and have done so for a very long time.

CodeRush from DevExpress

Ever since .NET was released, the only refactoring tool I have used is CodeRush from DevExpress. It works with VB.NET and C# in the .NET Framework, .NET Core, and .NET 5 projects. Here is a short description of the product.

> *CodeRush is an extension for Visual Studio that helps you get more work done with less effort. With sophisticated tools to help you craft better code, refactor, format code, find bugs, run tests, and instantly navigate through large software systems, nothing is faster than CodeRush.*

CodeRush speeds up my productivity and uses proper coding patterns. Use the link below to download your FREE copy today.

https://www.devexpress.com/rock-your-code

Do not procrastinate, this free offer expires on December 31, 2021. I mention CodeRush throughout this book.

Introduction

Companion Books

I have released companion books that are be meant to be read along with this book.

Rock Your Code: Code Performance for Microsoft.NET

How fast your code executes is very important for your users and back-end server processes. This is even more important for the future as more and more users, use your app or services. Thinking about performance while you are first writing the code will save tons of time and money in the future!

There are many ways to write the same block of code, some more performant than others. Short of requiring your users to buy faster machines with more memory and faster processors or the same for back-end servers, this book will show you the best practices when writing business apps, so your code can run as fast as possible and could lead to cost savings for your servers or cloud services.

This book discusses and shows common code performance guidelines for Microsoft .NET. Topics include general tips, string performance, reference type & structure performance, collection performance, internationalization & localization, and how to analyze code for performance problems, and more.

This new edition of the book includes data from over 3,400 benchmark tests and has brand new chapters on serialization for JSON and XML, collection performance under simulated workloads, and how to speed up performance using the dotNetTips.com NuGet packages. This book is written for Microsoft .NET Core 3 and Microsoft .NET version 4.8 using Visual Studio 2019. All examples in this book are in C#.

100% of all profit from the paperback version of this book will be donated to the Voice of Slum NGO in Delhi, India.
https://www.voiceofslum.org/

To order, go to Amazon.com!

Introduction

How to Use This Book

This book is written for C# developers using Visual Studio 2019. If you are not a C# developer, you can translate the examples in this book by going here: https://converter.telerik.com.

> ☑ If you would like to see more information about a specific topic or you find code or spelling errors, please email me at *dotnetdave@live.com* and I will fix it in the next edition.

Project Setup

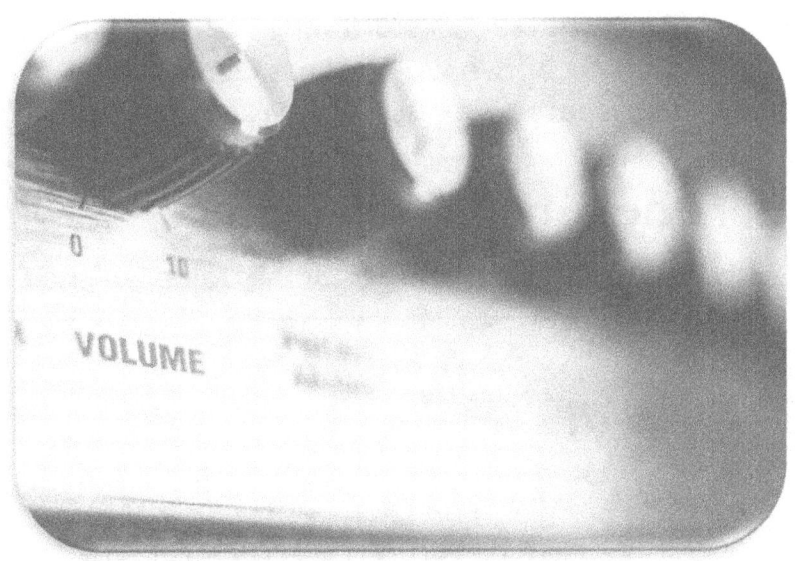

By default, Visual Studio does not set all the proper options to help you write rock-solid code when creating a new project. In this chapter, all the following recommendations are for Visual Studio 2019. If you have an older version, most of my recommendations should still work.

Application Information

Before creating a project, it is important to take a few minutes to think about the assembly name since that usually becomes the root or default namespace. This is the default name of the EXE or DLL created during the build process. You can learn about namespaces in the Assembly Layout chapter.

The name you choose should follow this format:

`<Company>.<Component>.dll`

Multiple `<Component>` names can be used separated by a period. For example:

`DevExpress.Pdf.Core`

`dotNetTips.App.Ads.DataAccess`

`dotNetTips.Utilities.Core.Windows`

`Microsoft.Build.Utilities.Core`

`System.Threading.Tasks`

`System.Web.Services`

Application Information

Project Setup

Assembly name is used to create the compiled file name. For example, the assembly name above will become **dotNetTips.Spargine.5.Extentions.dll**. **Default namespace** will become the root namespace for all of your classes.

.NET Package Information

Go to the **Package** tab and fill out the values as shown below.

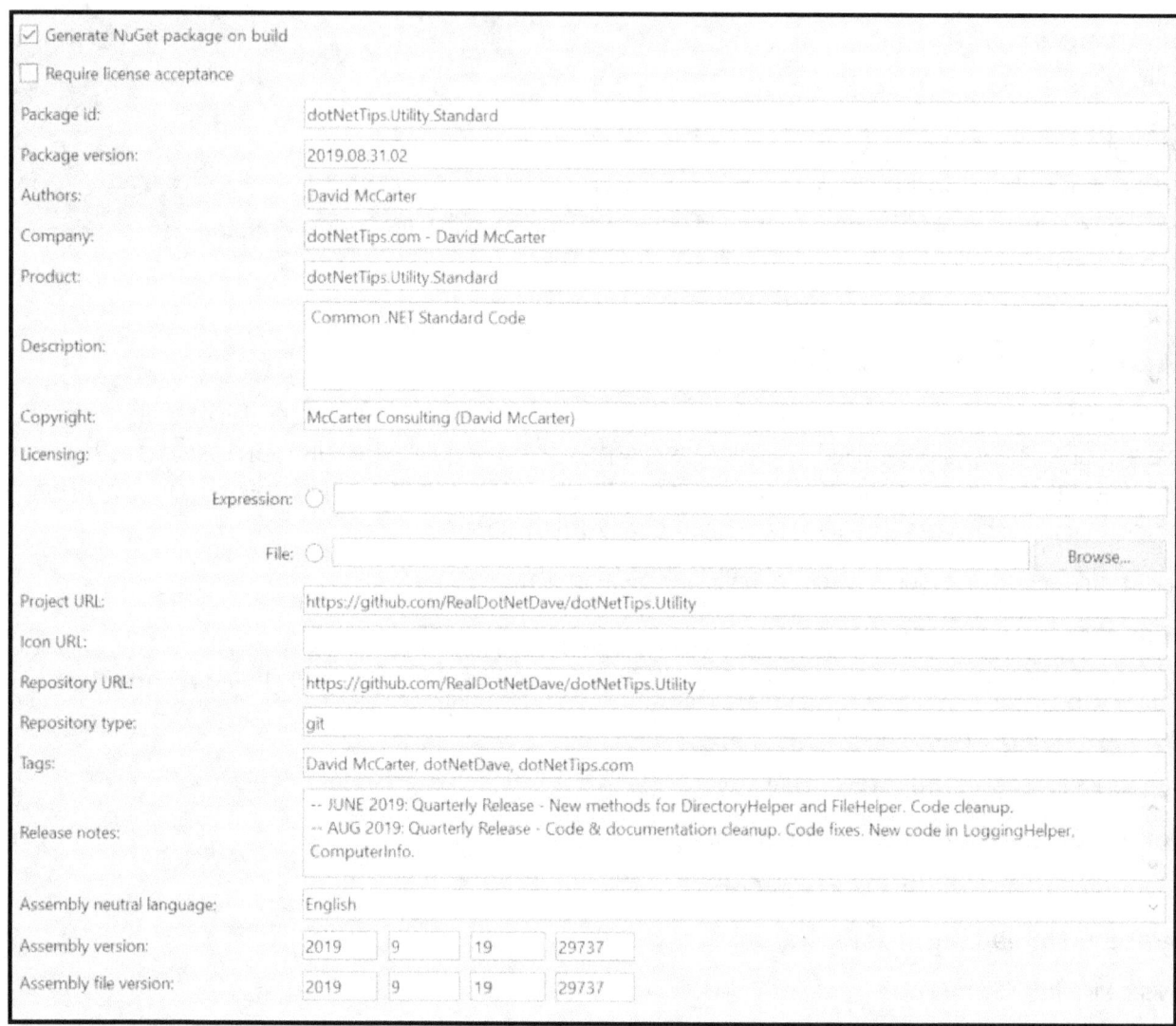

These settings are not only important for the version number, but other values are used by .NET for things like the proper location to store application data. With every major release of my NuGet packages, I always fill out **Release notes** since they will show up in the description of the package on the website.

Project Setup

Build Settings

These are instructions on what is important to fill out in the build settings.

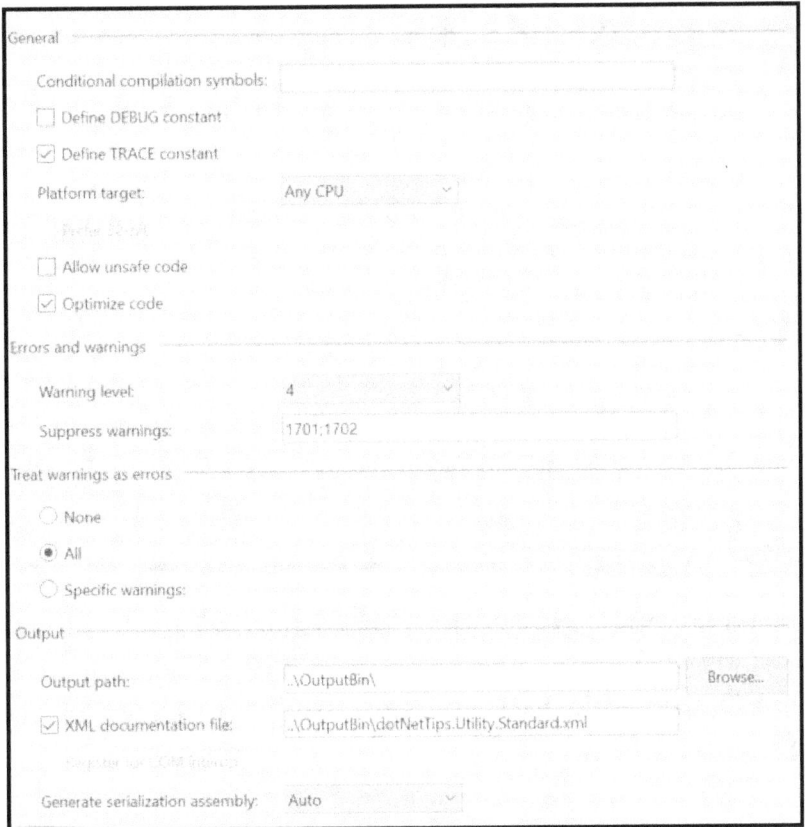

1. **Treat warnings as errors** in **Release** or **Debug Build**. This will make sure that warnings are also fixed. This is advisable because they could seriously affect the operation of the code. Below is an example from an in-production project.

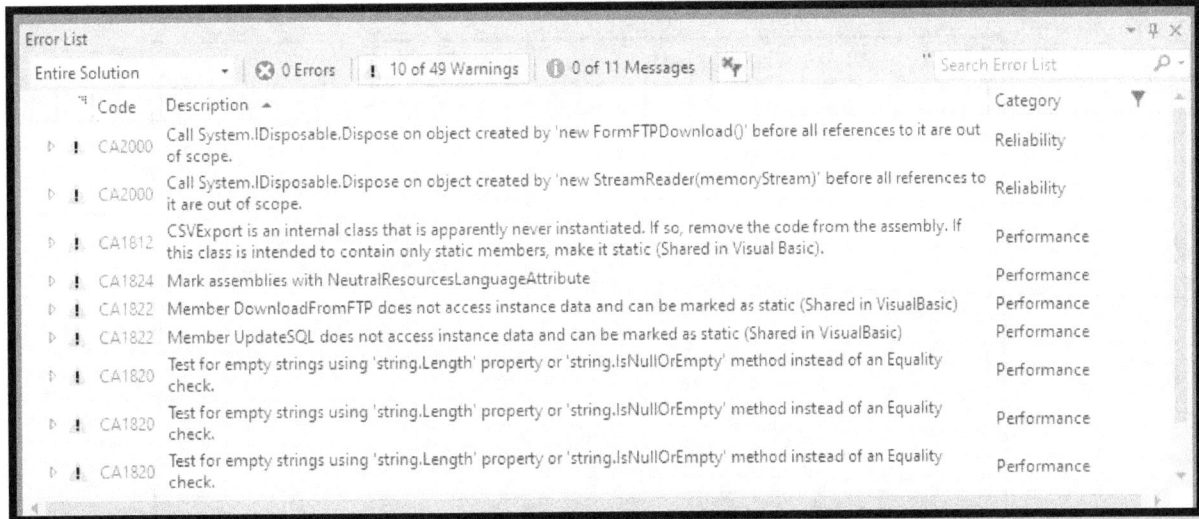

The most important warning in this list is `Dispose()` is not being called on multiple objects (discussed later in this book). Also, the code is not using

11

Project Setup

`string.IsNullOrEmpty()` which *is* a performance issue. I recommend setting these two warnings to **error**. It is easy to do in Visual Studio by **right-clicking** on the warning and by going to **"Set severity"**.

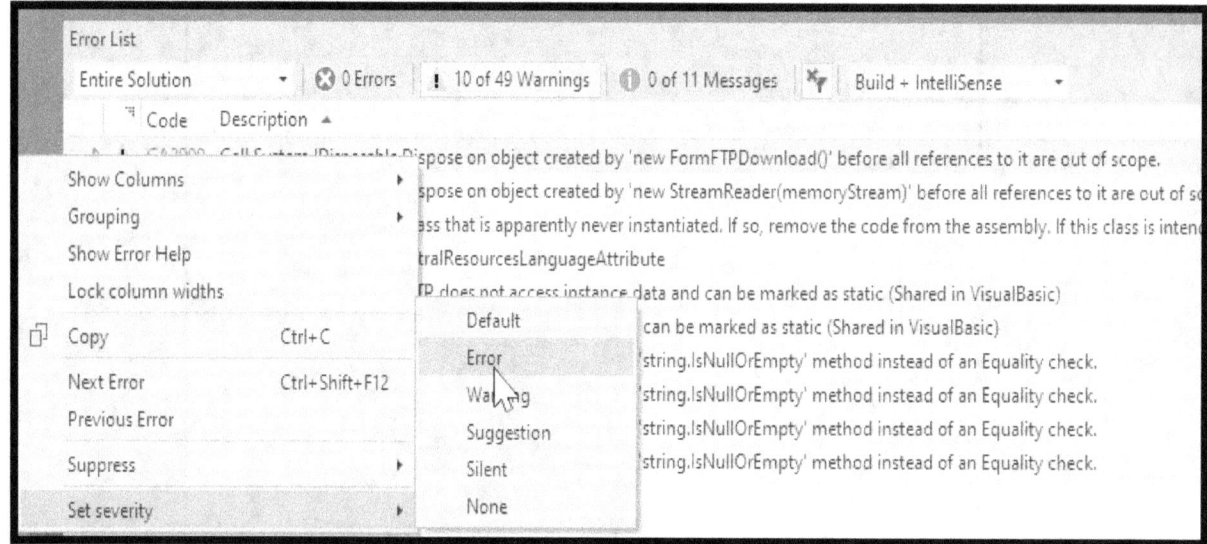

2. **XML Document File** should be named: `/comments.xml` (or the file name of your choice as I did in the graphic). This will output XML comments to the same directory as the **Output Path**. XML documentation and comments are discussed in the Code Style chapter.

Signing Settings

Signing your assemblies, especially DLL's is very important for many reasons. It is the only way to create a "unique" assembly in .NET that is digitally signed which means it is more secure.

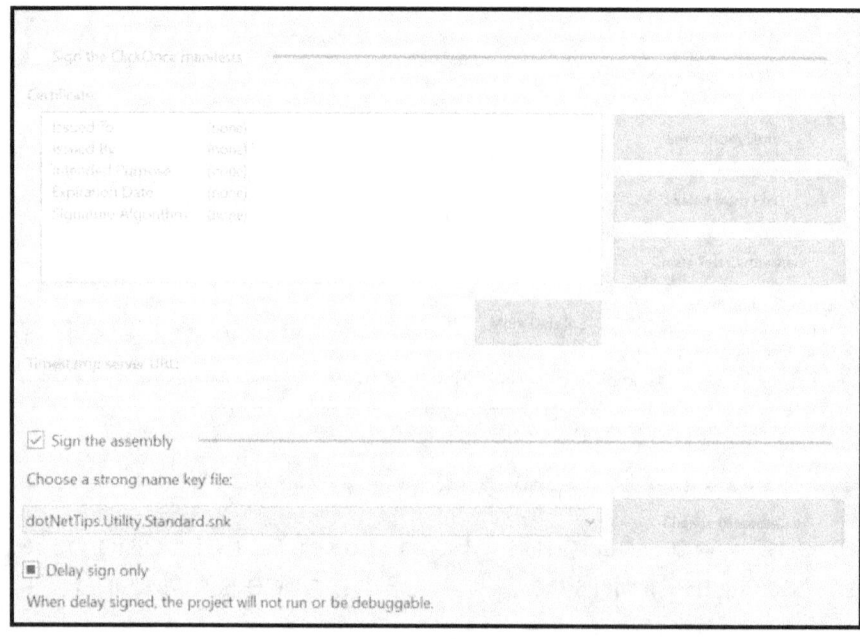

Project Setup

1. Always check "**Sign the assembly**" to create a strongly named key file. This makes sure the assembly:
    a. It is protected from spoofing (*the most important reason*)!
    b. It can more easily have Code Access Security (Clr) applied.

To learn more about signing, read the "Manage Assembly and Manifest Signing" post on the docs.microsoft.com site.

Analyzing Code for Issues

How do you find issues in your code? Many of these rules have been ingrained in my brain over the over 20 years I have been coding using .NET, but I still need to use tools to speed up this process or to find the ones I miss. Using tools that I describe in this section will *dramatically* decrease the time it takes to find issues, so you can get back to adding features so you can get more customers!

I am recommending these tools since they are the ones that I have used for many years and are part of my workflow *before* I commit.

Visual Studio Analyze

Analyze has been available in most of the Visual Studio editions for a long time and used to be based on FXCop[1]. Originally, FXCop was an internal Microsoft tool for the .NET team to analyze code. Much of the first edition of this book was taken from FXCop before it was released publicly. Analyzing .NET 5 code has dramatically changed, and I will walk you through it.

In .NET 5, instead of using FXCop, code style analysis is configured using a new file type called `.editorConfig`. EditorConfig[2] helps maintain consistent coding styles for multiple developers working on the same project across various editors and IDEs. The EditorConfig project consists of a file format for defining coding styles and a collection of text editor plugins that enable editors to read the file format and adhere to defined styles. EditorConfig files are easily readable, and they work nicely with version control systems.

Reading how all this works on the Microsoft Docs site is not easy to understand and is very time-consuming. I will try to break it down into the most important things that every team should implement.

---

[1] For more FXCop information go to: https://en.wikipedia.org/wiki/FxCop

[2] For more EditorConfig information, go to: https://editorconfig.org

Project Setup

Step 1: Analyze Setup

If you are reading this, *stop* and open all the solutions you are currently working on and do the following for any of your projects. Go to the project properties and click on **Code Analysis**.

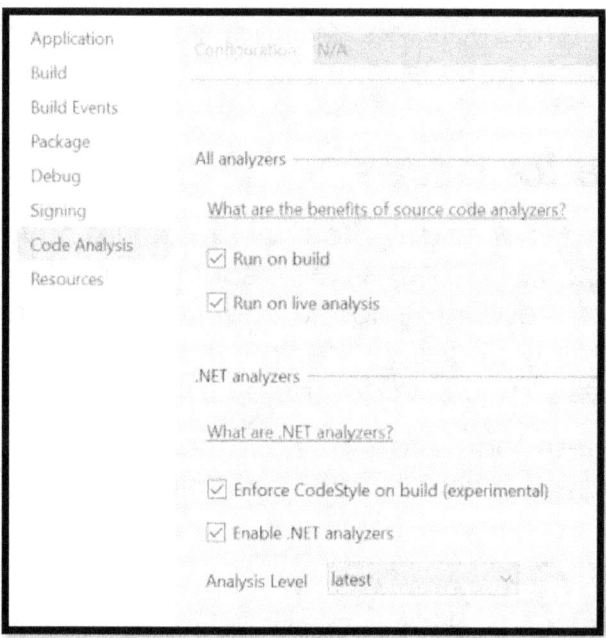

This will ensure that analysis will be done on every build. This is *very* important since it is much cheaper to fix bugs when writing the code as opposed to the user or QA finding it later.

1. Make sure to check "**Enforce CodeStyle on build**" (not default). More details about this later.

Step 2: Install EditorConfig Language Service Extension

Before we discuss the `.editorConfig` file used in code analysis, first install the EditorConfig Language Service[3] extension created by Mads Kristensen, Senior Program Manager at Microsoft. This extension will make it much easier to configure the `.editorConfig` file.

> ☑ Currently, this extension does not recognize all settings available for .editorConfig.

---

[3] EditorConfig Language Service:
https://marketplace.visualstudio.com/items?itemName=MadsKristensen.EditorConfig

Project Setup

Step 3: Create .editorConfig File

To create the **.editorConfig** file, **right-click** on the project, select **Add**, then **.editorConfig File**. The default setup only includes two minor rules.

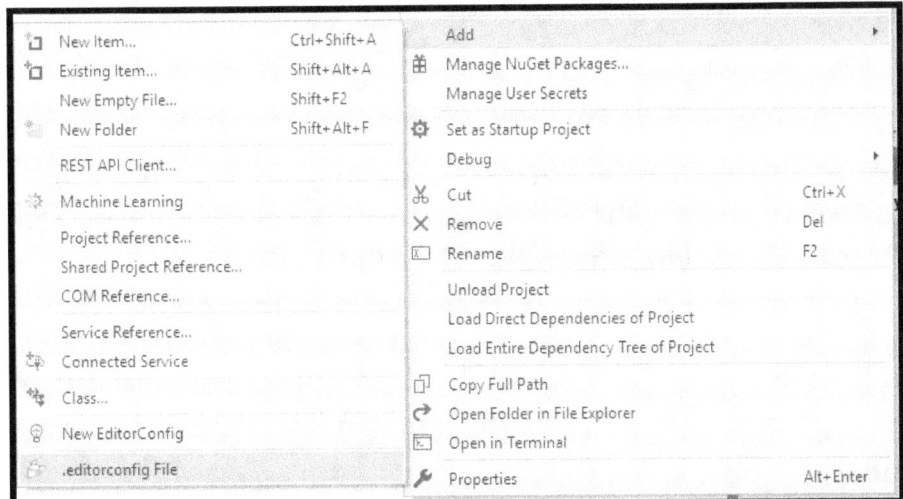

To add the missing rules, open the **.editorConfig** file, and **click** on the light bulb. Then select **Add Missing Rules**, then **All**. Unfortunately, this extension does not add all available rules. I have reported[4] this to the extension author.

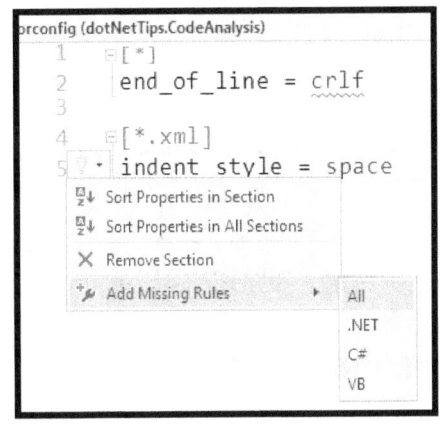

If you would like to see how my .editorConfig is set up, you can go to http://bit.ly/EditorConfig5.

Step 4: Running Code Analysis

There are two ways to run code analysis in Visual Studio.

Running During Build

In step 1, I showed that you should have **Run on Build** enabled. This is a must because dealing with issues while you are coding is far easier to fix and much, much cheaper. Now every time you build the project or solution, code analysis will fire off after the build and then the issues show up in the Error List window as shown below.

---

[4] Extension Issue Reported at: https://github.com/madskristensen/EditorConfigLanguage/issues/92

Project Setup

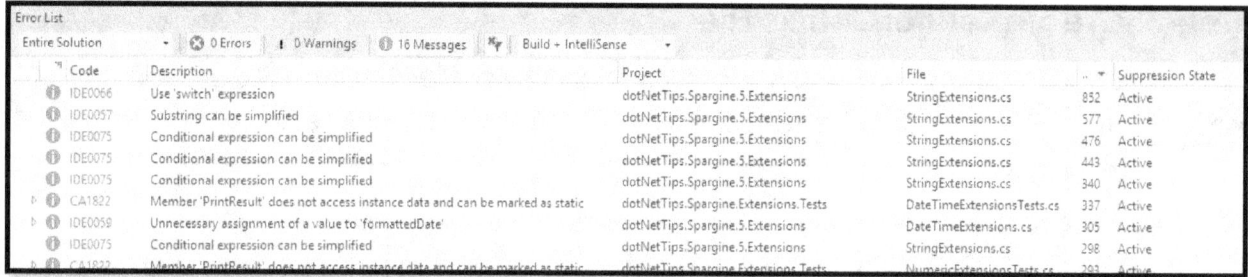

Clicking on each issue will take you to the code. If you need to know why the code has been flagged and how to fix it, then simply click on the code in the Code column and it will take you to the online documentation.

> ☑ Tip: To make sure all assemblies are analyzed, make sure to build using **Rebuild Solution**.

Running Using Analyze

The second way you can run code analysis (this is the way I use the most) is to manually run Analyze. Just go to **Analyze** on the top menu bar and then click on **Run Code Analysis**, then choose **On Solution**. This will build the solution and then run an analysis on the entire solution. The issues will show up the same way as in the previous method.

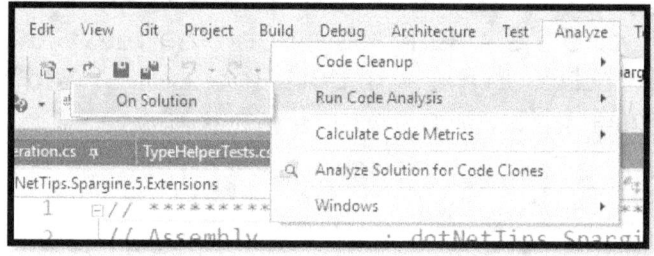

.editorConfig File

EditorConfig files use an INI format that is compatible with the format used by Python ConfigParser Library, but [and] are allowed in the section names. The section names are file path globs (case sensitive), like the format accepted by gitignore. Here is an example of some common settings.

```
csharp_style_var_for_built_in_types = true : warning
```

This setting is for C# and creates a warning if **var** is not used for built-in types. There are **none**, **silent**, **suggestion**, **warning,** and **error**.

The example below is are the settings to properly name interfaces.

```
dotnet_naming_rule.interface_should_be_begins_with_i.severity = error
dotnet_naming_rule.interface_should_be_begins_with_i.symbols = interface
dotnet_naming_rule.interface_should_be_begins_with_i.style = begins_with_i
```

What are all the available settings that work in Visual Studio? Sadly, there is not a single source for them. I have spent a lot of time searching the Microsoft Docs site and blog posts to find them all. If you would like to see the ones I have been able

Project Setup

to find, I have put them in the **.editorConfig** file that you can view here: http://bit.ly/EditorConfig5. Check back often to see if I have added new ones. Also, if there are any missing, please send me an email to let me know. I will add it to the file.

Pain Is Good

At every job I work at, setting up Analyze is the first thing I do when I am assigned to a project. Many times, the other developers turn it off after I check-in my changes to source control, saying that the build is taking too long or is "painful".

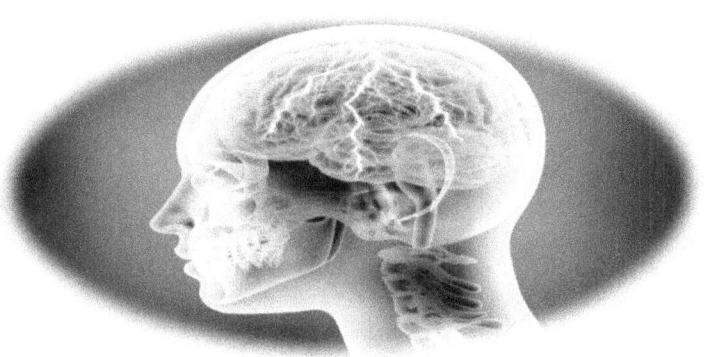

My response is "good"! It should be painful until the issues are fixed. I have been on projects that the solution exceeded the maximum number of violations and others that crashed Visual Studio!

Build Process

Scanning the code for issues can and *should* be added to your build process on the build server or for continuous integration. Do not release the code for testing by QA until the issues have been fixed or marked to ignore (by a lead on the team).

Release Build

Make sure that the "**Set Optimize Code**" is turned on (default behavior).

Build Events

It is now simple to create a NuGet package from your DLL projects. To test my NuGet packages before I upload them to the site, I use the build event script below to pack and copy them to a local folder.

```
if $(ConfigurationName) == Release (dotnet pack "$(ProjectPath)" --
no-build --include-source --include-symbols --output
"c:\dotNetTips.com\NuGet")
```

Then go to **"Manage NuGet Packages for Solution"** and create a package source that points to the folder (like the one above) as shown below.

Project Setup

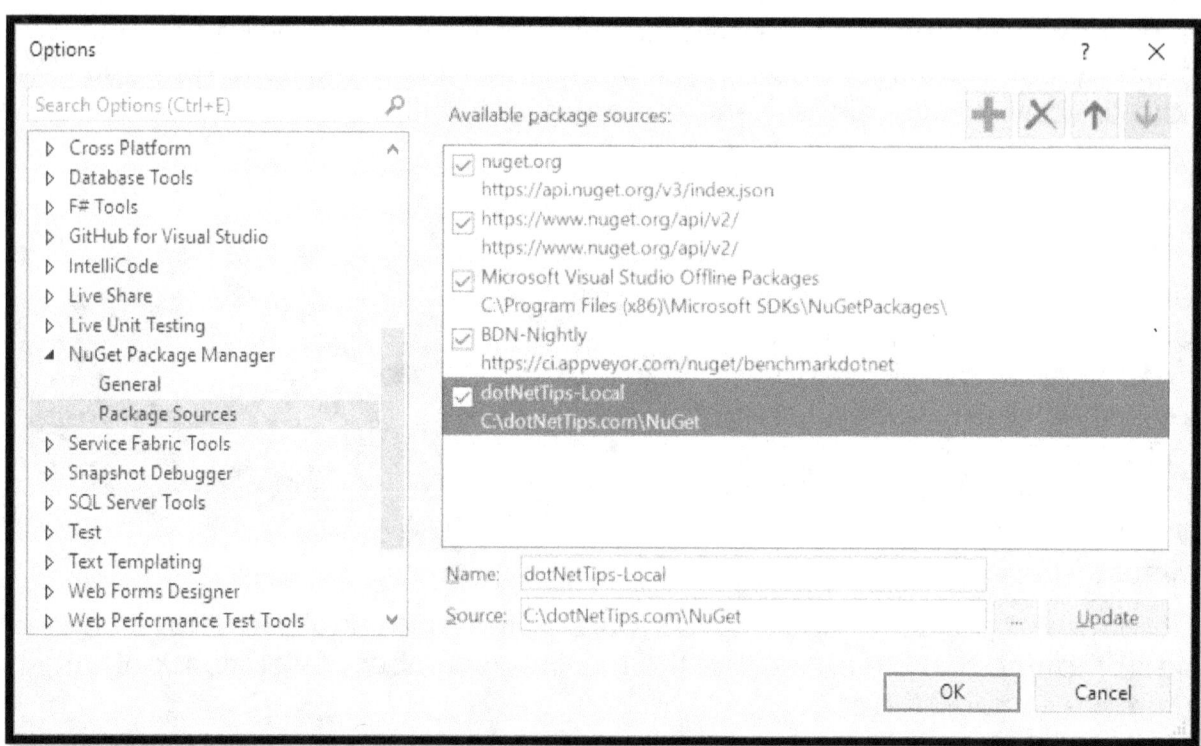

Source File Naming

Always use PascalCasing for naming source files. Do not use the underscore character and do not use casing to differentiate the names of files.

EXAMPLE

`CollectionExtensions.cs`

`DistinctBlockingCollection.cs`

`FileProgressState.cs`

`IUsers.cs`

`MessagesControl.vb`

Folder Structure

The folder structure should follow the namespaces you create. In C# this is easy, just create a new folder or sub-folder and add a file. C# will automatically put the correct namespace at the top of the class. In VB.NET, you need to do this manually.

Project Setup

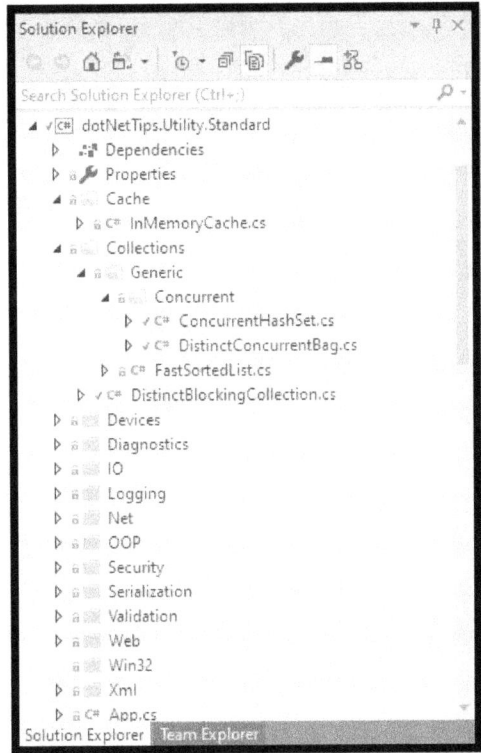

Assembly Layout

This chapter will discuss how to *properly* set up your assembly. I will provide examples of how methods should be ordered in a class, setting up interfaces, classes, destructors, and more.

General Tips to Get You Started

- Avoid explicit preprocessor definitions (**#define**). Use the project settings for defining conditional compilation constants instead.

- Name your application configuration file as **app.config** or **appsettings.json** and include it in the project.

- *Never* hardcode values that might change based on deployment such as connection strings, URLs, etc. The best place to put these in a .NET application is the **app.config** file for Windows applications and the **appsettings.json** for ASP.NET applications.

    *The .NET team did not include the Settings feature that was in the .NET Framework, so I created a type in my open-source assembly to mimic this feature in .NET 5 called **Config**. I hope you will check into it for your projects. More information can be found in Appendix B.*

- Populate all fields in the Packages tab such as **AssemblyCompany**, **AssemblyDescription**, and **AssemblyCopyright**. This is important for a strong-named assembly and more.

- Sign your assemblies, including the client applications. Also, sign interop assemblies with the project's **.snk** file.

.NET Framework Assemblies

Here is layout information for assemblies.

Element Order

To keep consistency across the code base, and to improve code readability, and helps in printing code, these rules enforce a standard element order for code files. For example, member variables (fields) within a class should be declared at the top, followed by delegates, events, and enumerations. These should be followed

Assembly Layout

by properties, and, finally, methods. This order is documented in StyleCop Rule SA1201:
github.com/DotNetAnalyzers/StyleCopAnalyzers/blob/master/documentation/SA1201.md

The order of file-level elements should be:

1. Using/Imports statements
2. Namespaces

The order of namespace-level elements should be:

1. Delegates
2. Enums
3. Interfaces
4. Structs
5. Classes

The order of class-level elements should be:

1. Fields
2. Constants
3. Constructors
4. Finalizers
5. Delegates
6. Events
7. Enums
8. Interfaces
9. Properties
10. Indexers
11. Methods
12. Structs

Within elements of the same type, they should appear in this order:

1. **public** elements
2. **internal** elements
3. **protected internal** elements
4. **protected** elements
5. **private** elements

Assembly Layout

> ☑ **Note**: The enumerations, interfaces, and structure elements appear both in namespace and class-level order above because these elements do not need to be located inside of a class.

Use **#region/#endregion** to group namespace-level and class-level elements. Use separate regions to organize **private**, **protected**, and **internal** members.

> ☑ Note: In most cases, there should only be one class, structure, or enum per class file.

Namespaces

Namespaces are used to organize your classes into logical working groups. They also allow the creation of duplicate class names, if needed, since the full name of the type contains the namespace. Also, if named correctly, namespaces make it easy for a developer to find the class they need to get their job done.

The general rule for naming namespaces is as follows:

```
<Company>.(<Product>|<Technology>)[.<Feature>][.<Subnamespace>]
```

I once worked at a company that when I got there the only namespace they defined in all their assemblies was named "Classes". I could not believe what I saw. It took about two months of refactoring to fix this, which included the creation of multiple re-usable assemblies.

Prefixing namespace names with a company name or other well-established brand avoids the possibility of two published namespaces having the same name. Use a stable, recognized product or technology name at the second level of a hierarchical name (not a company organization name). Lastly, if needed add a sub-namespace. Take time coming up with easy to discover namespaces. Internally at Microsoft, they have meetings just to come up with type and namespace names.

> ☑ **Note**: Make sure not to name the last part of the namespace the same name as a class contained within it.

GUIDELINES

- Use Pascal case. Use uppercase for very small words (2-3 characters in length).

EXAMPLE

DevExpress.XtraReports.UI

dotNetTips.Conference.Survey.DataAccess

Assembly Layout

dotNetTips.Spargine.Collections

Microsoft.AspNet.Identity

Microsoft.Azure.Mobile.Server.Tables

System.Data.Entity.Infrastructure.Annotations

If you are unsure what to name your namespaces, look at the .NET namespace names. This will also make it easier for any .NET programmer to find features quickly. Once the namespace goes into production, it will be very difficult if not impossible to change later down the road.

The folder structure for the project should be synced with the namespaces. For example, from one of my open-source assemblies for the **DistinctConcurrentBag** class, the namespace is **dotNetTips.Utility.Standard.Collections.Generic.Concurrent**.

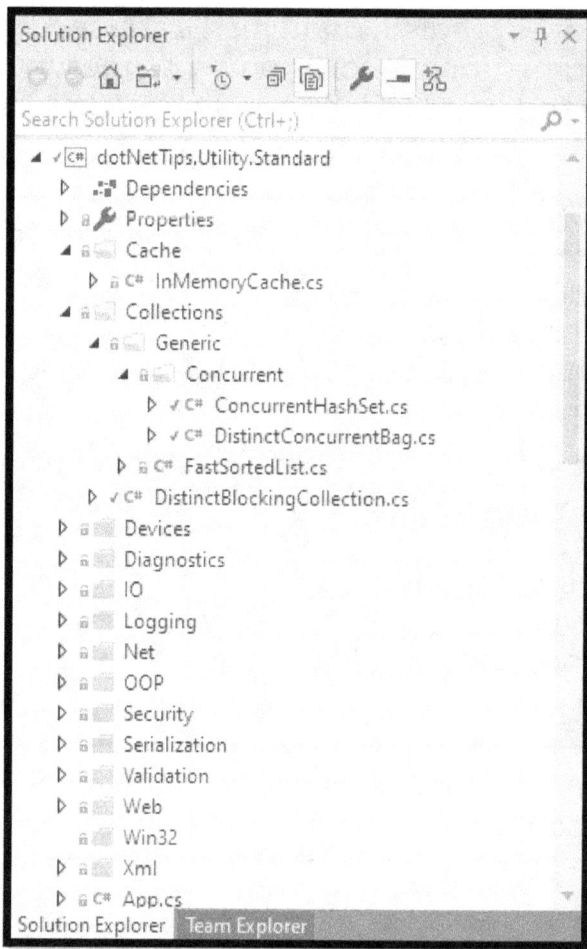

Syncing folders with namespaces make it *much* easier to find the class in IntelliSense and in the Solution Explorer.

Naming Standards

This chapter focuses on making source code easily understood by anyone who will read it. Source code will be changed or maintained, and no one wants to stare at a block of code for thirty minutes or longer trying to figure out what it is doing. Taking a little more time up front will save countless hours and money down the line.

Have you ever looked at the code in .NET using a decompiler tool such as Reflector from Red Gate? If you do, you will see that it all looks like it was written by the same person. This is because Microsoft implements very good standards and makes sure everyone follows them by using their free open-source tool called StyleCop. Well, they

did this well for the .NET Framework but not nearly as good for .NET Core and .NET 5. I hope that they work on this for future releases.

General Guidelines

Here is a list of things to keep in mind when naming types and variables in .NET.

- Create easily readable identifier names.
- Do not use abbreviations or contractions as part of identifier names.
- Do not use Hungarian Notation.
- Do not use underscores, hyphens, or any other non-alphanumeric characters. The only exemption to this is underscores for the beginning of a private field name.
- Favor readability over brevity.
- Only use acronyms that are widely accepted such as **HTML** or **XML**. How do you know if they are well known? If you search for it in a search engine like Bing, if the definition is not in the first few results, it is *not* well known.

Capitalization

There are two ways to name identifiers and they are PascalCasing (capital at the beginning of each word) or camelCasing (the first word starts with a lower case;

Naming Standards

the rest of the words start with a capital). Use Pascal case for all identifiers except for parameter names and local variable names.

Case Sensitivity

Never vary identifiers based on the case! Not all the .NET languages are case sensitive (such as VB.NET).

Classes

Classes are *the* building blocks for creating your types in .NET along with structures and interfaces. The following are guidelines to get you started.

GUIDELINES

- <u>Do not</u> begin with a prefix of "**C**".
- <u>Do not</u> begin with an underscore character "**_**".
- <u>Do not</u> put multiple types in a single file.
- Interfaces should always start with "**I**".
- Name with nouns or noun phrases.
- The file name should reflect the type it contains.
- When inheriting from a base class or implementing an interface, *in most cases*, the class should end in that base class name or interface name.

EXAMPLE

```
public class Button
public class XmlTraceListener : TraceListener
public sealed class MessageProcessor : IMessageProcessor
public class DistinctBlockingCollection<T> : BlockingCollection<T>,
                                             ICloneable<T>
```

Generic Classes

Generics are a very powerful tool for the programmer and allow strongly type parameters instead of using **Object**. Using generics can increase performance up to 200%, but with most things, naming is very important for readability.

When creating your generic type parameters use a descriptive name that starts with **T**, unless a single letter name is completely self-explanatory (this is rare).

Naming Standards

EXAMPLE

```
public IEnumerable<T> OrderBy<T>(IEnumerable<T> list,
                                 string sortExpression)
```

If the class or method supports a single generic type, then **T** should always be used. As you can see in the graphic to the right, .NET uses **TKey** to represent the key type and **TValue** to represent the value type.

Inheriting Classes

In *most* cases, if you inherit a class you should add the name of the base class as the suffix to the new class name. There are cases when you would not. Below are when you would.

When creating a custom **Attribute** class always suffix the class with **Attribute**. For example:

```
ObsoleteAttribute : Attribute
AttributeUsageAttribute : Attribute
```

When creating a custom **EventHandler** class, always add the suffix **EventHandler** to the names of types that are used in events. For example:

```
AssemblyLoadEventHandler : EventHandler
DataRowChangeEventHandler : EventHandler
```

When creating a delegate that is *not* an event handler, add the suffix **Callback** to the name. For example:

```
ValidatorCallback
TimerCallback
```

When creating a custom **EventArgs** class for use in an event handler, always suffix the class with **EventArgs**. For example:

```
AssemblyLoadEventArgs : EventArgs
DragEventArgs : EventArgs
```

When creating a custom **Exception** class, always add the suffix **Exception** to the name. For example:

```
ArgumentNullException : Exception
ArgumentOutOfRangeException : Exception
```

Naming Standards

When creating a custom class that implements one of the following types, add the suffix **Collection**.

`System.Collections.Generic.ICollection<T>`
`System.Collections.Generic.IEnumerable<T>`
`System.Collections.Generic.IList<T>`
`System.Collections.ICollection`
`System.Collections.IEnumerable`
`System.Collections.IList`

EXAMPLE

```
DesignerCollection : ICollection
ConfigurationPropertyCollection : List<ConfigurationProperty>
```

This is a list of types that you would *not* add the type name as a suffix to your type:

`CodeAccessPermission` (or `Permission`)	`Delegate`	`Dictionary`	`Stream`

Abstract Classes

Abstract classes follow the same rules as any other class except for these differences:

- Define a protected or an internal constructor.
- Do not use a public or protected internal constructor.

In many cases, I use abstract classes over an interface that is easier to version. There are more details and an example of an abstract class in the Class Design chapter.

Partial Classes

Partial classes are for use by code designers such as Windows Forms, Entity Framework, generated service proxies, and more. They are used to add custom code to a class in a way so that the designers do not overwrite it. In the graphic below, the designer class is **ConfigForm.Designer.cs** which should never be modified. The code that you write goes into the **ConfigForm.cs** file.

Naming Standards

☑ It is best practice to *avoid* creating partial classes in your code.

Static Classes

A static class is one that contains only static members. I usually use static classes when creating "helper" methods when it makes no sense to create an object just to call one method.

GUIDELINES

- Use static classes sparingly.

In C#, use **static** when declaring the class. In VB, use a module, not a class when a type contains **static** methods and properties.

☑ *Remember* to be careful using static fields in classes since they will not be destroyed (memory cleaned up) until the application process ends. Also, not used properly can cause data corruption.

Structures

Structures are used if instances of the type are small and short-lived or are embedded in other objects.

GUIDELINES

- A file name should reflect the type it contains.
- Avoid using reference types in structures such as **String**.
- Do not begin with an underscore character "_".
- Do not define a mutable value type.
- Do not put multiple types in a single file.
- If using value types, implement **IEquatable<T>**.
- Name with nouns or noun phrases.

With most types that I write, I use classes since they have more features and fewer limitations than structures.

29

Naming Standards

Interfaces

Interfaces are created if you need common methods, events, etc. to be supported by multiple types. In .NET, a type can implement any number of interfaces as it needs.

GUIDELINES

- A file name should reflect the type it contains.
- Always begin an interface with the letter "**I**".
- Do not begin with an underscore character "**_**".
- Do not put multiple types in a single file.
- Name interfaces with adjective phrases. Try to avoid nouns or noun phrases.

In many instances, using a base class is preferable to using an interface. Interfaces are proper in the following situations:

- Several unrelated classes want to support the protocol.
- These classes already have established base classes (for example, some are user interface (UI) controls, and some are XML Web services).
- Aggregation is not appropriate or practical.

In all other situations, class inheritance, including abstract class, is usually a better model. Once assemblies use an interface, it is usually difficult to change later. So, keep them to only a few definitions or none.

EXAMPLE

```
/// <summary>
/// ICloneable Interface
/// </summary>
/// <typeparam name="T">The type of T.</typeparam>
public interface ICloneable<T>
{
   /// <summary>
   /// Cones this instance.
   /// </summary>
   /// <returns>T.</returns>
   T Cone();
}

public interface IComparable<in T>
{
   // Interface does not need to be marked with the serializable
   // attribute, Compares this object to another object,
   // returning an integer that indicates the relationship. An
   // implementation of this method must return a value less
```

Naming Standards

```
    // than zero if this is less than object, zero if this is
    // equal to object, or a value greater than zero if this
    // is greater than object.
    int CompareTo([AllowNull] T other);
}
```

Checking Type for an Interface

Checking to see if a type implements an interface is as easy as using the code below.

EXAMPLE

```
var result = typeof(ILogger).IsAssignableFrom(typeof(SomeCotroller))
```

Interfaces with Implementation

Recently, .NET has implemented a limited way to include implementation in an interface. Below is an example from my open-source testing framework.

```
/// <summary>
/// Interface IPersonPlus
/// </summary>
[XmlRoot(ElementName = "IPersonPlus",
  Namespace = "http://dotNetTips.Utility.Standard.Tester.Models")]
public interface IPersonPlus : IPerson
{
  /// <summary>
  /// Gets the age.
  /// </summary>
  /// <value>The age.</value>
  [IgnoreDataMember]
  public TimeSpan Age => this.CalculateAge();

  /// <summary>
  /// Calculates the person's current age.
  /// </summary>
  /// <returns>TimeSpan.</returns>
  private TimeSpan CalculateAge() =>
                DateTimeOffset.UtcNow.Subtract(this.BornOn);
}
```

With this new feature in .NET, I found that using modifiers like protected, do not work.

Naming Standards

Constants

Use constant fields for constants that will never change. The compiler inserts the values of **const** fields directly into the calling code, which means that **const** values can never be changed without the risk of introducing a compatibility issue.

EXAMPLE

```
public const char FormFeed = '\f';
```

Access Modifiers

Every element declaration should begin with an access modifier keyword of **public**, **private**, **protected**, or **internal**. In C #, it is legal to declare an element without an access modifier, in which case the protection of the element defaults to private. However, to maintain consistency across the code base, it is recommended that *all* element declarations explicitly state their access modifier. This also makes for better readability.

> ☑ Member variables (fields) ***must not*** be declared **public** or **protected**. To expose member variables outside of a class, use a property. Constant member variables may be declared **public**.

Private Variables

Prefix private field variables with an underscore ("_"). While this goes against recommendations by StyleCop, the reason for this is to make it easy to find private variables from other members in the class in your code and IntelliSense.

```
Public Property EmailAddressType() As EmailAddressType
    Get
        Return _emailAddressType
    End Get
    Set(ByVal value As EmailAddressType)
        Me._emailAddressType = value
    End Set
End Property
    ''' <summary>
    ''' Contact
    ''' </summary>
    ''' <value>
    ''' <return>
    ''' <remark>
Public Property Name() As String
```

Naming Standards

Never create public fields. Instead, use private fields and expose them through properties or methods. This is made much easier (less coding on your part) with refactoring tools like ReSharper and CodeRush. If this is not done, then encapsulation is not implemented properly, therefore the type is not using good object-oriented design principles. This is discussed in detail in the Class Design chapter.

Make sure to use constant fields for constants that will never change. For example, the Math class defines **E** (2.7182818284590451) and **PI** (3.1415926535897931) as static constants. The compiler inserts the values of **const** fields directly into the calling code, which means that **const** values can never be changed without the risk of introducing a compatibility issue.

Public static read-only fields can be used for predefined object instances. For example, the **DateTime** class supplies static read-only fields, **MaxValue,** and **MinValue** that you can use to obtain **DateTime** objects set to the maximum or minimum time value.

Use nouns, noun phrases, or adjectives for field names. Make sure to not assign instances of mutable types to read-only fields. The objects created using a mutable type cannot be changed after they are created. For example, arrays and most collections are mutable types while **Int32**, **Uri**, and **String** are immutable types. For fields that hold a mutable reference type, the read-only modifier prevents the field value from being overwritten but does not protect the mutable type from modification.

EXAMPLE

```
//Field
private SqlConnection _connection;

//Property
public SqlConnection Connection
{
   get
   {
      return this._connection;
   }
   set
   {
      this._connection = value;
   }
}
```

Read-Only Fields

Read-only fields are similar constants except that their value can be changed only in the constructor.

Naming Standards

EXAMPLE

```
public class DbConnector
{
   private readonly string _connection;

   public DbConnector(string connection)
   {
      this._connection = connection;
   }

   public string Connection => this._connection;
}
```

Public Instance Fields

DO NOT USE, EVER create public instance fields! If you do, you are not following proper type encapsulation which is the first pillar of Object-Oriented Programming (OOP).

Declaration Keyword Order

In an element declaration, the access modifier should always appear first. Non-access modifier keywords (e.g., **static/ Shared**, **const**, etc.) should appear next, followed by the element name and type. For example, the following declarations would be considered correct:

```
private int _customerAge;
private static int _customerAge;
private static readonly int _customerAge;
```

However, the following declarations would be a violation:

```
static private int _customerAge;
```

Underscores

In C++, it was customary to preface all class variable names with **m_** to signify that these were member variables. In .NET, this is no longer necessary since all class member items are prefaced with this. All member items should be prefaced with an underscore.

EXAMPLE OF THE C++ STYLE

```
class Printer
{
   private int m_data;
   private string m_name;
```

34

Naming Standards

```
   public void PrintData()
   {
      Print(m_data, m_name);
   }
}
```

The correct way to write this code would be:

```
class Printer
{
   private int _data;
   private string _name;

   public void PrintData()
   {
      Print(this._data, this._name);
   }
}
```

Nullable Value Type Variables

Value types can easily be nullable by using **?**. They are very easy to use as shown below.

```
private readonly int? _nullableInt = 10;
```

To uses these to return the actual value or a default value can be used like this.

```
var result = this._nullableInt ?? 0;
```

Alternatively, the **GetValueOrDefault()** method could be used like this.

```
var result = nullableInt.GetValueOrDefault(0);
```

As you can see by my benchmark tests, null coalesce is much more performant!

Method	Mean	Error	StdDev	Median	Gen 0	Gen 1	Gen 2	Allocated
Nullable Int or Default Coalesce	0.0000 ns	0.0000 ns	0.0000 ns	0.0000 ns	0	0	0	0 B
Nullable Int or Default GetValueOrDefault()	0.2062 ns	0.0037 ns	0.0035 ns	0.2051 ns	0	0	0	0 B

Constructors

Supply a constructor for every class except for static classes. Since adding a class with Visual Studio does not create a constructor by default, one should be added

Naming Standards

even if it is only one with no parameters. This will prevent serialization issues in the future. Supply a **protected** constructor that can be used by types in a derived class.

Always use the **static** keyword when declaring a class when providing static member variables. This prevents the class from being created. With the addition of object initializers, parameters should be limited to data that is needed for the type to correctly work such as a database connection string or a file path.

Do not call methods in constructors or do anything that could cause an exception. Exceptions are difficult to catch when called from a constructor and could cause other issues. Only set property values in constructors. Do not use the **base.** reference unless invoking another constructor from within a constructor.

```
public class DivideByZeroException : ArithmeticException
{
   public DivideByZeroException(string message) : base(message)
   {}

   public DivideByZeroException(string message,
                                Exception innerException) :
                                base(message, innerException)
   {}
}
```

Finalizers (Destructors)

Avoid implementing a destructor if possible. The use of destructors is demoted since it introduces a severe performance penalty due to the way the Garbage Collector (GC) works. It is also a bad design pattern to clean up any resources in the destructor since you cannot predict at which time the destructor is called (in other words, it is non-deterministic). Note that destructors are not destructors as in C++. They are just a compiler feature to represent finalizers. If a destructor is needed, also use **GC.SuppressFinalize** so the object will be removed from memory faster.

Instead, implement **IDisposable** if a class uses unmanaged or expensive resources. If a class uses unmanaged resources such as windows handles, database connections, graphics, or other resources that must be disposed of as soon as possible, you must implement the **IDisposable** interface to allow class users to explicitly release such resources. The following code snippet shows the pattern to use for such scenarios.

EXAMPLE

```
public class TempFileManager : IDisposable
{
   private bool _disposed;

   public void Dispose()
```

Naming Standards

```
{
   this.Dispose(true);
   GC.SuppressFinalize(this);
}

protected virtual void Dispose(bool disposing)
{
   if (!this._disposed && disposing)
   {
      this.DeleteAllFiles();
   }

   this._disposed = true;
}

//Code removed for brevity
}
```

If another class derives from this class, then this class should only override the **Dispose()(bool)** method of the base class. It should not implement **IDisposable** itself, nor supply a destructor. The base class's destructor is automatically called.

Do not access any reference type members in the destructor. When the destructor is called by the Garbage Collector, it might be possible that some or all the objects referenced by class members are already garbage collected, so dereferencing those objects may cause exceptions. Only value type members can be accessed (since they live on the memory stack).

Do not throw exceptions from inside destructors. When you call an exception from inside a destructor, the runtime will stop executing the destructor, and pass the exception to the base class destructor (if any). If there is no base class, then the destructor is discarded. Allow a **Dispose** method to be called more than once without throwing an exception. The method should do nothing after the first call.

Events

When naming events think of the concept of before and after, using the present and past tense. For example, an event that is raised before a window is closed would be called **Closing** and one that is raised after the window is closed would be called **Closed**.

USAGE

- Name events with a verb or a verb phrase.
- Use **System.EventHandler<T>** instead of manually creating new delegates to be used as event handlers.

Naming Standards

- Do not use **Before** or **After** prefixes or suffixes to indicate pre-events and post-events.
- Name an event argument class with the **EventArgs** suffix.

EXAMPLE

```
public event EventHandler<EventArgs> Completed;

protected virtual void OnCompleted(object sender, EventArgs e)
{
   EventHandler<EventArgs> handler = Completed;

   if (handler != null)
   {
      handler(sender, e);
   }
}
```

Name this method **On<EventName>**, where **EventName** should be replaced with the name of the event. Raise events through a protected **virtual** method. If a derived class wants to intercept an event, it can override such a virtual method, do its work, and then decide whether to call the base class version. Since the derived class may decide not to call the base class method, ensure that it does not do any work required for the base class to function properly.

EXAMPLE

The sender parameter should be of type **Object**, and the **e** parameter should be an instance of or inherit from **EventArgs**.

```
private void DoWork()
{
   this.OnCompleted(this, new EventArgs());
}
```

Enumerations

Enumerations are usually used to avoid "magic numbers" and should always contain more than one value.

GUIDELINES

- *Always* add the **FlagsAttribute** to a bit field **Enum** type.
- Do not supply explicit values for **Enums** (unless necessary).
- Do not specify a type for an **Enum** (the default is an Int32).
- Do not use an **Enum** suffix on **Enum** type names.

Naming Standards

- In a non-flag **Enum**, the 0 value of an **Enum** should always be the default value or not-chosen value such as **None**.
- Use a singular name for most **Enum** types but use a plural name for **Enum** types that are bit fields.
- Use abbreviations sparingly for **Enums** and their values.

EXAMPLE

```
//Incorrect
public enum Color
{
    None = 0,
    Red = 1,
    Green = 2,
    Blue = 3
}
```

```
//Correct
public enum Color
{
    None,
    Red,
    Green,
    Blue
}
```

Properties

Properties support the first pillar of Object-Oriented Programming, which is encapsulation. Always use properties, *never public or protected fields*!

GUIDELINES

- Allow properties to be set in any order. The object should never depend on a predefined order to work properly. If there are properties that must be set, use constructor parameters.
- Avoid throwing exceptions from property getters.
- Do not use write-only properties because they tend to be confusing. Use a method instead.
- Name a property that returns an **Enum** the same name as the **Enum**.
- Name Boolean properties with an affirmative phrase like "**CanSeek**" or "**IsValid**".

Naming Standards

- Preserve the previous state of a property if the setter throws an exception.
- Properties that return arrays or collections should be plural or a singular name followed by "**List**" or "**Collection**".
- Provide default values for all properties. Prevents security holes and inefficient designs.
- Throw the **InvalidOperationException** exception if a call to a property **set** accessor or method is not proper given the object's current state.
- Use nouns or noun phrases to name properties.
- Use a property rather than a method when the member is a logical data member.
- You should use a read-only property when the user cannot change the property's logical data member. Usually, these read-only properties are set via a parameter in a constructor.

CONSIDER

- Name a property the same name as its type. For example, **Color**.
- Providing events that are raised when certain properties are changed. Such an event should be named **<Property>Changed**, where **<Property>** should be replaced with the name of the property with which this event is associated.
- Using an auto-implement property if change events, data validation, etc. is not needed. Make sure to set their default values in the constructor.

PROPERTY NAMING EXAMPLE

```
BackColor
CurrentEmployees
NumberOfItems
```

PROPERTY EXAMPLE

```
private int _value;
private int _minimum = Int32.MinValue;
private int _maximum = Int32.MaxValue;

public Int32 Value
{
   get { return _value; }

   private set
   {
      if (this.Value != value)
      {
         if ((value <= this._maximum) & (value >= this._minimum))
```

Naming Standards

```
      {
          this._value = value;
          this.OnValueChanged();
      }
    }
  }
}

//Code removed for brevity
}
```

Always validate the value of a property during the setter, not in another section of the type!

If you are not validating data or throwing an event in a property, then it is okay to use auto property, but they should be used sparingly.

```
public DateTime BirthDate { get; private set; }
```

There are more property examples in The Complete Person Type appendix.

Methods

Often, developers do not know if they should create a property or a method in a class. Both have similar uses, so consider these guidelines when choosing a method.

GUIDELINES

- Calling the member twice in succession produces different results.
- Obtaining a property value using the **get** accessor would have an observable side effect.
- Only a **set** accessor would be supplied. Write-only properties tend to be confusing.
- The member is **static** but returns a value that can be changed.
- The member returns a copy of an internal array or another reference type.
- The operation is a conversion, such as **Object.ToString()**.
- The operation is expensive enough that you want to communicate to the user that they should consider caching the result.
- The order of execution is important.

EXAMPLE

```
GetCharAt()
RemoveAll()
ShowDialog()
```

Methods with return values should have a name describing the value returned.

Naming Standards

EXAMPLE

Consider a method name that is a verb or a verb phrase.

```
public static ImmutableArray<OneDriveFolder> LoadOneDriveFolders()
{
    //Code removed for brevity
}
```

Avoid methods with more than five arguments. Use structures, classes for passing multiple arguments. Always mark **public** and **protected** methods as **virtual** in a non-sealed class. Avoid explicit code exclusion of method calls (**#if**...**#endif**), instead, use conditional methods.

EXAMPLE

```
public class Save
{
    [Conditional("registered")]
    public void SaveData()
    {
        //Code removed for brevity.
    }
}
```

Avoid providing static methods that alter the static state. In common server scenarios, the static state is shared across requests, which means multiple threads can execute that code at the same time. This opens the possibility of threading bugs and data corruption. Consider using a design pattern that encapsulates data into instances that are not shared across requests.

Method Overloading

Method overloading occurs when a class contains two methods with the same name, but different signatures (different parameters or parameter types). All variants of an overloaded method shall be used for the same purpose and have similar behavior. If you must provide the ability to override a method, make only the most complete overload virtual and define the other operations in terms of it. Using the pattern below requires a derived class to only override the virtual method. Since all the other methods are implemented by calling the most complete overload, they will automatically use the new implementation provided by the derived class.

```
public void CopyFile(string sourceFileName,
                    string destinationFileName)
{
    CopyFile(sourceFileName, destinationFileName, true);
}
```

Naming Standards

```
public virtual void CopyFile(string sourceFileName,
                             string destinationFileName,
                             bool overwrite)
{
   FileSystem.CopyFile(sourceFileName, destinationFileName,
                       overwrite);
}
```

> ☑ Using method overloading is preferred to optional parameters.

Named Parameters

If it is not obvious when looking at a call to a method what the parameters mean, then use named parameters when calling a method.

```
CopyFile(@"C:\\temp\tempfile.txt", @"D:\\temp\tempfile.txt",
         overwrite:true);
```

Using proper naming standards for variable names help to avoid this in most cases.

Methods with Variable Numbers of Arguments

You might want to expose a method that takes a variable number of arguments. For managed class libraries, use **params** for this construct. For example, use the following code instead of several overloaded methods.

GUIDELINES

- If an overload takes a variable argument list, the list must be the last parameter.
- If the overload takes out parameters, by convention these should appear as the last parameters.

```
void Format(string formatString, params object [] args)
```

Using **params** is easier to the code methods with a variable number of values but you can still use just an array as shown below.

```
void Format(string formatString, object [] args)
```

I wondered if these two different ways of doing this were more performant than the others and based on my benchmark tests, they are almost the same.

Naming Standards

Performance Results

Method	Mean	Error	StdDev	Gen 0	Gen 1	Gen 2	Allocated
Array Parameter	8.092 ns	0.1225 ns	0.1146 ns	0.0035	0	0	32 B
Params Parameter	8.408 ns	0.0117 ns	0.0109 ns	0.0035	0	0	32 B

Resources

In about any program, especially larger enterprise applications, it is very important to put *all* strings such as user messages, menu text, images, and more into a resource file. No matter what your boss says, it is very likely that someday down the road they will come to you and say that the program needs to be translated into another language. Now moving all the resources at this point will be a huge task and you will kick yourself for not doing it in the beginning. There is a lot more to globalization, but here we are just going to talk about resources. Globalization of small projects can take months and larger enterprise applications will take many, many months.

> ☑ This does not apply to windows forms and controls placed on them. Instead, use the Language property to localize forms.

Guidelines

Use Pascal case for the resource keys.

- Provide descriptive rather than short identifiers (as with most naming in .NET)
- Only alphanumeric characters in naming resources.

Menu Example

```
MenusFileMenuCloseText
```

User Message Example

```
UserMessageBackupComplete
```

Putting information into resources could also speed up the performance of the assembly. The only thing that I do not put in resources is strings for use in exception messages and logging since only developers read them.

Coding Style

In this chapter, I will show the best way to do element name case, variable names, parenthesis placement, LINQ, Tuples, exceptions, performance, XML commenting for classes (very important), and much more. Using these standards is very important for any team to produce code that is easy to understand and modify in the future.

Element Name Case

Elements should *always* begin with an upper-case letter or a lower-case letter, depending on the type of element. Variable names must always begin with a lower-case letter. The following element types must always begin with an upper-case letter.

Classes	Const variables	Delegates
Enums	Events	Methods
Namespaces	Properties	Structs

<u>Do not</u> use names that require case sensitivity. Components must be fully usable from both case-sensitive and case-insensitive languages. Case-insensitive languages (such as VB.NET) cannot distinguish between two names within the same context that differ only by case. Therefore, you must avoid this situation in the components or classes that you create.

Variables

Avoid single-character variable names, such as **i** or **t**, use **index** or **temp** instead. Do not abbreviate variable words (such as **num**, instead of a **number**). Always use predefined types rather than aliases in the **System** namespace.

EXAMPLE

object instead of **Object**

string instead of **String**

int instead of **Int32**

Coding Style

Constants

Never hard-code a numeric value, always declare a constant instead. Replacing these later in case of changes is error-prone and unproductive. Let's say, your application can now handle 3540 users instead of the 427 hardcoded into your code in 50 lines scattered throughout your 25,000 line project (this is a real-world example). Instead, declare a constant variable that contains the number:

EXAMPLE

```
public class Math
{
   public const double PI = 3.14159265358979323846;
}
```

Local Variables

Private or local variables should be clear as to the value they will contain. Declare a local variable as close as possible to its first use.

EXAMPLE

```
firstName
employeeData
```

Accessing Class Members

For readability, preface all calls to class members with **this.**, and place **base.** before calls to all members of a base class. This way you know exactly where the method that is being called is from the current type or the base class.

```
class Processor
{
   public void ProcessData()
   {}
}

class AnalyticsProcessor: Processor
{
   public void AnalyzeData()
   {}

   // Correct usage of this. and base.
   public void Good()
   {
      this.AnalyzeData();
      base.ProcessData();
```

Coding Style

```
   }

   // Incorrect usage.
   public void Bad()
   {
      AnalyzeData();
      ProcessData();
   }
}
```

Objects

Check **all** reference type objects to see if they implement the **IDisposable** interfaces by looking for the **Dispose()** method. If the object has this method, call it <u>as soon as your code is done using it</u>. Calling the **Dispose()** method or the **using** statement (see below) will free up system resources and can improve performance.

EXAMPLE 1

```
using (var sourceStream = File.Open(file.FullName, FileMode.Open))
{
   if (File.Exists(newFileName))
   {
      File.Delete(newFileName);
   }

   using (var destinationStream = File.Create(newFileName))
   {
      sourceStream.CopyTo(destinationStream);
      destinationStream.Flush();
   }
}
```

EXAMPLE 2 – C# 8+

There is a newer way of using **IDisposable** types as shown below.

```
public static T Clone<T>(this object obj)
   where T : class
{
   using var stream = new MemoryStream();

   var formatter = new BinaryFormatter();

   formatter.Serialize(stream, obj);
   stream.Seek(0, SeekOrigin.Begin);
```

Coding Style

```
    return formatter.Deserialize(stream) as T;
}
```

I think it makes it easier to read using the original way of disposing of objects with the using statement, so it just comes down to style. I wondered if one is more preformat than the other. As you can see from my benchmark tests below, there is not much of a difference.

Method	Mean	Error	StdDev	Gen 0	Gen 1	Gen 2	Allocated
USING STATEMENT C#8 +	430.147 ns	0.6842 ns	0.6400 ns	0.3166	0.0014	0	2920 B
USING STATEMENT	430.663 ns	0.9368 ns	0.8763 ns	0.3161	0.0014	0	2920 B

Creating Objects Safely

There many ways of creating an in-memory object of a type. Developers typically use this way of creating an object *safely*.

```
public T CreateNormal<T>()
  where T : class
{
  var instance = Activator.CreateInstance<T>();

  if (instance is T)
  {
    return instance;
  }
  else
  {
    return null;
  }
}
```

This can also be done using a ternary expression.

```
public T CreateTernary<T>()
  where T : class
{
  var instance = Activator.CreateInstance<T>();

  return (instance is T) ? instance : null;
}
```

Another way is by using a switch statement.

```
public T CreateSwitchCase<T>()
  where T : class
{
  var instance = Activator.CreateInstance<T>();
```

Coding Style

```
    switch (instance)
    {
      case T _:
        return instance;
      default:
        return null;
    }
}
```

All three of these methods produce the same result but is one more performant over the others? As you can see from benchmarks tests, all three are close to the same speed.

Method	Mean	Error	StdDev	Gen 0	Gen 1	Gen 2	Allocated
Normal	43.255 ns	0.1238 ns	0.1033 ns	0.0129	0	0	120 B
Switch Case	40.111 ns	0.1025 ns	0.0959 ns	0.0129	0	0	120 B
Ternary	40.986 ns	0.1039 ns	0.0972 ns	0.0129	0	0	120 B

Checking an Object for an Interface

Always check the result of an **as** operation. If you use the **as** operator to obtain a certain interface reference from an object, always ensure that this operation does not return **null**. Failure to do so may cause a **NullReferenceException** at a later stage if the object did not implement that interface.

Casting

Only implement casts that operate on the complete object. In other words, do not cast one type to another using a member of the source type. For example, a **Button** class has a string property **Name**. It is valid to cast the **Button** to the **Control** (since **Button** is a **Control**), but it is not valid to cast the **Button** to a **string** by returning the value of the **Name** property.

Strings

Strings are one of the most widely used types in programming. In this section, I will discuss reducing memory and properly comparing strings for globalization.

Using StringBuilder to Reduce Memory

When building a long string, *always* use **StringBuilder**, *not* **string**. Strings are immutable, which means that when you concatenate two strings to each other, you effectively create a new string and copy the contents of the other two into it.

Coding Style

The more strings are concatenated; the more copying is performed which may result in a dramatic performance loss. This is due to strings not being removed from memory *until* there is a garbage collection.

Either create a **StringBuilder** object or use the **String.Format()** method (which uses the **StringBuilder** internally). The following example illustrates this.

EXAMPLE

The following is an example of using **StringBuilder** from one of the methods in my open-source project.

```
public static string ToDelimitedString<T>(this IEnumerable<T> list,
                                char delimiter)
{
  if (list.HasItems() == false)
  {
    throw new ArgumentNullException(nameof(list), $"{nameof(list)} 
                                is null or is empty.");
  }

  var sb = new StringBuilder();

  list.ToList().ForEach(item =>
  {
    if (sb.Length > 0)
    {
      sb.Append(delimiter.ToString(CultureInfo.CurrentCulture));
    }

    sb.Append(item.ToString());
  });

  return sb.ToString();
}
```

Let us look at the performance of **StringBuilder**. The benchmark results below compare concatenating a string (from an array) using **+=** and **StringBuilder.Append()**.

Method	Word Count	Mean	Error	StdDev	Gen 0	Gen 1	Gen 2	Allocated
+=	5	102.863 ns	0.1145 ns	0.1071 ns	0.0564	0	0	520 B
+=	10	294.827 ns	1.0264 ns	0.8013 ns	0.1998	0	0	1848 B
+=	25	1,227.410 ns	2.5736 ns	2.4074 ns	1.1196	0	0	10320 B
+=	50	4,192.439 ns	7.9328 ns	7.0322 ns	4.2725	0.0076	0	39448 B
StringBuilder	5	176.503 ns	0.4582 ns	0.4062 ns	0.078	0	0	720 B

Coding Style

Append							
StringBuilder Append	10	286.208 ns	0.8199 ns	0.7269 ns	0.1292	0	0	1200 B
StringBuilder Append	25	556.918 ns	1.0695 ns	1.0004 ns	0.2422	0	0	2232 B
StringBuilder Append	50	1,020.255 ns	1.3770 ns	1.2207 ns	0.4406	0	0	4080 B

These results show that the StringBuilder is more performant and uses less memory the more words that are combined.

Other useful methods from StringBuilder are **AppendLine()** and **AppendFormat()**. There is also **ObjectPool** that can be used with StringBuilder as shown below.

```
var objectPool = new DefaultObjectPoolProvider();
var stringBuilderPool = objectPool.CreateStringBuilderPool();

for (int arrayCount = 0; arrayCount < stringArray.Count;
arrayCount++)
{
  var sb = stringBuilderPool.Get();
  sb.AppendLine(stringArray[arrayCount]);
  stringBuilderPool.Return(sb);
}

return stringBuilderPool.ToString();
```

I wondered if there is a performance increase using **ObjectPool**. Based on my benchmark tests using you can see the overall difference is very little but using **ObjectPool** allocates a lot less memory.

Method	Word Count	Mean	Error	StdDev	Gen 0	Gen 1	Gen 2	Allocated
ObjectPool + AppendLine()	5	274.247 ns	0.2698 ns	0.2523 ns	0.0496	0	0	456 B
ObjectPool + AppendLine()	10	428.836 ns	0.4640 ns	0.3623 ns	0.0491	0	0	456 B
ObjectPool + AppendLine()	25	970.903 ns	1.3582 ns	1.1342 ns	0.0477	0	0	456 B
ObjectPool + AppendLine()	50	1,912.566 ns	5.4471 ns	5.0952 ns	0.0496	0	0	456 B
AppendLine()	5	216.356 ns	0.3189 ns	0.2827 ns	0.0794	0	0	736 B
AppendLine()	10	357.596 ns	1.0041 ns	0.8901 ns	0.1345	0	0	1240 B
AppendLine()	25	719.308 ns	1.2069 ns	1.0078 ns	0.2527	0	0	2328 B
AppendLine()	50	1,343.041 ns	2.0031 ns	1.8737 ns	0.4654	0	0	4280 B

Alternatively, you can use **String.Format()** is shown next.

Coding Style

EXAMPLE

```
string message = String.Format("The error {0} occurred at {1}.",
                               errorMessage, DateTime.Now);
```

With the latest version of .NET, you can also use string interpolation as shown below.

```
string message = $"The error {errorMessage} occurred at
{DateTime.Now}."
```

Since it's more difficult to use string interpolation with globalization/ localization, I recommend using it only with error or logging messages.

The below results are from using these methods including globalization.

Method	Mean	Error	StdDev	Gen 0	Allocated
Interpolation	549.7519 ns	0.4383 ns	0.3886 ns	0.0134	128 B
string.Format()	556.7002 ns	0.6563 ns	0.5818 ns	0.0134	128 B
string.Format() with CurrentCulture	558.7112 ns	1.4156 ns	1.2549 ns	0.0134	128 B
string.Format() with CurrentUICulture from Resources	650.2028 ns	0.8191 ns	0.7261 ns	0.0134	128 B
string.Format() from Resources)	632.6471 ns	1.9806 ns	1.8526 ns	0.0134	128 B

Comparing Strings

In Microsoft .NET there are many ways to compare strings. I would say that most of the code I analyze, I see it done one of these two ways:

```
bool result = email1 == email2;
bool result = email1.Equals(email2);
```

Is this the best way to compare strings? The quick answer is NO. While this works, it does not take into consideration localization and globalization. I have seen many developers convert the strings to lower or uppercase characters which do affect performance and might not have the results they expect. So, let us see how to properly compare strings while thinking about globalization and performance.

Here is how Wikipedia defines localization and globalization:

> In computing, internationalization and are means of adapting computer software to different languages, regional peculiarities, and technical requirements of a target locale. Internationalization is the process of designing a software application so that it can be adapted to various languages and regions without engineering changes. Localization is the process of adapting internationalized software for a

Coding Style

specific region or language by translating text and adding locale-specific components.

I would say that over 90% of the code projects that I analyze when a company hires me does not take this into account. In this global economy that we live in, this must be built into every line of code, especially dealing with strings that the user ends up seeing. Project Managers and developers who do not do this from the beginning of the project will end up costing the company a lot of money later. Changing a project to handle multiple languages and locals later will be *very* painful, costly, and delay the project for many months... even for small projects. I have been through this process many times in my career.

Let us set a baseline for performance that I will refer to later. Here is the performance when using `==` or `Equals()` to compare two strings.

Method	Mean	Error	StdDev	Gen 0	Gen 1	Gen 2	Allocated
==	4.0384 ns	0.0217 ns	0.0193 ns	0	0	0	0 B
Equals()	4.3945 ns	0.0198 ns	0.0185 ns	0	0	0	0 B

As you can see, the performance of these two ways of comparing strings is very close in performance.

string.Compare()

Using `string.Compare()` for globalization works the best when considering performance based on the benchmarking I have done. Before I show you an example, I need to show the different string comparison globalization choices that can be used.

Comparer	Description
CurrentCulture	Compare strings using culture-sensitive sort rules and the current culture.
CurrentCultureIgnoreCase	Compare strings using culture-sensitive sort rules, the current culture, and ignoring the case of the strings being compared.
InvariantCulture	Compare strings using culture-sensitive sort rules and the invariant culture.
InvariantCultureIgnoreCase	Compare strings using culture-sensitive sort rules, the invariant culture, and

Coding Style

Comparer	Description
	ignoring the case of the strings being compared.
Ordinal	Compare strings using ordinal (binary) sort rules.
OrdinalIgnoreCase	Compare strings using ordinal (binary) sort rules and ignoring the case of the strings being compared.

I would say that for most of the strings I am comparing, I use either **CurrentCultureIgnoreCase** or **IvariantCultureIgnoreCase**. Here is an example:

```
bool result = string.Compare(email1, email2,
              StringComparison.CurrentCultureIgnoreCase) == 0;
```

There are 16 overloaded methods for **string.Compare()** that makes it very flexible for a variety of comparison tasks, including sorting.

Performance

Now, let us look at the performance of **string.Compare()**. As you can see from the benchmark tests below, using **Ordinal** is close to the speed of using one of the equals shown earlier. I hope that the .NET team continues to work on performance since this type of comparison is used a lot in applications.

Method	Mean	Error	StdDev	Gen 0	Gen 1	Gen 2	Allocated
Compare(Ordinal)	3.2278 ns	0.0062 ns	0.0055 ns	0	0	0	0 B
Compare(OrdinalIgnoreCase)	6.2539 ns	0.0207 ns	0.0194 ns	0	0	0	0 B
Compare(InvariantCulture)	32.4761 ns	0.1748 ns	0.1364 ns	0	0	0	0 B
Compare(InvariantCultureIgnoreCase)	33.6297 ns	0.0121 ns	0.0101 ns	0	0	0	0 B
Compare(CurrentCultureIgnoreCase)	39.1685 ns	0.0608 ns	0.0508 ns	0	0	0	0 B
Compare(CurrentCulture)	39.4016 ns	0.0677 ns	0.0633 ns	0	0	0	0 B
Compare()	40.4257 ns	0.0458 ns	0.0429 ns	0	0	0	0 B

The takeaway from this section is even though using **Compare()** with a string comparison is less performant than one of the other methods mentioned, it is very important to code this way for globalization. I highly recommend benchmarking your code to see what works best for your project and requirements.

I have also written articles about code performance on dotNetTips.com http://bit.ly/dotNetTipsPerf and in my code performance book.

Coding Style

Arrays

Always use zero-based arrays. Always explicitly initialize an array of reference types using a **for** loop.

```
public class Person{}

Person[] people = new Person[100];

for(int index = 0; index < people.Length; index++)
{
   people[index] = new Person();
}
```

Using Array.ForEach()

Here is a tip for you. If you are doing a simple foreach against a collection like this:

```
foreach (var se in this._scheduledItems)
{
   se.Verified = false;
}
```

You can easily change it to one line using **Array.ForEach()** and a Lambda expression:

```
Array.ForEach(this._scheduledItems.ToArray(), p =>
                                        p.Verified = false);
```

Parenthesis Placement

The following parenthesis styles are common:

```
if (count > 1)
{
   count += 1;
}

if(count > 1)
{
   count += 1;
}

if ( count > 1 )
{
   count += 1;
}
```

Coding Style

```
if( count > 1 )
{
   count += 1;
}
```

The rule enforced for code is that no extra spaces should ever be placed around parenthesis, except following an **if**, **while**, **for**, **foreach**, **lock**, **catch**, **switch**, **case**, **return**, or **in** statement. For example, the following lines are correct.

```
return ((i + 2) - j);
catch (Exception ex)
while (true)
```

However, the following are *not*.

```
return ( ( i + 2 ) - j );
catch (Exception ex );
while(true )
```

> ☑ Parenthesis placement is automatically formatted in VB by its code editor. In C#, you can use **Ctrl+K**, **Ctrl+D** which will properly format the entire file.

Bracket Placement

The most diverse and emotional style decision in programming today involves the positioning of brackets. There are many bracket placement styles in use. For example:

```
if (count > 1)
{
   count += 1;
}

if (count > 1) {
   count += 1;
}

if (count > 1)
   {
   count += 1;
   }

if (count > 1) {
   count += 1;
   }
```

The positioning of brackets has a dramatic effect on the readability of code. When a developer comes across code with an unfamiliar bracket placement style, they

Coding Style

normally find it much harder to understand and maintain. For these reasons, there is a need to standardize on a uniform set of rules for bracket placement style.

Code brackets must always appear on a line by themselves, as in the first **if** statement is shown above. Secondly, any **if** statement that covers two or more lines must use brackets. This makes the following code illegal.

```
if (count > 1)
   ++count;
```

This type of code has historically been shown to cause maintainability problems down the road when an unsuspecting developer wishes to add another line to the body of the *if-statement* and unwittingly produces the following code:

```
if (count > 1)
   count += 1;
   Print("This count is {0}", count);
```

Of course, the call to **Print** is not actually within the *if-statement* and will always be executed.

If an if-statement fits all on one line, no brackets are needed. For example:

```
if (count > 1) count += 1;
```

The following, however, is illegal because the statement spans across multiple lines:

```
if (count > 1 &&
    num > 0) count += 1;
```

To write this code correctly, add brackets:

```
if (count > 1 && num > 0)
{
   count += 1;
}
```

Parameters

Use descriptive parameter names. Parameter names should be descriptive enough such that the name of the parameter and its value can be used to decide its meaning in most scenarios. Do not prefix parameter names with Hungarian type notation.

Guidelines

- Always validate arguments passed to **public**, **protected,** or explicitly implemented members.
- Do not use a Boolean unless you are sure there will never be a need for more than two values (how can you be sure?). If a Boolean must be used, then

Coding Style

consider using **TriState** (from the dotNetTips.com NuGet package) since it includes the value **UseDefault**.

- Use enumerations if a member would otherwise have two or more Boolean parameters. Enumerations add significant readability to member signatures.

CONSIDER

- If the member is security-sensitive, make a private copy of the mutable object and use the copy for validation and processing. This applies only to mutable data. Immutable data, such as **Uri** objects, does not need to be copied.
- Use a name based on the parameter's meaning rather than the parameter's type.

EXAMPLE

```
public void UpdateUser(int userId, string userName)
{
   if (userId <= 0)
   {
      throw new ArgumentOutOfRangeException(nameof(userId));
   }

   if (string.IsNullOrEmpty(username))
   {
      throw new ArgumentNullException(nameof(userName));
   }

   //Code removed for brevity
}
```

When calling a method with parameters that might not be obvious in the call, always used named parameters.

EXAMPLE

```
CopyFile(@"C:\\temp\tempfile.txt", @"D:\\temp\tempfile.txt",
         overwrite:true);
```

Using proper naming standards for variable names help to avoid this in most cases.

Passing Parameter Values

By default, in .NET, all parameters are passed by value. But there are differences in how this works depending if the value is a value type or a reference type.

Coding Style

With value types, a copy of the value is sent into the method. Therefore, if the value needs to be changed when the method returns, then use the **ref** keyword or an **out** argument.

With reference types, a copy of the location of the data in the memory heap is passed, not a copy of the data itself. Due to this adding **ref** does not do anything. If the data is changed in the method, then the caller to that method will also see the changes. The only way to not modify the data so the calling method would see it is to clone it.

Passing Parameters

Here are guidelines for passing parameters.

GUIDELINES

- Avoid using **out** or **ref** parameters.
- Do not pass reference types by reference.

Parameter Arrays

Consider adding the **params** keyword if you expect the end-users to pass a small number of elements.

GUIDELINES

- Always make sure to check the parameter array for **null** before processing it.
- Consider providing special overloads and code paths for calls with a small number of arguments in extremely performance-sensitive APIs. You should only do this if you are going to special case the entire code path, not just create an array and call the more general method.
- Consider using the **params** keyword in a simple overload, even if a more complex overload cannot use it. Only if it makes sense that the other overloads might not implement it.
- Do not use parameter arrays if the array is modified by the member taking the parameter array parameter. Instead use an array as the type for a parameter.
- Do not use parameter arrays if the caller would always already have the input in an array.

Blank Lines

This simple rule maintains that there should never be two or more blank lines in a row in any code file. This improves consistency and readability across the codebase.

Coding Style

Indentation

Maintain strict indentation. Always use tabs for indentation. You can set up how many spaces a tab occupies to your liking in Visual Studio by going to **Tools → Options → Text Editor → All Languages → Tabs**. On this screen, select the **Keep Tabs** option.

Control Flow

Do not change a loop variable inside a **for** loop block. Updating the loop variable within the loop body is considered confusing, even more so if the loop variable is modified in more than one place. Update loop variables close to where the loop condition is specified. This makes understanding the loop much easier.

All **switch/case** statements shall have a default label as the last case label. A comment such as "no action" is recommended where this is the explicit intention. If the default case should be unreachable, an assertion to this effect is recommended. If the default label is always the last one, it is easy to locate.

Use simple assignment or initialization instead of selection statements (e.g., **if**, **switch/Select Case**) whenever possible. Consider the following example.

EXAMPLE

```
public void PrintAnswer(string answer)
{
   if ("no" == answer)
   {
      Console.WriteLine("You answered with No");
   }
   else if ("yes" == answer)
   {
      Console.WriteLine("You answered with Yes");
   }
   else
   {
      // This block is required, even though you might
      // not care of any other answers than "yes"
      // and "no".
   }
}
```

Avoid multiple or conditional return statements. One entry, one exit is a sound principle and keeps control flow simple. However, in some cases, such as when preconditions are checked, it may be good practice to exit a method immediately when a certain precondition is not met.

Coding Style

Do not use selection statements (**if**, **switch**) instead of a simple assignment or initialization. Express your intentions directly. For example, rather than...

```
bool pos;

if (val > 0)
{
   pos = true;
}
else
{
   pos = false;
}
```

Or slightly better...

```
bool pos = (val > 0) ? true : false;
```

Write...

```
bool pos;
pos = (val > 0); // single assignment
```

Or even better...

```
bool pos = (val > 0); // initialization
```

Tuples

.NET now supports tuples. If you are unfamiliar with them, this is a short description.

> *Tuples are types that you define using a lightweight syntax. The advantages include a simpler syntax, rules for conversions based on the number (referred to as cardinality) and types of elements, and consistent rules for copies, equality tests, and assignments. As a tradeoff, tuples do not support some of the object-oriented idioms associated with inheritance.*

In a nutshell, methods and properties can only return a single value. If you want to return multiple values, a class or structure must be used. Tuples allow methods to return any number of variables without requiring the creation of a class or structure. In the latest versions of .NET, we can now also use named variable tuples. This should be the preferred way to use them.

EXAMPLE

Here is an example using a Tuple from my open-source project.

```
public static IEnumerable<(string FileName, string ErrorMessage)>
```

61

Coding Style

```
                DeleteFiles(this IEnumerable<string> files)
{
   Encapsulation.TryValidateParam<ArgumentNullException>(
                files != null, nameof(files));

   var errors = new List<(string FileName, string ErrorMessage)>();

   var result = Parallel.ForEach(source: files, body: (fileName) =>
   {
      try
      {
         File.Delete(fileName);
      }
      catch (Exception ex) when (ex is ArgumentException ||
            ex is ArgumentNullException ||
            ex is DirectoryNotFoundException ||
            ex is IOException ||
            ex is NotSupportedException ||
            ex is PathTooLongException ||
            ex is UnauthorizedAccessException)
      {
         errors.Add((FileName: fileName, ErrorMessage:
                        ex.GetAllMessages()));
      }
   });

   return errors.AsEnumerable();
}
```

Here is how to use this method.

```
var deletedFiles = FileHelper.DeleteFiles(files.Select(
                                    p => p.FullName));
foreach (var deletedFile in deletedFiles)
{
   Console.WriteLine($"FileName: {deletedFile.FileName},
                  Error: {deletedFile.ErrorMessage},");
}
```

As you can see, using named tuples is very easy to use and read. But do not go crazy with them. If you are needing more than 2 or 3 values in the response, then using a class or structure might be a better way to go.

LINQ

Language-Integrated Query (LINQ) is one of my favorite features in .NET. It makes writing queries so much easier, especially for XML, JSON, or object collections. Even though Visual Studio auto-formats the query statements, there is even a better way to make them more readable.

Formatting

Auto formatting for LINQ queries has gotten better in Visual Studio 2019. But I still prefer the way I started formatting these queries a while ago.

EXAMPLE

This is how Visual Studio formats LINQ statements.

```
var query = from
    p in people
            where (p.Age.TotalDays / 365) > 30 &&
            p.City == "Los Angeles"
            select new
            {
                Name = string.Format("{0} {1}", p.FirstName,
                                                p.LastName),
                Email = p.Email
            };
```

After working with LINQ ever since it came out, I have come up with the following formatting that I like better because it is easier to read:

```
var query = from
                p in people
            where
                (p.Age.TotalDays / 365) > 30 &&
                p.City == "Los Angeles"
            select new
            {
                Name = string.Format("{0} {1}", p.FirstName,
                                                p.LastName),
                Email = p.Email
            };
```

Indent on each LINQ keyword like **from**, **where,** etc., and then as it makes sense in the **select** statement. Also, put each logic operator on its own line. This is a short LINQ statement but when it gets to be a very large one this formatting makes it much easier to read.

Formatting Lambda Expressions

Visual Studio does not auto-format Lambda expressions, so I came up with my own formatting.

Coding Style

EXAMPLE

This is an example of how it looks like in Visual Studio.

```
var query = people.Where(a => (a.Age.TotalDays / 356) > 30).Where(c => c.City == "Los
  Angeles").Select(s => new { Name = string.Format("{0} {1}", s.FirstName, s.LastName), Email =
  s.Email });
```

I have come up with my way of formatting Lambda's which is a lot easier to read.

```
var query = people.Where(a => (a.Age.TotalDays / 356) > 30)
              .Where(c => c.City == "Los Angeles")
              .Select(s => new
              {
                  Name = string.Format("{0} {1}", s.FirstName,
                                                  s.LastName),
                  Email = s.Email
              });
```

This follows the same rules that I use for LINQ statements.

Object Initializers

Object initializers are a straightforward way to declare an object and set its properties at the same time. This not only makes it easier to see (if you use the style below) but there is not a need to type the variable name over and over when setting properties.

EXAMPLE

```
var options = new MessageListRequest
{
   DateSent = dateSent.Date.ToUniversalTime(),
   To = phoneNumber,
   DateSentComparison = ComparisonType.GreaterThanOrEqualTo
};
```

Exceptions

Any code that might cause an exception (accessing files, using objects like **DataSets,** etc.) should perform validation before operating on that object so an exception is not thrown. For example, call **File.Exists** to avoid a **FileNotFoundException**.

EXAMPLE

```
public void CompressFile(string sourceFileName,
                         string destinationFileName)
{
   if (File.Exists(sourceFileName))
   {
      // Code removed for brevity
   }
}
```

> ☑ Checking objects for **null** before using them will dramatically reduce exceptions!

Event handlers in Visual Studio use an "**e**" parameter for the event parameter to the call. To ensure we avoid conflict, use "**ex**" as a standard variable name for an **Exception** object.

EXAMPLE

```
catch (Exception ex)
{
   // Handle Exception
}
```

In the **catch** statement that throws an exception, always throw the original exception to maintain the stack location of the original error. i.e., do not throw a "new exception".

```
catch (Exception ex)
{
   MessageBox.Show(ex.Message);
   throw; //Same as thrown exception;
}
```

Only catch and re-throw exceptions if you want to add additional information and/or change the type of the exception into a more specific exception. In the latter case, set the **InnerException** property of the new exception to the caught exception.

Allow callers to prevent exceptions by providing a method or property that returns the object's state. For example, consider a communications layer that will throw an **InvalidOperationException** when an attempt is made to call **Send()** when no connection is available. To prevent such a situation, provide a property such as **Connected** to allow the caller to determine if a connection is available before attempting the operation.

Coding Style

Avoid error code as methods return values. Before creating custom exception objects, first check to see if there is one that could be used from the .NET Framework like **IndexOutOfRangeException**, **InvalidOperationException**, **NotSupportedException**, **ArgumentException**, **ArgumentNullException,** or **ArgumentOutOfRangeException**.

Trapping Exceptions

Ever since .NET was released, this is the normal way of coding **Exception** trapping, something very important in your code to prevent the app or service from going down.

```
try
{
    //Code that could cause an Exception
}
catch (ArgumentNullException argNullEx)
{
    return argNullEx.Message;
}
catch (ArgumentOutOfRangeException argOutOfRangeEx)
{
    return argOutOfRangeEx.Message;
}
```

The newer and easier way of trapping exceptions is by using the **When()** clause like this:

```
try
{
    //Code that could cause an Exception
}
catch (Exception ex) when (ex is ArgumentNullException ||
                           ex is ArgumentOutOfRangeException)
{
    return ex.Message;
}
```

As you can see, using the **When()** clause while trapping *similar* exceptions can decrease the amount of code needed to deal with it.

Exceptions in Reusable Assemblies

In the Application Design chapter, I state that most code (up to 90%) should be in reusable assemblies (DLL's). In these types of assemblies, the only exceptions that should be trapped in the **catch()** clause should be exceptions that you can do something with them.

Coding Style

EXAMPLE

Here is an example from my open-source logging assembly.

```
try
{
   this.AdditionalInformation.Add(new AdditionalInformationItem(
           "Process.Id", UnsafeNativeMethods.GetCurrentProcessId()
           .ToString(CultureInfo.InvariantCulture)));
}
catch (SecurityException ex)
{
   this.AdditionalInformation.Add(new AdditionalInformationItem(
           "Process.Id", string.Format(
           CultureInfo.InvariantCulture,
           Properties.Resources.IntrinsicPropertyError,
           new object[] { ex.Message })));
}
```

As you can see, I am not trapping the **Exception** type in the **catch**. Instead, if there is a **SecurityException** thrown in the **try**, which would be in the call to **GetCurrentProcessId()**, then I add to the error message to a collection.

Here is another example.

```
try
{
   adminSqlConnection.Open();
}
catch (SqlException ex)
{
   adminSqlConnection.Close();
   throw new ActivationException("Unable to get activation code.
                                  User does not have permission.",
                                  ex);
}
```

In this example, if opening a connection to SQL Server fails, then in the **catch**, I close the connection and then throw the proper exception type which is an **ActivationException**. When an **Exception**, always make sure to include the original **Exception** as the inner **Exception** (the **ex** in the code above) otherwise the stack trace will be lost which is *very* important for logging to make it easier to track down the problem.

Other things you can do in the **catch** could be cleaning up things like file handles, delete temporary files, or do a retry. If an exception is thrown that is not handled, it should be allowed to bubble up to the application layer. This is so they can be logged, notify the user, and change program flow. If you look at any of my open-

Coding Style

source assemblies, there are barely any **try/ catch** blocks because I want the calling application to handle them.

Never catch the following **Exception** types in reusable assemblies since they do not give enough information to the calling code.

- ⊗ `System.Exception`
- ⊗ `System.ApplicationException`
- ⊗ `System.SystemException`

Most of the .NET libraries from Microsoft document what exceptions that could be thrown from the call.

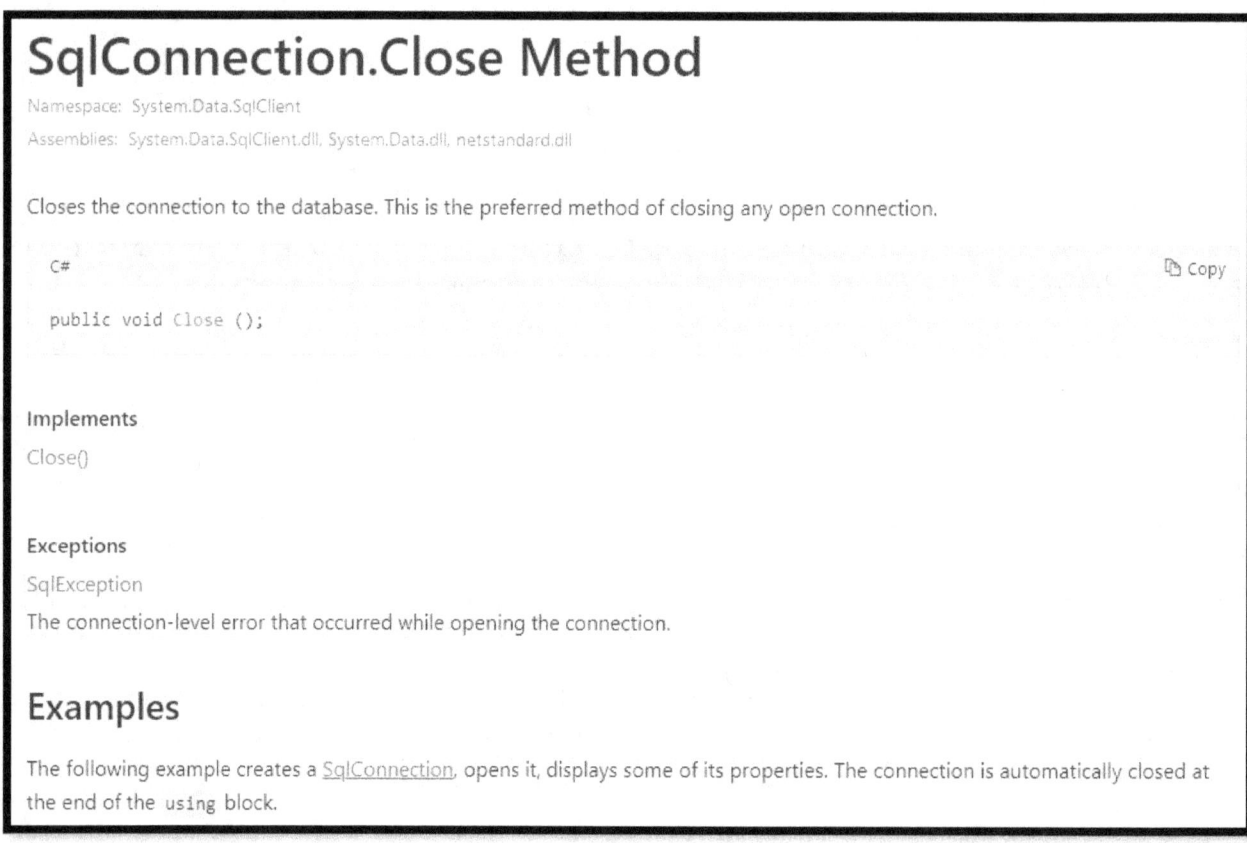

Therefore, all the code that you write must include in the XML comments for the method, what exceptions could be thrown, if any.

> ☑ **Never** log exceptions in reusable assemblies (unless the **ILogger** interface is passed in the type constructor). If you do, then you are tightly coupling it to the logging framework that you chose, which might not be the logging framework that someone else in your company uses. This is even worse if you do this in open-source assemblies.

Coding Style

Exceptions in Applications

Now, let us discuss trapping **Exceptions** in applications. Make sure to wrap any code that could cause an exception (which is about everything) with **try/ catch** blocks.

The three most important reasons are:

- ✓ Notify the user. Make sure to not use **Exception.Message**!!!
- ✓ Log the Exception (more coming up later)
- ✓ Change program flow

> ☑ **Never** use the `try/ catch` code block to validate a value!

EXAMPLE

This is an example from the code I wrote for a local university.

```
try
{
    _da.PatientVideoMissingUpdate(missingVideo);
}
catch (Exception ex)
{
    LogWriter.WriteException(ex, TraceEventType.Error, "Error
                            updating patient, missing video
                            information.");
}
```

In the code above, it is logging the exception using my open-source assembly. The last parameter of **WriteException** is the *user-friendly* message that is automatically displayed based on project type.

> ☑ In the application layer, it is okay to trap **Exception**.

Throwing Exceptions

Now, let's discuss throwing exceptions. At a contract I was working on, I received an email from one of the developers asking why I marked the code below that needs to be fixed. There are multiple throwing exception violations. Let us see if you can spot the issues. *There are other issues with this code, just stick to the issues dealing with exceptions.*

Coding Style

```
try
{
   Id = Customer.GetByName(cust, request.CustomerName).CustomerID;
}
catch (DataException ex)
{
   if (ex.Number == DataException.DataErrorEnum.NoDataFound)
   {
      throw new DataException("Customer with the specified name not
                              found.",
                (int)DataException.DataErrorEnum.NoDataFound);
   }
   else
   {
      throw ex;
   }
}
catch
{
   throw new ApplicationException("Unable to create new customer");
}
```

How many issues did you find? Let's look at the first issue on down. The first is this line of code.

```
throw new DataException("Customer with the specified name not
            found.", (int)DataException.DataErrorEnum.NoDataFound);
```

The issue with the throwing of a new **DataException** is that the original exception is not defined as the inner exception. Without doing so, the original message and stack trace is lost, which is *very* important when logging the exception in another block of code. I question their custom exception design by requiring callers of this code to know the meaning of the number that comes from the enumeration. I would have included the **enum** as a property type or just created multiple **Exception** types, one representing each number.

The second issue is in this line of code.

```
throw ex;
```

This violates Microsoft Design Guideline: (CA2200) Rethrow to preserve stack details. Rethrowing the exception, as shown above, will lose the stack trace defined in **ex**. Again, the entire stack trace is *important* when logging in the application. This code should be changed to simply this:

```
throw;
```

Coding Style

The third issue is in this line of code.

```
throw new ApplicationException("Unable to create new customer");
```

This violates Microsoft Design Guideline: (CA2201) *Do not raise reserved exception types*. The reserved exception types are the **System.Exception**, **System.ApplicationException** and **System.SystemException** because they do not give enough information to the calling code and the user. Instead, either throw a more derived type that already exists in the framework or create your type that derives from **Exception**. These three exceptions should only be used in a try/catch block in the application layer when it is unknown what exceptions might be thrown by the code being called. In the case of calling code in .NET, most are documented. A custom exception should have been used here.

Unfortunately, I found over 900 violations of this type in only 293K lines of code that I analyzed for this project. There is a lot of refactoring that needs to be done! Laziness is got a good excuse for bad code design.

Documenting Exceptions Thrown in a Method or Property

Code should *always* document the explicit exceptions a method or property can throw. Describe the recoverable exceptions by using the **<exception>** XML comment tag. Explicit exceptions are the ones that a method or property explicitly throws from its implementation and which users can catch. Exceptions thrown by .NET Framework classes and methods used by this implementation do not need to be listed here.

EXAMPLE

Here is an example from one of my open-source assemblies.

```
/// <summary>
/// Compares value to the enumeration.
/// </summary>
/// <param name="obj">The object to compare.</param>
/// <returns>System.Int32.</returns>
/// <exception cref="ArgumentNullException">Object cannot be null.
/// </exception>
public int CompareTo(object obj)
{
   if(obj is null)
   {
      throw new ArgumentNullException(nameof(obj));
   }

   return this.Value.CompareTo(((Enumeration)obj).Value);
}
```

Coding Style

> ☑ Documenting exceptions like this is *very easy* if you install the **free** GhostDoc extension for Visual Studio from Submain.com.

Custom Exceptions

If you create custom Exception types, suffix custom exception classes with **Exception**. Do not use one of the reserved exception types as the base type. Instead derive the custom exception from **Exception** (in most cases) or other types such as **ArgumentException**. Provide common constructors for custom exceptions. It is advised to provide the three common constructors that all standard exceptions provide as well. These include:

```
LoginException()
LoginException(string message)
LoginException(string message, Exception innerException)
```

Do not throw an exception from inside an exception's constructor. Throwing an exception from inside an exception's constructor will stop the construction of the exception being built, and hence, preventing the exception from being thrown. The other exception is thrown, but this can be confusing to the user of the class or method.

Logging Exceptions

It is *very* important to log *every* exception in the application layer (EXE's) which also includes:

- ✓ ASP.NET
- ✓ Azure Functions
- ✓ Azure WebJobs
- ✓ And more

This is so they can be reviewed by the development team to fix issues. If it is not logged, it cannot help to find out what went wrong. Exceptions should only be logged by the application layer, not DLL's. *Never, ever DLL's*. The simple answer to that is it would be tightly coupling a logging system to reusable assemblies.

I typically use the logging system I wrote back in the .NET 2.0 timeframe or Log4Net. Do not write your own! Microsoft .NET has been around long enough that there is no reason to write one. Make sure you pick a framework that also supports logging events such as performance information, report clicks, etc. With the latest version of .NET, you can even log from your applications (even WinForms) to Azure Application Insights which is a great feature of Azure!

Coding Style

EXAMPLE

Here is an example of trapping exceptions that I wrote for my free app for developers called dotNetTips.Dev.Utility.App.

```
private void StartServices()
{
   foreach (var service in _services.Where(p =>
            p.ServiceActionResult == ServiceActionResult.Stopped))
   {
     try
     {
       var result = Services.StartService(service.ServiceName);

       LogWriter.WriteEntry($"Restarted the {service.ServiceName}
                             service. Result:{result}",
                            TraceEventType.Information);
     }
     catch (Exception ex)
     {
       LogWriter.WriteException(ex, TraceEventType.Error, $"Error
                                with starting service
                                {service.ServiceName}.");
     }
   }
}
```

In the example above, if the call to **StartService** succeeds, then I log the event so I can easily see in the application log which services were restarted. If there was an exception, then I log it using **WriteException** where I pass in the **Exception**, event type, and the message.

This example is from an Azure Function that I wrote.

```
[FunctionName("ProcessAdClick")]
public static void Run([ServiceBusTrigger("adclicks",
           Connection = "ServiceBusQueueConnection")]
           string queueItem, ILogger log,
           [CosmosDB(databaseName: "Ads", collectionName:
           "adclicks", CreateIfNotExists = true,
           ConnectionStringSetting = "AdsDBConnection")]
           out dynamic document)
{
   log.LogInformation("Starting ProcessAdClick function at {0}.",
                      DateTime.UtcNow);

   try
   {
     if (string.IsNullOrEmpty(queueItem) == false)
```

Coding Style

```
    {
        log.LogInformation("Processing ad click {0}.", queueItem);

        document = JsonConvert.DeserializeObject<AdClickMessage>
                                            (queueItem);
    }
    else
    {
        log.LogError("Could not process item.", string.Empty);

    }
}
catch (Exception ex)
{
    log.LogError(ex, "Error processing ad click in the
                    ProcessAddClick function.");
    throw;
}
}
```

In Azure Functions, the reference to Azure Application Insights is passed in the **log** parameter. In the **else** in the **try** block, I log an error if the string coming from the Azure Queue is empty. In the **catch**, I log the exception and then throw it. The reason I am throwing the exception is so the function does not automatically remove the item from the queue, so it can be reprocessed.

> ☑ More information on logging exceptions, including global **Exception** handling, can be found in my book called *Rock Your Code: Defensive Programming for Microsoft.NET*.

XML Commenting

It is ***very important*** to use XML commenting in all your projects to document the intent of the class and its fields, properties, and methods. XML documentation headers for all public members should be kept up to date with the code. XML documentation headers will be a valid XML construct containing a summary at a minimum. Each method parameter will be included in the header, and a returns tag will be present if the member is a method that has a return value. If the header is invalid or does not match the item it describes, it will be a violation of this standard.

Use **//** for comments or **///** for XML commenting blocks. Do not use blocks of **//--------** or **//********.**

Indent comments at the same level of indentation as the code you are documenting. All comments should pass spell checking. Misspelled comments indicate sloppy development. Each file shall contain a header block. The header block should consist of the following which adheres to the required format for StyleCop.

```
// *************************************************************
// Assembly         : dotNetTips.Spargine.5.Extensions
// Author           : David McCarter
// Created          : 05-11-2020
//
// Last Modified By : David McCarter
// Last Modified On : 09-10-2020
// *************************************************************
// <copyright file="StringBuilderExtensions.cs" company="David
McCarter - dotNetTips.com">
//     McCarter Consulting (David McCarter)
// </copyright>
// <summary>StringBuilder Extensions.</summary>
// *************************************************************
```

Use XML tags for documenting types and members. All public and protected types, methods, fields, events, delegates, etc. shall be documented using XML tags. Using these tags will allow IntelliSense to provide useful details while using the types. Also, automatic documentation generation tooling relies on these tags. Section tags define the different sections within the type documentation.

> ☑ Use the (free) Visual Studio extension from Submain.com called GhostDoc that can dramatically speed up the process of doing XML documentation... if you use proper naming standards.

Section Tags

Below are the different section tags that can be used in XML commenting.

Section Tags	Description	Location
`<completionlist>`	**I cannot find any documentation on this tag.**	
`<example>`	Contains examples (code or text) related to a member or a type	Type or member
`<exception>`	Lists the exceptions that a method or property can throw	Method, Event, or Property

Coding Style

Section Tags	Description	Location
`<include>`	Let's you refer to comments in another file that describe the types and members in your source code.	
`<inheritdoc>`	Inherit XML comments from base classes, interfaces, and similar methods. This eliminates unwanted copying and pasting of duplicate XML comments and automatically keeps XML comments synchronized.	
`<list>`	Used to define the heading row of either a table or definition list. When defining a table, you only need to supply an entry for the term in the heading.	
`<overloads>`	Provides a summary for multiple overloads of a method	The first method in an overload list
`<para>`	The text of the paragraph.	
`<param>`	Describes the parameters of a method	Method
`<permission>`	Allows you to document the access of a member. The PermissionSet class lets you specify access to a member.	
`<remarks>`	Describes preconditions and other additional information.	Type or member
`<returns>`	Describes the return value of a method.	Method
`<seealso>`	Adds an entry to the See Also section	Type or member
`<summary>`	Short description.	Type or member
`<typeparam>`	Used in the comment for a generic type or method declaration to describe a type	

Coding Style

Section Tags	Description	Location
	parameter. Add a tag for each type parameter of the generic type or method.	
`<typeparamref>`	Use this tag to enable consumers of the documentation file to format the word in some distinct way, for example in italics.	
`<value>`	Describes the type of data a property accepts and/or returns	Property

Inline Tags

Inline tags can be used within the section tags.

Inline Tags	Description
`<see>`	Creates a hyperlink to another member or type.
`<paramref>`	Gives you a way to indicate that a word in the code comments, for example in a <summary> or <remarks> block refers to a parameter. The XML file can be processed to format this word in some distinct way, such as with a bold or italic font.

Markup Tags

Markup tags are used to apply special formatting to a part of a section.

Markup Tags	Description
`<code>`	Changes the indentation policy for code examples
`<c>`	Changes the font to a fixed-wide font (often used with the <code> tag)
`<para>`	Creates a new paragraph
`<list>`	Creates a bulleted list, numbered list, or a table.
`<b>`	Bold typeface
`<i>`	Italics typeface

Coding Style

EXAMPLE

```
/// <summary>
/// Creates the collection with the specified items.
/// </summary>
/// <param name="items">The items.</param>
/// <param name="ensureUnique">if set to <c>true</c> [ensure
///    unique].</param>
/// <returns>Collection&lt;T&gt;.</returns>
/// <exception cref="ArgumentNullException">Items is null or has
///    no items.</exception>
public static Collection<T> Create(IEnumerable<T> items,
                                   Tristate ensureUnique)
```

> ☑ In an inheritance hierarchy, do not repeat the documentation but use the **<see>** tag to refer to the base class or interface member.

Hungarian Naming

In C++ or VB6 (and earlier) code, it is common to use Hungarian Notation to call out the type of variables. In .NET, this is no longer necessary since Visual Studio provides this information in a tooltip, IntelliSense, and variables are always strongly typed. Instead, developers should take care to use variable names that describe the purpose of the variable, rather than its type.

EXAMPLE OF CODE USING HUNGARIAN NOTATION

```
public class Customer
{
   private int intAge;
   private string strName;
}
```

THE PROPER WAY

```
public class Customer
{
   private int _age;
   private string _firstName;
}
```

Any variable name that starts with one to three lower-case letters followed by an upper-case letter will be considered Hungarian notation and is a violation. In some cases, variable names that do not contain Hungarian notation still follow this format, however. For instance, a variable that describes the current operating system version might be named **osVersion**.

Class Design

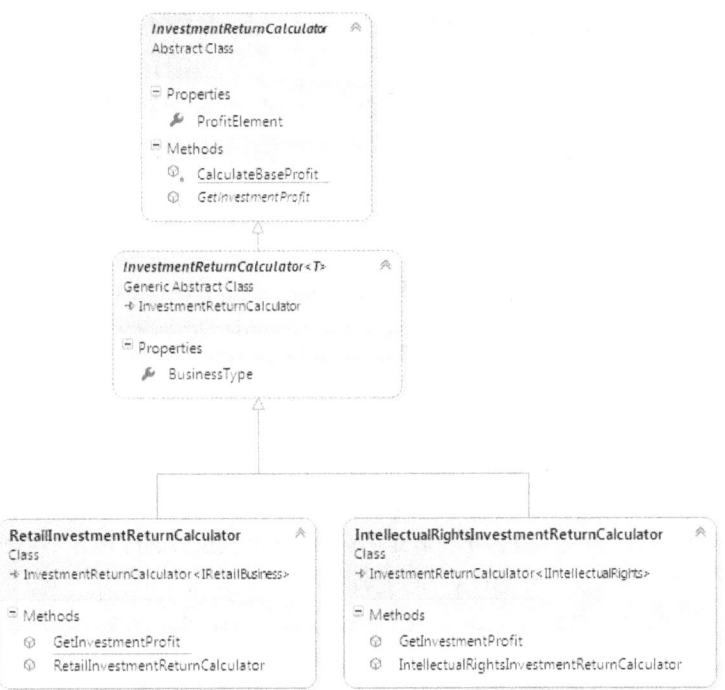

This chapter will discuss properly designing classes, starting with Object-Oriented Programming. I will also discuss proper model class design, methods to overload, serialization, abstract classes, and more.

Object-Oriented Programming

Before I get into the code for this chapter, I want to stop and talk about Object-Oriented Programming (OOP). OOP was invented back in the late 1950s. First, let us look at the definition of OOP from Wikipedia.

> *Object-oriented programming (OOP) is a programming paradigm based on the concept of "objects", which can contain data, in the form of fields (often known as attributes), and code, in the form of procedures (often known as methods). A feature of objects is an object's procedures that can access and often modify the data fields of the object with which they are associated (objects have a notion of "this" or "self"). In OOP, computer programs are designed by making them out of objects that interact with one another. OOP languages are diverse, but the most popular ones are class-based, meaning that objects are instances of classes, which also determine their types.*

For most of my career, I have been using OOP when I write any type of application. In *my* experience, OOP produces more stable code and applications. In many of the projects I see fail, one of the main reasons when it comes to the code is the lack of OOP or implemented improperly.

OOP is the single most design principle that you need to know to implement in your projects. I have interviewed many software engineers straight out of a computer science degree that cannot explain OOP. Heck, even beginner, intermediate, and even senior developers have a hard time explaining it.

There are three main pillars of OOP and they are *encapsulation, inheritance,* and *polymorphism*.

Class Design

1. **Encapsulation**: If a class disallows calling code from accessing internal object data and forces access through methods only, this is a strong form of abstraction or information hiding known as encapsulation.
2. **Inheritance**: Allows classes to be arranged in a hierarchy that represents "is-a-type-of" relationships. This allows a class to "inherit" functionality from another class.
3. **Polymorphism**: This is when calling code can be agnostic as to whether an object belongs to a parent class or one of its descendants.

In this chapter, I will focus mostly on encapsulation since most of the code I analyze does not get this correct. When I speak at conferences, I ask how many programmers practice OOP, usually, most hands go up. After I talk about the proper way to do encapsulation, almost all those hands go down. My feeling is that if there is not even proper encapsulation in the code, I have little faith that inheritance or polymorphism will be done properly. Does your team practice proper OOP? If you answered yes, I will ask again at the end of this chapter.

This is not an OOP book, so if you are new to it or need to brush up on it, go to https://en.wikipedia.org/wiki/Object-oriented_programming

Encapsulation – The First Pillar of OOP

Encapsulation is the first pillar of OOP. Wikipedia defines it as:

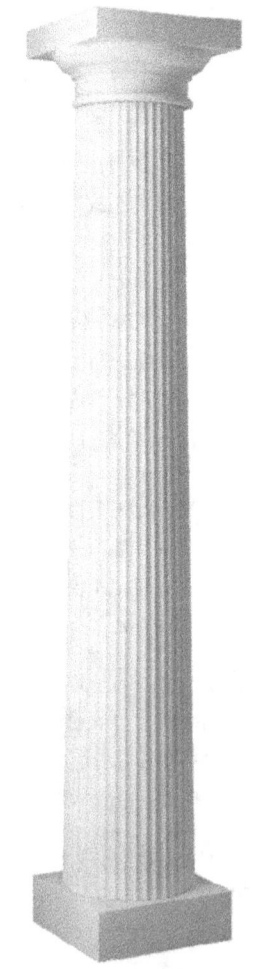

> *Encapsulation is an object-oriented programming concept that binds together the data and functions that manipulate the data, and that keeps both safe from outside interference and misuse. Data encapsulation led to the important OOP concept of <u>data hiding</u>.*
>
> *If a class does not allow calling code to access internal object data and permits access through methods only, this is a strong form of abstraction or information hiding known as encapsulation. Some languages (Java, for example) let classes enforce access restrictions explicitly, for example denoting internal data with the private keyword and designating methods intended for use by code outside the class with the public keyword. Encapsulation prevents external code from being concerned with the internal workings of an object. This facilitates code refactoring, for example allowing the author of the class to change how objects of that class represent their data internally without changing any external. It also encourages programmers to put all the code that is concerned with a certain set of data in the same class, which organizes it for easy comprehension by*

Class Design

other programmers. Encapsulation is a technique that encourages decoupling.

The two words from their definition I would like to highlight is "Data Hiding". Any code that calls the class should <u>only</u> be able to get to the data it *encapsulates* via methods and properties. Also, all data coming into the class should be validated before continuing to the processing code. This is VERY important... bad data in, bad data out. If that bad data makes it to the database, then it is *very* tough to fix and *very* costly.

Poor Class Design

I have many examples of poor class design, but the worse one that I can remember is the one below that I still use in conference sessions from a *real* in-production project. This is what it looks like.

```
public class OrderData
{
    public string ORDER;
    private string facilityID = "";
    public string OrderNumber = "";
    public string openClosed = "";
    public string transType = "";
    public string dateOpened = "";
    public string dateClosed = "";
    public string dateShop = "";
    public OrderData(string _ORDER)
    {
        this.ORDER = _ORDER;
    }

    //Remainder of code removed for brevity
}
```

This code, from a real in-production project, had <u>198 public string fields</u> (no other data types) and NO properties (the best way to validate data other than methods). Also, every time data was sent into this type, over 300 exceptions were thrown... I wonder why? Let us go over the main issues.

1. All the data for the class was held in those 198 *public* fields. This completely breaks encapsulation, the first pillar of any OOP class design (discussed below).
2. All the fields are strings! The proper type for the data should always be used like **DateTimeOffset**, **Integer**, etc.
3. Poor coding standards. The standard even changes from field to field!
4. No documentation.

Number 1 & 2, of course, are the most important, but so are the other two.

Class Design

Data Hiding

By practicing good OOP design, it is *your* job as the developer to properly implement encapsulation, which is all about data hiding. The only way that code outside of the class or type can get or set the data is to go through methods and properties. For the rest of this chapter, I will be using an example type called **Person** (as seen below) and you will see how it changes as we go along.

```
public class Person
{
    public DateTime BornOn { get; set; }
    public string Address1 { get; set; }
    public string Address2 { get; set; }
    public string CellPhone { get; set; }
    public string City { get; set; }
    public string Country { get; set; }
    public string Email { get; set; }
    public string FirstName { get; set; }
    public string HomePhone { get; set; }
    public string Id { get; set; }
    public string LastName { get; set; }
    public string PostalCode { get; set; }
}
```

This example class closely follows the way that I see how over 90% of model classes being designed. But this *still* is not proper OOP design since there is not any data validation. The whole purpose of encapsulation is not only hiding the data but making sure it is correct in the first place! Never allow bad data into the class, <u>ever</u>!

Unless your model classes will take any length of string, or incorrect dates, incorrect number values, etc. (and I am sure they should not do this), then you need to validate the data! *Never* rely on the database to validate your data since that would be a big performance issue. Also, new document-based databases like Cosmos DB do not have typed columns, so there is not a way to do it unless you want to write a lot of back-end scripts.

Validating the Data

Unless your code does not care about the value of the data (for example I will not do this for Boolean values), then the first lines of any public or protected property and method *must* validate the data. Here is how I would write the **Address1** property in **Person**.

Class Design

```
public string Address1
{
    get
    {
        return this._address1;
    }
    set
    {
        // 1.Validate that the current & new value aren't the same.
        if (this._address1 == value)
        {
            return;
        }

        // 2. Validate that value isn't null
        if (string.IsNullOrEmpty(value))
        {
            throw new ArgumentNullException(nameof(Address1),
                "Value for Address1 cannot be null or empty.");
        }

        // 3. Validate that the value is within range
        if (value.Length < 10 || value.Length > 256)
        {
            throw new ArgumentOutOfRangeException(nameof(Address1),
                "Address must be between 10 - 256 characters.");
        }

        this._address1 = value;
    }
}
```

Let us go through the validation and why it is important.

1. The first validation is to make sure that the new value is different from the current value. Why set the same value twice? This can be a performance issue. Also, many model classes used in apps, throw change events when data is modified, so this is very important for those types of classes.

2. Validate that we have a string! As you should know, a null value in a string can crash the application if code in the class calls a **String** method like **Length**. This is to make sure the string is not null or is empty.

3. Finally, is the length of the string itself. Most databases set the string length, so you need to mimic this in the code before it gets to the database. This is even important for databases like Cosmos DB since each document has a maximum size limit. Sending any string length could cause an error.

Of course, your validation for #3 will be different based on business rules. If you follow what I wrote in my Reuse, Reuse and More Code Reuse! article on

Class Design

dotNetTips.com, these model classes should always but put in a reusable assembly (away from the database context) so they can be used by any layer of your application. That way any code that uses it will have the same validation... no code duplication!

Encapsulating Business Logic in Class Properties

I will explain how I recently helped one of the other junior developers on the team I work in and ended up teaching my entire team about the *proper* way to implement encapsulation in class properties.

Implementing New Business Rules

When the team member contacted me, he showed me a class like the one below.

```
public class PropertyDemo
{
    public string BillingStartDate { get; set; }
    public string EventDate { get; set; }
}
```

The new business rule he was told to implement was that if **BillingStartDate** is greater than the **EventDate**, then the **EventDate** should be set with the **BillingStartDate** value. I gave him advice and said that the check should be done in the property setter. After a few days, he showed me the modifications like the example below.

```
public class PropertyDemo
{
    public string BillingStartDate { get; set; }
    private string _eventDate;
    public string EventDate
    {
        get
        {
            if (DateTime.Parse(BillingStartDate) >
                DateTime.Parse(_eventDate))
            {
                return BillingStartDate;
            }
            else
            {
                return _eventDate;
            }
        }
        set
        {
            _eventDate = value;
        }
```

Class Design

```
    }
}
```

While this solves the new business rule, it's *not* implementing encapsulation the way I would implement it. Let me explain why.

Encapsulating Properties

Since encapsulation is the first pillar of OOP, my #1 rule for encapsulation states:

All data coming into a class (type) MUST be validated!

This goes back to the old saying "*Bad data in, bad data out*". This is especially true for databases, and as developers, we need to make sure that does not happen. The place to implement rules like this one is to encapsulate that logic in the class and for properties, in the setter. Also, it makes better sense when thinking about performance, to determine if **EventDate** should be set to **BillingStartDate** once in the setter, not every time the getter is called.

When I told my teammate this, he said that it would only happen once due to deserializing the data from JSON. While that could be true *now*, this might not be valid in the *future*. I told him, when designing classes, you cannot count on what order the properties would be set and there is no guarantee that there is even a value in **BillingStartDate**. The .NET Framework did have a way to do this easier with Code Contracts, but unfortunately, the Visual Studio team has abandoned that project, with no replacement. I hope they bring it back in the future (I have submitted a ticket to Microsoft to try to get this done).

My teammate said he was told to put the logic in the property getter. Unfortunately, I had a hard time explaining why I do not prefer this to my team… until I showed them the code that I re-worked and explained it.

Fixing the EventDate Property

Fixing the **EventDate** property includes a few things with the first one validating the data in the property setter.

1. Make sure the data encapsulated in the type is always valid, so I will move the logic into the setter.
2. Using **DateTime.Parse** will cause an exception if the date string is not formatted correctly. This is very important since the type of these properties is a string. If it were my project, these properties would use **DateTimeOffset**.
3. This change will force a change in the **BillingStartDate** property that I will discuss in the next section.

This is how I ended up changing this property:

Class Design

```csharp
public string EventDate
{
    get
    {
        return _eventDate;
    }
    set
    {
        if (_eventDate == value)
        {
            return;
        }

        //If we have a valid event date
        if (DateTime.TryParse(value,
                            CultureInfo.CurrentCulture,
                            DateTimeStyles.None,
                            out DateTime eventDate))
        {
            _eventDate = value;

            // If we have a valid billing start date
            if (DateTime.TryParse(BillingStartDate,
                            CultureInfo.CurrentCulture,
                            DateTimeStyles.None,
                            out DateTime billingStartDate))
            {
                //Set event date to billing start date if greater
                if (billingStartDate > eventDate)
                {
                    _eventDate = BillingStartDate;
                }
            }
        }
        else
        {
            throw new ArgumentNullException(nameof(value),
                                        "Invalid event date.");
        }
    }
}
```

As you can see, I am using **DateTime.TryParse** since it does not throw an exception if the string is an invalid date. I even included globalization settings to make sure that this property will work "if" the project is needed to work properly with different languages in the future. Also, I only allow the logic if **BillingStartDate** is greater than **EventDate** if there is a valid date. If this were my project, I would encapsulate most of the code in the setter in a private method. Also, after working on this, I have added a new extension method for **DateTime** called **Max** in my open-source NuGet package. But we are not done.

Fixing the BillingStartDate Property

Now that we moved the logic to the setter in **EventDate**, what if **BillingStartDate** changes after the **EventDate** is set? Well, we need to write some logic around that too. Here is the new property code.

```
public string BillingStartDate
{
    get
    {
        return this._billingStartDate;
    }
    set
    {
        if (this._billingStartDate == value)
        {
            return;
        }

        //Validate that the billing start date is valid.
        if (DateTime.TryParse(value,
                              out DateTime billingStartDate))
        {
            this._billingStartDate = value;

            //Set Event date if billing start date is greater than
            //event date
            if (DateTime.TryParse(this.EventDate,
                                  out DateTime eventDate))
            {
                if (billingStartDate > eventDate)
                {
                    this._eventDate = value;
                }
            }
        }
        else
        {
            throw new ArgumentNullException(nameof(value),
                          "Invalid billing start date.");
        }
    }
}
```

Class Design

As you can see, I implemented similar logic in this property as in the **EventDate** property. This is the *proper way to implement encapsulation*! Well, at least it is correct for me.

As you can see, we added a lot more code to the properties that will make sure that not only the business logic is encapsulated in the property, but it also ensures that the properties only store proper dates in the backing fields.

If you are new to encapsulation or need to learn how to do it better, I hope this has helped. I also write about this subject a lot on this website.

Constructors

All classes in .NET require a constructor so that they can be created. When a class is created using Visual Studio, it does not automatically add an empty constructor. If you do not implement one, then the compiler will add an empty constructor for you during the build process. This is referred to as the "magic constructor" since it is magically added for you. If you want to use a constructor to set data, then that can be done like this.

```
public Person(string id, string email)
{
   this.Id = id;
   this.Email = email;
}
```

My rule for constructors is that the data set in the parameters are *required* for the type to work properly. For **Person**, I am making **Id** and **Email** required. I also use this for other types of classes such as data context classes where the connection string is required.

I would like to point out that I am using the properties to set the data, not directly setting the private fields. This way the data set in the constructor goes through the same validation as outside code setting the properties.

When you create a constructor like this, the compiler will not add the "magic constructor" anymore. The empty constructor is *required* for serialization. You need to add it yourself like this, especially if it is a model class.

```
public Person()
{}
```

If this empty constructor is not added, then deserialization for the type will not work. I never add constructors to make it easy for someone to set data. Since we now have object initialization in .NET, there is not a reason to. Here is an example of how to use it.

Class Design

```
var person = new Person("ASODIDADLVOD109A", "dotnetdave@live.com")
{
   FirstName = "David",
   LastName = "McCarter"
};
```

When I design types (usually models) like this, I want to require users of the type to send in the email address and id and not use the empty constructor. There is a way to hide from IntelliSense the empty constructor like this.

```
[EditorBrowsable(EditorBrowsableState.Never)]
public Person()
{}
```

Using the **EditorBrowsable** attribute will hide the constructor, or any other method, from types outside of the assembly that the model is located in.

Implement IComparable & IComparable<T> Interfaces

By default, when objects are compared in .NET, reflection is used, which can affect the performance of that type. To make the ordering of objects better in a collection, it is recommended to implement the **IComparable** and **IComparable<T>** interfaces.

Microsoft documentation states the following about this interface:

> *Defines a generalized comparison method that a value type or class implements to create a type-specific comparison method for ordering or sorting its instances.*

The definition of **Person** now looks like this.

```
public class PersonProper : IComparable, IComparable<PersonProper>
```

For **PersonProper**, I am implementing the two methods from the interfaces like this.

```
public int CompareTo(object obj)
{
   if (obj == null)
   {
      return 1;
   }

   var other = obj as Person;

   if (other == null)
   {
      throw new ArgumentException(nameof(obj) + " is not a " +
                                  nameof(Person));
```

Class Design

```
   }

   return CompareTo(other);
}

public int CompareTo(Person other)
{
   if (other == null)
   {
      return 1;
   }

   int result = 0;
   result = _email.CompareTo(other._email);

   if (result != 0)
   {
      return result;
   }

   return result;
}
```

As you can see in the second **CompareTo()** method, I am only showing comparing the email address. All the properties are compared in the actual class shown in Appendix E.

Performance Increase

Implementing these two interfaces *can* increase performance when sorting a collection of that type. In the chart below, the performance is benchmarked by comparing a **Person** class without these interfaces against the **PersonProper** class that implements these interfaces.

Method	Count	Mean	Error	StdDev	Median	Gen 0	Gen 1	Gen 2	Allocated
OrderBy() - Person	50	12,469.0 ns	175.68 ns	146.70 ns	12,538.9 ns	0.1831	0	0	1736 B
OrderBy() - Person	100	34,774.8 ns	33.35 ns	29.57 ns	34,765.2 ns	0.3052	0	0	3136 B
OrderBy() - Person	250	96,503.6 ns	296.52 ns	247.61 ns	96,471.3 ns	0.7324	0	0	7336 B
OrderBy() - Person	500	229,654.5 ns	4,459.37 ns	3,723.78 ns	231,550.3 ns	1.4648	0	0	14336 B
OrderBy() - Person	1000	489,974.1 ns	4,491.46 ns	3,750.57 ns	490,113.2 ns	1.9531	0	0	28336 B
OrderBy() - Person	2000	1,225,011.6 ns	2,503.65 ns	2,090.66 ns	1,224,739.1 ns	0	0	0	56336 B
OrderBy() - Person	3000	1,810,249.0 ns	3,579.48 ns	2,989.03 ns	1,810,613.3 ns	0	0	0	84312 B
OrderBy() - PersonProper	50	14,538.8 ns	97.07 ns	86.05 ns	14,556.2 ns	0.1831	0	0	1736 B

Class Design

OrderBy() - PersonProper	100	29,474.9 ns	39.59 ns	37.03 ns	29,480.0 ns	0.3357	0	0	3136 B
OrderBy() - PersonProper	250	94,679.1 ns	231.86 ns	205.54 ns	94,597.5 ns	0.7324	0	0	7336 B
OrderBy() - PersonProper	500	232,407.6 ns	262.48 ns	219.18 ns	232,468.1 ns	1.4648	0	0	14336 B
OrderBy() - PersonProper	1000	356,922.2 ns	202.50 ns	179.51 ns	356,900.8 ns	2.9297	0	0	28336 B
OrderBy() - PersonProper	2000	1,217,037.0 ns	3,028.12 ns	2,832.50 ns	1,215,789.8 ns	0	0	0	56336 B
OrderBy() - PersonProper	3000	1,298,486.7 ns	19,858.14 ns	18,575.32 ns	1,307,963.5 ns	0	0	0	84312 B

As you can see, implanting these two interfaces can increase performance, so why not implement them as a regular practice?

> ☑ Without implementing these two interfaces, calling **Sort()** on a collection will cause an error!

Overloading GetHashCode()

Overloading the **GetHashCode()** method, could be a performance increase and you can choose what data will be used to create the hash code. Here is how I did it for **Person**.

```
public override int GetHashCode()
{
    HashCode.Combine(Email, Id);
}
```

As you can see, I am only using the data for the email address and id for the hash code. Overriding **GetHashCode()** is simple when using refactoring tools.

Making Classes Easier to Debug

Next, I will show you how to make your type easier to use when debugging. Here is why; let us say I have a collection of **Person** and I want to look at its values. Below is the default experience in Visual Studio.

```
var collection = people;
              Count   ● people Count = 5
                   ● [0]    {dotNetTips.OOP.Design.Models.Article2.Person}
                 ▷ ● [1]    {dotNetTips.OOP.Design.Models.Article2.Person}
                 ▷ ● [2]    {dotNetTips.OOP.Design.Models.Article2.Person}
                 ▷ ● [3]    {dotNetTips.OOP.Design.Models.Article2.Person}
                 ▷ ● [4]    {dotNetTips.OOP.Design.Models.Article2.Person}
                 ▷ ● Raw View
```

Class Design

As you can see, by default, it shows the full type name. Not very useful is it? Well, there is a new attribute called **DebuggerDisplay** that you can use to fix this.

```
[DebuggerDisplay("{Email}")]
public class Person : IComparable, IComparable<Person>
```

Using **DebuggerDisplay**, I can set what properties will be used for the display while debugging.

```
var collection = people;
              Count   people Count = 5
                      [0]    "DOTNETDAVE@LIVE.COM"
                      [1]    "DSMITH@LIVE.COM"
                      [2]    "DJONES@LIVE.COM"
                      [3]    "KCARPENDER@LIVE.COM"
                      [4]    "SSMITH@LIVE.COM"
                      Raw View
```

As you can see, this is much more useful and anyone using this type will thank you!

Override ToString()

While you are at it, you should override **ToString()**. As with debugging, **ToString()** will just return the type name that is not very useful. Here is how I did it for **Person**.

```
public override string ToString()
{
    return $"{Id} - {Email}";
}
```

The result from calling **ToString()** would look like this:

"3f1640265c844b908bcc31028ae3f238 - dotNetDave@live.com"

Class Design

Serialization

Serialization is something important to think about for good model class design, even though it is not part of OOP. If you implement what I discuss, other developers using these models will appreciate the little bit of extra work.

> *In computer science, in the context of data storage, serialization is the process of translating data structures or object state into a format that can be stored (for example, in a file or memory buffer) or transmitted (for example, across a network connection link) and reconstructed later (in a different computer environment).*
>
> *It goes on to add this for OOP: Serialization of object-oriented objects does not include any of their associated methods with which they were previously linked. Wikipedia*

Since this section focuses on model classes, the Wikipedia definition fits well since these types of objects need to be serialized to be sent via web-based APIs, ASP.NET view models, and even for document databases like Cosmos DB since its internal storage is JavaScript Object Notation (JSON). I even serialize configuration objects to and from disk for apps that I write to store app and user data.

Let us improve `Person.cs` to include what it needs to properly serialize to and from JSON and XML.

Serializing to JSON

I would say that the way most objects these days that get serialized would be using JSON. I would also say, that with over 266 million downloads, the Newtonsoft.JSON NuGet package is the most popular library to do JSON serialization.

Using this package, it only takes one line of code like this.

```
var json = JsonConvert.SerializeObject(people);
var people = JsonConvert.DeserializeObject<List<Person>>(json);
```

If we serialize a `List<Person>` with two items (with fake data), this is what it looks like in JSON.

Class Design

```
[
  {
    "Address1": "yJuDoux_HGTsXod",
    "Address2": "qAUPPFylqn",
    "BornOn": "2005-12-14T12:55:24.2371442-08:00",
    "CellPhone": "681-064-3138",
    "City": "COgx^xpxdFMhFup",
    "Country": "OjpX\\AXEPDCl[[e",
    "Email": "cskccwnrg@cr.es",
    "FirstName": "ukEpbcSWkRPAHka",
    "HomePhone": "072-236-5678",
    "Id": "06ba87e0e0cc4a51a8dc00c827ad401a",
    "LastName": "eKXt\\MU]xJ[dPTNuSFGL",
    "PostalCode": "82268"
  },
  {
    "Address1": "Ft^JaGY^vA]W\\df",
    "Address2": "xUqiuNjH[D",
    "BornOn": "2005-12-14T12:55:24.2423257-08:00",
    "CellPhone": "733-337-0770",
    "City": "Q\\Gla`j_M`^sW_s",
    "Country": "bbLaBUmDFlgBF_K",
    "Email": "mfbwia@vxkwm.org.uk",
    "FirstName": "\\`ecV]OEHU]Ktu`",
    "HomePhone": "807-472-7275",
    "Id": "a34f3777518e49e2acd62775e5503621",
    "LastName": "^YAAt_dyBDxNnJWS]DM^",
    "PostalCode": "17147"
  }
]
```

Fixing JSON Formatting

One thing we need to do is to fix the JSON property name casing since it is not compliant with JSON coding standards. In the OOP world, properties start with an uppercase (PascalCasing) and in the JSON world, they should start with a lower case (camelCasing). It is easy enough to do with attributes.

First, we need to add the **DataContract** attribute to the class like this:

```
[DataContract(Name = "person")]
public class Person : IEquatable<Person>, IComparable,
                     IComparable<Person>
```

Then we need to add the **DataMember** attribute to all the properties we want to serialize like this:

```
[DataMember(Name = "address1")]
public string Address1
```

Class Design

I would like to point out that you can use these two attributes to change horribly named data properties from API endpoints from companies like Salesforce to proper OOP naming. Here is an example:

```
[DataMember(Name = "Total_Units_Sold__c")]
public double UnitsSold
```

Making a property required is also easy too:

```
[DataMember(Name = "email", IsRequired = true)]
public string Email
```

Now, with these attributes, the JSON looks like this:

```
[
  {
    "address1": "gVpEAP_pLyRmnYY",
    "address2": "k\\^sqrx\\Dp",
    "bornOn": "2005-12-14T12:52:08.6788613-08:00",
    "cellPhone": "887-720-6030",
    "city": "HCHNugsfZcnknZc",
    "country": "\\slC[htlOFRfCws",
    "firstName": "`hWWQiTQxKxSB[B",
    "homePhone": "113-161-8082",
    "lastName": "NQrHdAqhaDGTWJtHbnr\\",
    "postalCode": "37228",
    "id": "3f1640265c844b908bcc31028ae3f238",
    "email": "rvlwon@wjykqw.net"
  },
  {
    "address1": "mOPddKKZxTyeL\\l",
    "address2": "x^t][sSF\\f",
    "bornOn": "2005-12-14T12:52:08.6852134-08:00",
    "cellPhone": "346-363-7213",
    "city": "ybaCU[AFiYqwrWJ",
    "country": "G`uYv[InxKk\\FNu",
    "firstName": "FREHmWwrHArMWCo",
    "homePhone": "452-157-8818",
    "lastName": "pmcqdytqnT_sjdmJgmYD",
    "postalCode": "26616",
    "id": "81b195b94cb14ee0bf91716cfc3c4b6e",
    "email": "gveq@qlbbkmdiedplkw.ly"
  }
]
```

Serializing to XML

So that you do not leave out applications that still use XML as their format (which there are a lot and will continue to be for a long time), for now, you should make

Class Design

sure that your model classes support it. Here is the code to serialize and deserialize XML (available in my dotNetTips.Utility.Standard NuGet package).

```
public static string Serialize(object obj)
{
   using (var writer = new StringWriter())
   {
      using (var xmlWriter = XmlWriter.Create(writer))
      {
         var serializer = new XmlSerializer(obj.GetType());
         serializer.Serialize(xmlWriter, obj);
         return writer.ToString();
      }
   }
}

public static T Deserialize<T>(string xml)
{
   using (var sr = new StringReader(xml))
   {
      var xs = new XmlSerializer(typeof(T));
      return (T)xs.Deserialize(sr);
   }
}
```

If we serialize a **List<Person>** to XML, it will look like this:

```
<?xml version="1.0" encoding="utf-16"?>
<ArrayOfPerson xmlns:xsi="http://www.w3.org/2001/XMLSchema-instance" xmlns:xsd="http://www.w3.org/2001/XMLSchema">
  <Person>
    <Address1>B[adUUt^r]SrhRq</Address1>
    <Address2>qkbll`gUk[</Address2>
    <BornOn />
    <CellPhone>468-244-4428</CellPhone>
    <City>KIqLScmLgZegq]O</City>
    <Country>PTsLiTFoJoevOWy</Country>
    <Email>jmkekoaq@lormhbesmjdicaxqy.org.uk</Email>
    <FirstName>lWVSgitVYI1\hRo</FirstName>
    <HomePhone>774-811-5255</HomePhone>
    <Id>a5938cd190ee4c49a532bbe83644744f</Id>
    <LastName>EThWhg_nggOQ^o`VwZCv</LastName>
    <PostalCode>73438</PostalCode>
  </Person>
  <Person>
    <Address1>Qcr`H^pMJJwiaiK</Address1>
    <Address2>WqlWXqoVbt</Address2>
    <BornOn />
    <CellPhone>708-847-5728</CellPhone>
```

Class Design

```
        <City>EIFZC^YPfP\gwcP</City>
        <Country>ybC^T[MPfOXuQeS</Country>
        <Email>mgfucctrpjeysmfraqo@iqlufffqtqvikx.org</Email>
        <FirstName>VtPlFOlSUtX_jRX</FirstName>
        <HomePhone>112-642-4284</HomePhone>
        <Id>16738e0a16e34469bf80f2c43bb527d2</Id>
        <LastName>rrYKdbIdSsaWL^ANPgcu</LastName>
        <PostalCode>84820</PostalCode>
    </Person>
</ArrayOfPerson>
```

Houston, We Have A Problem

As you can easily see in the XML, the value for the **BornOn** property is missing. This is because the serializer in .NET does not support the **DateTimeOffset** type. I guess the .NET team never went back and fixed this issue when it was added, but we can!

Before we get to that fix, let us start with adding the **Serializable** and **XmlRoot** attributes to the class.

```
[Serializable]
[XmlRoot(ElementName = "Person")]
public class Person : IEquatable<Person>, IComparable,
                      IComparable<Person>
```

There are a few ways to fix this missing **BornOn** value. We are going to implement it quickly by adding a new property like this:

```
[EditorBrowsable(EditorBrowsableState.Never)]
[IgnoreDataMember]
[XmlElement("BornOn")]
public string BornOnForXml
{
   Get
   {
      return BornOn.ToString("o");
   }
   Set
   {
      BornOn = DateTimeOffset.Parse(value);
   }
}
```

I added the **EditorBrowsable** attribute to hide this property from other assemblies. Then I added the **IgnoreDataMember** so the JSON serialization will ignore this

Class Design

property. Then I added the **XmlElement** attribute to use **BornOn** as the element name in XML. I also added **XmlElement** to the rest of the properties.

Then we need to hide the **BornOn** property from XML serialization like this:

```
[XmlIgnore]
public DateTimeOffset BornOn
```

You can also use the **XmlElement** attribute to make the property required.

```
[XmlElement(IsNullable = false)]
public string Id
```

The final XML looks like this:

```
<?xml version="1.0" encoding="utf-16"?>
<ArrayOfPerson xmlns:xsi="http://www.w3.org/2001/XMLSchema-
instance" xmlns:xsd="http://www.w3.org/2001/XMLSchema">
  <Person>
    <Address1>fSrGUNBGo`G[xiT</Address1>
    <Address2>YbTErOSHxE</Address2>
    <BornOn>2005-12-14T14:42:35.5808138-08:00</BornOn>
    <CellPhone>257-531-5721</CellPhone>
    <City>Is^y[yW\Hv[FApm</City>
    <Country>HETrESKsBEaL_WW</Country>
    <Email>vlspiramhqbxbr@fskkr.net</Email>
    <FirstName>Zgk^K`EUdsqqACd</FirstName>
    <HomePhone>158-720-2817</HomePhone>
    <Id>d3580c8684884098ac1bc656a87190a8</Id>
    <LastName>xy\utmrEj\nU\eNDijyM</LastName>
    <PostalCode>41738</PostalCode>
  </Person>
  <Person>
    <Address1>TDloXg\PAsNjsPb</Address1>
    <Address2>EjsJsx`ngQ</Address2>
    <BornOn>2005-12-14T14:42:35.5873074-08:00</BornOn>
    <CellPhone>334-364-7782</CellPhone>
    <City>lDVuskEaDhfus\u</City>
    <Country>OgxEXnOF^yPxpPT</Country>
    <Email>fscidsoqfnolscythouuei@fioxxjtdbayndy.us</Email>
    <FirstName>WvxCpBUwPIsxjxe</FirstName>
    <HomePhone>440-447-7643</HomePhone>
    <Id>525f843089a740cb8ab15888add465fe</Id>
    <LastName>]xquclOQiQivqftttjiv^</LastName>
    <PostalCode>74074</PostalCode>
  </Person>
</ArrayOfPerson>
```

One more thing, the XML serializer will try to serialize the private fields in the class, so we need to tell it to ignore them like this:

```
[NonSerialized]
private string _address1;
```

Summary

I would like to note that with both JSON and XML, the attributes also allow you to order the properties, but I could not get them to work. In JSON, they did not seem to have any effect. With XML, when I set the order, the serialized object would come back blank.

As you can see, there is much more to building good model classes than just implementing properties. Wouldn't it be a great value add to Visual Studio if it made designing classes like this easier? Maybe that should be the next extension from Mads Kristensen who builds a lot of my favorite Visual Studio extensions.

This example class is now over 600 lines. You can view the complete type (called **PersonProper**) by going to Appendix E.

Abstract Classes

Abstract classes are a popular way to design classes that must be inherited. Here is how Wikipedia defines it:

> *In programming languages, an abstract type is a type in a nominative type system that cannot be instantiated directly; a type that is not abstract – which can be instantiated – is called a concrete type. Every instance of an abstract type is an instance of some concrete subtype. Abstract types are also known as existential types.*

> *An abstract type may provide no implementation or incomplete implementation. In some languages, abstract types with no implementation (rather than an incomplete implementation) are known as protocols, interfaces, signatures, or class types. In class-based object-oriented programming, abstract types are implemented as abstract classes (also known as abstract base classes), and concrete types as concrete classes. In generic programming, the analogous notion is a concept, which similarly specifies syntax and semantics, but does not require a subtype relationship: two unrelated types may satisfy the same concept.*

In most cases, I prefer abstract classes over an interface since they have more features and can contain implementation along with methods and properties that must be implemented.

Class Design

EXAMPLE

Here is an example of an abstract class I wrote for a former company I worked for. I designed the **JobHandler** class below for use in a Windows scheduling service that I also wrote. The scheduling service could look at any assembly and run any type that inherited **JobHandler**. Along with the abstract methods and properties, I also wanted to include the common code that all the **JobHandler**'s could use.

For example, if there was an error in one of the **JobHandler**'s, the code could simply call the **OnExceptionNotification** method which would fire the **ExceptionNotification** event that would be handled (logged) by the scheduling service.

```
public abstract class JobHandler
{
   protected JobHandler()
   {
      this.Configuration = new JobHandlerConfiguration();
      this.CreateConfiguration();
   }

   public event EventHandler<ExceptionNotificationEventArgs>
                     ExceptionNotification;

   public abstract string Name { get; }

   public abstract Guid Id { get; }

   public abstract JobHanderTypes JobHandlerType { get; }

   public abstract void Invoke(object state);

   protected abstract void CreateConfiguration();

   protected virtual void OnExceptionNotification(Exception ex,
                     System.Diagnostics.TraceEventType
                     severity, string additionalInfo)
   {
      this.ExceptionNotification.Raise
                  <ExceptionNotificationEventArgs>(this,
                  new ExceptionNotificationEventArgs()
                  { HandlerName = this.ToString(),
                  HandlerException = ex, Severity = severity,
                  EventName = this.EventName,
                  AdditionalInfo = additionalInfo });
   }
```

Class Design

```
    protected virtual void OnEventNotification(string message,
                    System.Diagnostics.TraceEventType
                    severity, string additionalInfo)
    {
        this.EventNotification.Raise<EventNotificationEventArgs>
                    (this, new EventNotificationEventArgs()
                    { HandlerName = this.ToString(),
                    Message = message, Severity = severity,
                    EventName = this.EventName,
                    AdditionalInfo = additionalInfo });
    }

    //Remainder of the code removed for brevity
}
```

Here is how I designed this abstract class.

- **Protected Constructor**: I implemented the **JobHandler()** constructor as protected which means only the inheriting type can call it.
- **Abstract Properties**: I created **Id**, **Name,** and **JobHanderTypes** as read-only abstract properties, which means the inheriting type must implement them.
- **Abstract Methods**: **Invoke()** and **CreateConfiguration()** methods are abstract which means the inheriting type must also implement them.

Here is how I implemented the **JobHandler** class that would run code that would maintain our SQL Server database.

```
public sealed class DatabaseMaintenanceJobHandler : JobHandler
{
    public override void Invoke(object state)
    {
        this.RemoveOldQueueRecords();
        this.MiscDatabaseMaintenance();
    }

    public override string Name
    {
        get { return "SQL Database Maintenance"; }
    }

    public override Guid Id
    {
        get
        {
            return new Guid("{30000000-AAA-458a-A337-04F2A8CB9ADE}");
        }
    }
```

Class Design

```
    public override JobHanderTypes JobHandlerType
    {
       get { return JobHanderTypes.System; }
    }

    protected override void CreateConfiguration()
    {
       this.Configuration.CustomSettings.Add(
           new JobHandlerCustomSetting(SettingDaysToKeep,
           CustomSettingType.Number)
           { Caption = "Days to Store Event Logs", Value = 5 });
    }

    //Remainder of the code removed for brevity
}
```

As you can see, **DatabaseMaintenanceJobHandler** implements the abstract methods and properties from **JobHandler**.

Record Classes

If you think about how *most* model classes work, especially if they are used for a web API, since they are "disconnected", the data is not changed once set. For .NET 5, the team at Microsoft came up with a new class type called **record**. This new class type makes it much easier to create *immutable* classes that act like structures. The **record** classes achieve this by using the new **init** keyword for property setters.

Using **record** classes is very easy. This is how the person class used throughout the book would look like.

```
[DebuggerDisplay("{Email}")]
public record Person
{
  public string Email
  {
    get
    {
      return this._email;
    }
```

Class Design

```
    init
    {
        if (string.IsNullOrEmpty(value))
        {
            throw new ArgumentNullException(nameof(this.Email),
                "Value for Email cannot be null or empty.");
        }

        this._email = value.Length > 50 ?
            throw new ArgumentOutOfRangeException(nameof(this.Email),
            "Email length is limited to 50 characters.") : value;
        }
    }
  }
}
```

As you can see, the class definition uses **record** and the setter is changed to **init**. That is, it!

Setting the data can only be set during object initialization as shown below.

```
var person = new Person("dotnetdave@live.com", "ASDFLAKUDJAS120")
{
  Address1 = "1234 Main Street",
  // Code removed for brevity
};
```

Since these classes are immutable, if the client-side requested the data via an API and wants to change the data, well that was made easier by using the **with** the keyword as shown below.

```
var personNew = person with
{
  Address1 = "555 Main Street"
};
```

I recommend using the new **record** class for all your model classes.

Encapsulating Logic

Encapsulation in a type, such as a collection, can also include logic, not just data. Let us say you have a type called **OrderCollection** that contains a collection of **Order**. By design, there cannot be any orders with duplicate ids or even order data. Sure, that can be done by creating proper indexes in the database, and it should. But there are two issues with this way of thinking.

1. Indexes can hurt the performance of the database, especially inserts. They can also take up a lot of room on a disk drive.

Class Design

2. As a developer, I should not need to look at the documentation or the database to figure out what constitutes a unique order. What if I do not have access to see that info in the database? The more likely scenario is it is not documented. Even if it is, the documentation is likely to be out of date.

What makes a unique order should be encapsulated into the type, so all I must do as the consumer of that type is something like this:

```csharp
public sealed class OrderCollection: List<Order>
{
   public static OrderCollection Create(IEnumerable<Order> orders)
   {
      if (orders == null)
      {
         throw new ArgumentNullException(nameof(orders),
                                    "Orders cannot be null.");
      }

      var ordersAdded = new OrderCollection()

      foreach (var order in orders.Where(o => o != null))
      {
         ordersAdded.Add(order);
      }

      return ordersAdded;

   }
}
```

As you can see, the way to create a collection of **Orders** from a collection is to use this method. In this example, I am just checking to make sure that the order is not already part of the collection in memory.

Here is the code for the **Add()** method:

```csharp
public void Add(Order order)
{
   if (order != null && base.Contains(order) == false))
   {
      base.Add(order);
   }
}
```

I am checking to make sure that the order is not null and is not already in the collection, but other logic can be easily added here. Also, it would be easy to add an **OnAdded()** method to notify other objects through an event that an order has been added or **OnRemoved()**, etc., you get the idea.

Class Design

Now that we have a collection of **Orders**, what if I want to retrieve a list of the open or closed orders? What data in **Order** indicates that it is an open or closed order? As the consumer of the type, I *should not need to know* this. If you ask 5 of your colleagues what is an open order, you might get 5 different answers. Usually, I just see fingers wave at someone else with the statement like "ask that person".

As the architect of the type, it is *YOUR JOB* to encapsulate this logic into the type. Take the example below:

```
public IEnumerable<Orders> OpenOrders()
{
   var openOrders = base.Where(o => o.ClosedOn.HasValue()
                              == false);
   return openOrders.AsEnumerable();
}
```

In the example above, I am checking to see if the **ClosedOn()** property has a value. is simple but could easily be more complicated. A better way would be to have an **IsClosed()** or **Status()** property that has a private setter. This forces the encapsulation of this logic.

There are many patterns to help with encapsulation too. Such as Fluid Validation and more. Encapsulating this type of logic into the type is much better for code maintenance. If there is a bug or a change in the logic, there is only one place to change it (and test it) instead of throughout many projects. Just a little more time when architecting the type will save your company a lot of time and money down the road.

Do Your Projects Properly Implement OOP?

Now that I have explained how to properly implement encapsulation and more, do you believe your team practices proper OOP? I would be interested to know. Please email me if you have any comments or questions.

Defensive Programming

The purpose of the chapter is to help you stop exceptions *before* they happen or part of what I call "*Defensive Programming*". If you adhere to not only what I describe in this book but what you and your fellow team members come up with, I guarantee that you will produce better code. Also, you will not be visited by the people in quality assurance very often or need to release an "emergency" patch to your product. Let us face it... who likes working late or on weekends?

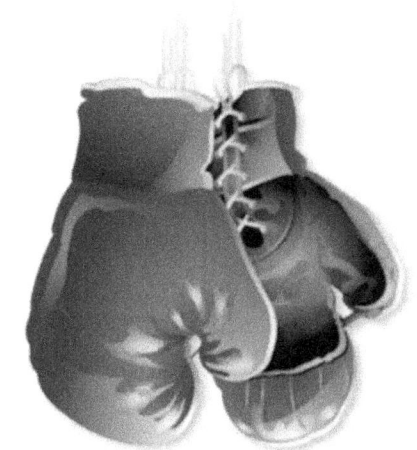

Did you know that over 68% of software projects fail? There are many reasons for this from unclear requirements, poor design, bad or spaghetti code, and more! Unfortunately, I have seen teams improperly implement Agile and now I see the documentation of requirements and design fall far short if they even exist at all!

I asked a few of my fellow developers what defensive programming means to them. This is what they said.

> "Anticipating and minimizing effects of potential problems even if you don't think they will normally arise." Dave Noderer – Microsoft MVP

> "Thinking as much as possible before even writing a single line of code. And yes, an enormous amount of unit tests." Oleksandr Valetsky

> "It means writing real exception handlers which deal with the stuff that might happen--the stuff you don't expect could possibly go wrong--but invariably does, but only after the app is deployed and you're on a beach in Australia." William Vaughn – Microsoft MVP

> "Assume that every function which can fail - will fail, so you must handle the failure (even if that means shutting down your app). Assume that all input is hostile until you have investigated it well enough to determine that it is acceptable - discard all unacceptable input. Assume that you fouled up somewhere else in your program, and the code you are working on today needs to be looking for that foul-up. Assume that hardware will fail, disk drives will fill, memory will be unavailable, and networks will be unresponsive or flooded with attackers and corrupted data - verify everything you rely upon. Assume that your underlying operating system and framework changes underneath you in a way that breaks your code - write tests to check that your assumptions remain true. A few tests in production

Defensive Programming

> *code for known fragile components, and many tests in your regression suite to ensure that the latest updates do not kill your application. Assume you missed something important."* Alun Jones

> *"Sometimes it's about dropping the last 3% of cleverness, that typical what's goanna bite you in the ass afterward."* Erik Hougaard

This is a description of defensive programming:

> *"Defensive programming is a form of defensive design intended to ensure the continuing function of a piece of software under unforeseen circumstances. The idea can be viewed as reducing or eliminating the prospect of Finagle's Law having effect. Defensive programming techniques are used especially when a piece of software could be misused."*

If you are not familiar with Finagle's Law, it states:

> *"Anything that can go wrong, will at the worst possible moment".*

This is so true! I would add those moments include Friday afternoons when you might be trying to start the weekend early or right before an important demo or trade show.

There are three things to keep in mind when practicing defensive programming:

1. Overall quality
2. Making the source code comprehensible
3. Making the software behave in a predictable manner

I will be discussing these topics in this chapter.

The Cost of Fixing Bugs

A long time ago, I found a study that shows the cost of fixing bugs (see below) and has been showing it in conference sessions ever since. I call this my "money" slide since management seems to only care about that, not quality and some even do not think too much about the users. So, in those conference sessions, I tell attendees to take a photo of this chart and then paste it to their managers' doors! If this does not show management why code quality is important, I am not sure what else would, sort from massive numbers of customer loss.

Defensive Programming

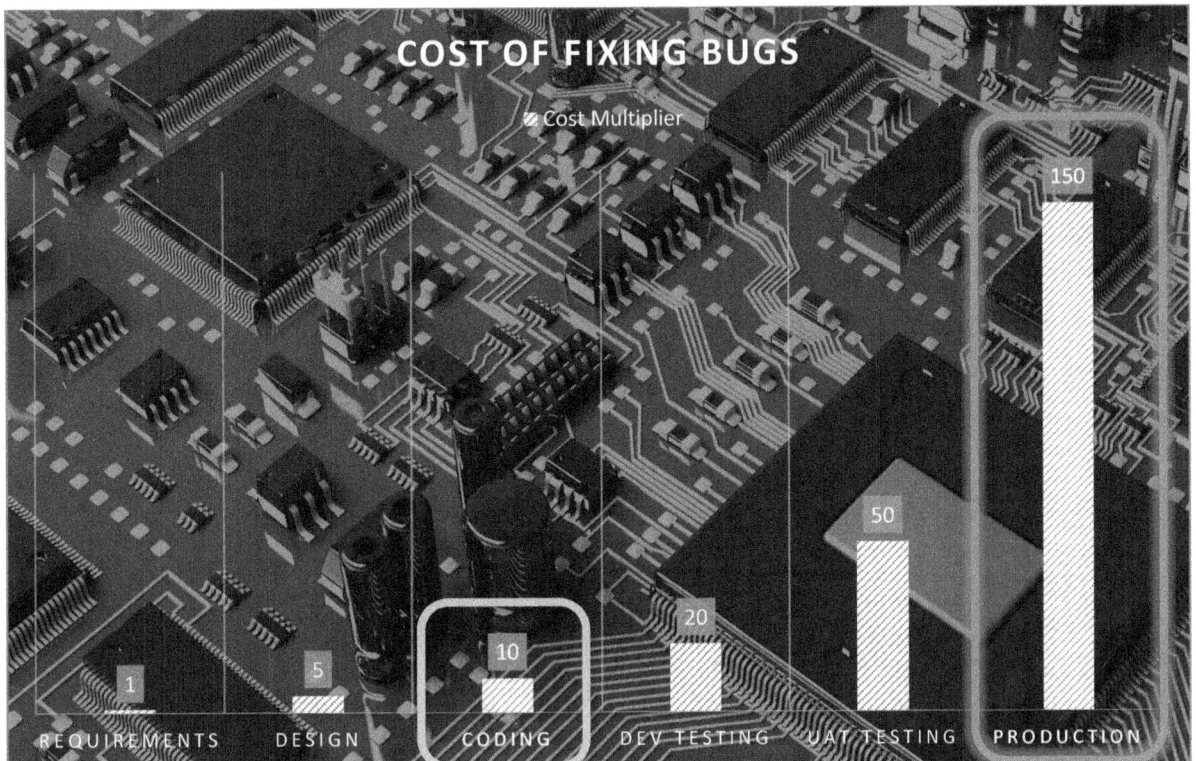

You might look at this chart and say, "You can fix bugs before I start coding?" and the answer is 100% yes! I want to point this out since I see less and less well-documented requirements and design in the past 10 years for many reasons. If I do get one of those documents, it is usually very poorly written. So, it is very, very important to do this before anyone sits down and start banging out code. I have tweeted many times this statement, "If you are spending most of your day coding, you are doing it wrong!".

When you sit down to code, it is already 10 times the cost to fix an issue that was not caught in the first two phases. If a user finds it, then that fires off a long list of tasks that must be completed before the user will get the fix. It is never good to upset users since they pay the bills.

If a bug or issue is found by users, here is just some of what could happen.

1. The user calls or sends a support request to technical support. Then that person could spend a lot of time, maybe hours just gathering enough information to fix it and hopefully offer the user a workaround.
2. Once the issue is logged then it usually goes to a "bug triage" group to be assigned to the correct team.
3. Then that team investigates the issue to gather more information. If it truly is a bug, then that issue needs to be added to a release and a developer.
4. Then the developer finally gets to work on it that could take a long time depending on the complexity.
    a. The developer needs to:

Defensive Programming

      i. Create, run, and fix any unit test issues.

      ii. Code needs to be analyzed for issues.

      iii. If the fix will be in the main release, the performance and memory testing should be done.

5. Then Quality Assurance is assigned to test the fix. This includes pushing the fix to DEV and QA servers.
6. Then the fix is pushed and tested on the UAT testing.
7. If the fix passes UAT testing, then the fix will need to be pushed to production servers. If the code is for a client app, then that will need to be pushed out to the users.

I am sure I am missing a few steps and those steps will be different at every company. I want to state again, bugs **always** cost more to fix later! Especially if it is found by the user in production or UAT testing.

> *At one company I worked at when our biggest partner found an issue, I was on a call where my boss said they would see it fixed in about six months! They were very unhappy with that timeline.*

Introduction

Practicing defensive programming is not that hard once you get used to it and use tools to help find issues. Fortunately, with every release of .NET and Visual Studio, this gets easier as you will see in this chapter. Just remember:

> *Any code that might cause an exception such as accessing files, using objects such as **DataSets** should always check the object for null so an exception is not thrown.*

Seems like a no-brainer, right? You would be surprised by the amount of code that I see at the workplace, on websites, and more that does not follow this *simple* practice. Another way to think of the statement above is to remember that just because the variable is typed as **DataSet** does not mean one was returned by the method or any tables are present, or the table contains any rows. If you keep this in mind, you will be on the right track.

Here are the rules to keep in mind:

- Write clean *understandable* code.
- Write code that is *easy* to test.
- Write methods with a single purpose and produces a *predictable* result. Use method overloading if needed.
- Write most of your code, around 90%, in *portable* or *.NET Standard* reusable DLL's.

Defensive Programming

One codebase I worked on had 1,700 unit tests and not one of them tested for encapsulation! None of the 3,300 types in this solution even implemented encapsulation properly.

How do you know how many unit tests you need to just test encapsulation? It is pretty easy by analyzing your code to determine its cyclomatic[5] complexity. That is the minimum number of unit tests you need, just to test encapsulation. In .NET projects, if you have the version of Visual Studio with Analyze built-in, simply click on Analyze - Calculate Code Metrics.

How do you easily write unit tests for encapsulation? In the .NET Framework, it is easy using IntelliTests that is included in Visual Studio 2015 - 2019. Sadly, this feature does not work for .NET 5 projects so you will need to do this manually. Make sure to use the new Live Unit Testing feature in Visual Studio. Since this feature takes a lot of CPU time away while you code, I only turn it on when I am making sure I have 100% code coverage for methods and properties.

Stop Exceptions Before They Happen

With a little more work, it is not too hard to stop exceptions from happening. Here is why you need to:

- Exceptions *dramatically* affect the performance of your application.
- Unhandled Exceptions can cause your application to *die a horrible death* that will:
    - Corrupt data!
    - Upset your customers!
    - Upset your boss!

This and subsequent chapters will show you how I have been practicing defensive programming for a long time and hopefully, you will too.

Rule #1 – Code that Can Cause Exceptions

Any code that might cause an exception (which is most code) should check the object/ value or validate so an **Exception** is *not* thrown. For example:

- Check an object for null. Whenever a method is called, the first thing that should be done when the call returns is to check the variable (of reference types) to make sure it is not **null**. The new null-conditional operator (**?**) can

---

[5] Cyclomatic Complexity reference: https://en.wikipedia.org/wiki/Cyclomatic_complexity

Defensive Programming

also be used to make other checks easier. For example: `If(dataSet?.Tables.Count > 0)`.
- Check a string for null or empty/ whitespace.
- Call **File.Exists** to avoid a **FileNotFoundException.**
- Check a **DataSet** for rows.
- Check an array for bounds.

These are just some of the things to keep in mind. Don't worry, the more you practice these rules, the less you will need to think about it.

Performance

.NET has added a new way to check for null. Before, we used this common way to check for null:

```
if(person == null)
```

Now we can use:

```
if(person is null)
```

Does one perform better than the other? Based on my benchmark tests, they do not.

Method	Mean	Error	StdDev	Gen 0	Gen 1	Gen 2	Allocated
String == null	288.037 ns	0.3978 ns	0.3721 ns	0.0157	0	0	144 B
String Is Null	287.794 ns	0.3032 ns	0.2836 ns	0.0153	0	0	144 B

Rule #2 - Parameters

We are going to explore parameters since they are used everywhere in programming. In constructors, methods, properties, structures, and more. When designing types always remember...

ALL DATA IS BAD UNTIL YOU VERIFY IT FIRST!

This my #1 mantra. If you always remember this, then I guarantee that you will create better, exception-free code. Encapsulation is the practice of data hiding. If you do not validate parameters, then bad data will get into the type and possibly the database (which is very difficult to fix). *Bad data in, bad data out* and that will cause a lot more exceptions.

A partial explanation of encapsulation on Wikipedia states:

> *Hiding the internals of the object protects its integrity by preventing users from setting the internal data of the component into an invalid or inconsistent state. A benefit of encapsulation is that it can reduce*

Defensive Programming

system complexity, and thus increase robustness, by allowing the developer to limit the interdependencies between software components.

Parameter Validation Rules

1. *Always* check for valid parameter argument values.
2. *Perform* argument validation for every public and protected method or property.
3. *Throw* meaningful exceptions to the calling code for invalid parameter arguments. Use the **System.ArgumentException** class, or a class derived from it such as **System.ArgumentNullException.**

```
public static void AddIfNotExists<T>(this ICollection<T> list,
                    params T[] values)
{
    if (values is null || values.Length == 0)
    {
        throw new ArgumentException($"{nameof(values)} is null
                or empty.", nameof(values));
    }

    foreach (var value in values)
    {
        list.AddIfNotExists(value);
    }
}
```

This extension method validates to make sure that the list of values to add to the collection is not null and there are items in it. Validation should happen on every parameter that could cause an issue (which is usually all reference types and many value types).

Here is another example from my open-source assembly and NuGet package. As you can see, I am checking every parameter except for Boolean which is the only built-in type that I feel is safe from this sort of validation.

```
/// <summary>
/// Sends mail.
/// </summary>
/// <param name="fromAddress">From email address.</param>
/// <param name="subject">Subject.</param>
/// <param name="message">Message.</param>
/// <param name="bodyHtml">Sets message is HTML.</param>
/// <param name="sendAddresses">Send email addresses.</param>
public void SendMail(EmailAddress fromAddress, string subject, string message, bool bodyHtml, List<EmailAddress>
    sendAddresses)
{
    Encapsulation.TryValidateParam<ArgumentNullException>(fromAddress.IsNotNull(), nameof(fromAddress));
    Encapsulation.TryValidateParam(subject, nameof(subject));
    Encapsulation.TryValidateParam(message, nameof(message));
    Encapsulation.TryValidateParam(sendAddresses, nameof(sendAddresses));
```

Defensive Programming

The **Encapsulation.TryValidateParam()** method is from my open-source assembly and discussed in more detail in Appendix B.

Rule #3 - Enumerations

Never assume that **Enum** arguments will be in the defined range. It is valid to cast *any* integer value into an **Enum** even if the value is not defined.

```
public void SetColor(Color color)
{
    if (Enum.IsDefined(typeof(Color), color) == false)
    {
        throw new ArgumentOutOfRangeException(nameof(color),
                "Value is not defined in the enum.");
    }

    //Code removed for brevity
}
```

The code above uses reflection that could be a slight performance issue but is *much* easier to maintain.

Rule #4 – Casting Types

Never assume a type supports an interface or base class, instead defensively query for that type by using "**as**" since it does not throw an **Exception**.

```
public interface ILogger
{
    void Save(string message);
    void File(string fileName);
}

//Code to validate interface
ErrorLogger logger = new ErrorLogger();
var loggerTest = logger as ILogger;

if(loggerTest != null)
{
    loggerTest.Save("Test Message");
}
```

Rule #5 – Let Type Checking Work for You

Remember that example from before that had 198 public string fields from the Class Design chapter? Well, this is how I would have approached re-writing it.

Defensive Programming

```csharp
public class Order
{
    private DateTime? _closedOn;
    private DateTime? _customerPickupOn;
    private OrderType _orderType;
    private ReplacementType _replacementType;
    private string _orderNumber;
    private TransactionType _transactionType;

    public string OrderNumber
    {
        get
        {
            return _orderNumber;
        }
        set
        {
            if (string.IsNullOrEmpty(value))
            {
                throw new ArgumentNullException();
            }

            _orderNumber = value;
        }
    }

    public bool IsClosed { get; private set; }

    public TransactionType TransactionType
    {
        get
        {
            return _transactionType;
        }
        set
        {
            if (System.Enum.IsDefined(typeof(TransactionType),
                value) == false)
            {
                throw new ArgumentOutOfRangeException();
            }

            _transactionType = value;
        }
    }

    public int EmployeeId { get; set; }
```

Defensive Programming

```csharp
    public DateTime OpenedOn { get; set; }

    public DateTime? CustomerPickupOn
    {
        get
        {
            return _customerPickupOn;
        }
        set
        {
            if (value < this.OpenedOn)
            {
                throw new ArgumentOutOfRangeException(
                        nameof(CustomerPickupOn),
                        "Value must be later than OpenedOn");
            }

            _customerPickupOn = value;
        }
    }

    public DateTime? ClosedOn
    {
        get
        {
            return _closedOn;
        }
        set
        {
            if (value < this.OpenedOn)
            {
                throw new ArgumentOutOfRangeException(
                        nameof(ClosedOn), "Value must be
                        the same or later than OpenedOn.");
            }

            _closedOn = value;
            this.IsClosed = true;
        }
    }

    public OrderType OrderType
    {
        get
        {
            return _orderType;
        }
        set
        {
```

Defensive Programming

```csharp
            if (!System.Enum.IsDefined(typeof(OrderType),
                value))
            {
                throw new ArgumentOutOfRangeException("Value
                        in not defined in the enum.");
            }

            _orderType = value;
        }
    }

    public ReplacementType ReplacementType
    {
        get
        {
            return _replacementType;
        }
        set
        {
            if (!System.Enum.IsDefined(typeof(ReplacementType),
                value))
            {
                throw new ArgumentOutOfRangeException("Value
                        in not defined in the enum.");
            }

            _replacementType = value;
        }
    }
}
```

As you can see from the code above, I changed most of the code to use proper types, like **bool**, **enum**, **DateTime**, and added validation where appropriate.

Rule #6 – Check Resources

This is one that I usually never see. Always check resources before accessing them. For example:

- Ensure access to the database server.

- Ensure access to the network/ internet. Just because the ethernet cable is plugged in does not mean the computer has access.

- Ensure access to websites before trying to download anything.

- Ensure the user is still connected (ASP.NET) by using **HttpResponse.IsClientConnected.** Make sure to set reasonable timeouts.

Defensive Programming

If resources cannot be accessed, then do not let the method continue and make sure to notify the user when appropriate and always log the issue. For example, ping a network resource before connecting to it.

```
public static bool IsHostAvailable(string hostNameOrAddress)
{
    Encapsulation.TryValidateParam(hostNameOrAddress,
                                   nameof(hostNameOrAddress));

    using (var pinger = new Ping())
    {
        var result = pinger.Send(hostNameOrAddress, 300);

        return result.Status == IPStatus.Success;
    }
}
```

You could also disable menus/ buttons if there is not a connection to the resource. Here is an example of how to be notified if the network availability has changed.

```
NetworkChange.NetworkAvailabilityChanged +=
  NetworkChange_NetworkAvailabilityChanged;

private static void NetworkChange_NetworkAvailabilityChanged(
                 object sender,
                 NetworkAvailabilityEventArgs e)
{
    Trace.Write($"Network availble: {e.IsAvailable}");
}
```

Rule #7 – Users

If you write code on the user experience layer, having them enter data will be one of the biggest headaches you will have to deal with. If they can screw up entering data, they will! So, do not let them enter it wrong in the first place. *Do not* use text boxes unless necessary. Use checkboxes, drop-down lists, option buttons, sliders, etc. A little more time will pay off. This applies to Windows, web, and mobile applications.

> *About 25% of the hours spent writing an application are spent figuring out ways the end-user will do something wrong." Brian Humes*

Rule #7.1 – Validate User Input

Make sure to validate data on the client-side to make their experience better. But *also* make sure to validate again when the data reaches the server via a web service etc. This is very important since data can be hacked between the client and the server. This could also lead to fewer calls to web servers.

Defensive Programming

Client-side validation is easy to do in ASP.NET web app. Make sure to call the **Page.Validate** and **Page.IsValid** on the server-side to ensure things were not hacked between the client and server.

```
protected void SubmitButton_Click(Object sender, EventArgs args)
{
    Page.Validate();

    if (Page.IsValid == true)
    {
        //Page is valid. Continue processing
    }
    else
    {
        //Page is invalid. Notify user.
    }
}
```

Make Validation Easier

To help with making validation/ encapsulation easier, I have added a new class called **Encapsulation** for my open-source projects. The method to call is **TryValidateParam()**.

Here is how to use it using a Boolean statement.

```
public bool Contains(T item)
{
    Encapsulation.TryValidateParam<ArgumentNullException>(
                                    item != null, nameof(item));
    //Code removed for brevity
}
```

With this example of **TryValidateParam()**, always provide an exception type that derives from **ArgumentException** when validating parameters.

TryValidateParam() is overloaded over many more times to properly validate types such as strings, enums, collections, numbers, and more. Here is another example.

```
void ICollection<T>.CopyTo(T[] array, int arrayIndex)
{
    Encapsulation.TryValidateParam(array, nameof(array));

    //Code removed for brevity
}
```

Defensive Programming

Dealing with Exceptions

Let us face it, no code is perfect, so exceptions *will* happen. It is very important to properly deal with exceptions which include logging them. Again, a little more time will be a huge payoff. There are two very important differences on how to deal with exceptions, one is on the application layer the other is the rest... DLL's.

Rule #1 – The Application Layer

Make sure to wrap code that could cause an exception (which is just about everything) with try/ catch blocks.

The three most important reasons are:

1. Log the Exception (more coming up later).
2. Notify the user. Make sure to never show **Exception.Message** to the user.
3. Change the program flow.

☑ Make sure you do not use try/ catch to validate a value!

```
try
{
  _da.CustomerVideoMissingUpdate(missingVideo);
}
catch (Exception ex)
{
  LogWriter.WriteException(ex, TraceEventType.Error,
    "Error updating customer, missing video
      information.");
}
```

In the code above, it is logging the **Exception** using the dotNetTips.Utility.Logger assembly. The last parameter is the *user-friendly* message that is automatically displayed based on project type.

Rule #2 – Trap Exceptions Globally

With rule #1 above, we all know that mistakes happen, and developers will forget to add try/ catch blocks. To make sure the exception is caught, it is very important

Defensive Programming

to trap them at a global level. .NET does not include global exception handling, but each application framework does, except for console apps.

Three common ways to do this are using:

1. **app.UseExceptionHandler** in the **ConfigureErrorHandling** method in **Startup.cs** for ASP.NET.
2. **DispatcherUnhandledException** in WPF
3. **ThreadExceptionEventHandler** using **Application.ThreadException** in Windows Forms

EXAMPLE

Here is an example of how to set up global Exception trapping in Windows Forms apps.

```
[STAThread]
static void Main()
{
  Application.SetHighDpiMode(HighDpiMode.SystemAware);
  Application.EnableVisualStyles();
  Application.SetCompatibleTextRenderingDefault(false);
  Application.Run(new Form1());
  Application.ThreadException += Application_ThreadException;
}

private static void Application_ThreadException(object sender,
                    System.Threading.ThreadExceptionEventArgs e)
{
  Log.Logger.Fatal(e.Exception, "Critical: Unhandled Error!");
}
```

In past projects I worked on with my logging assembly, any exception marked as critical gets immediately emailed to the development team. This could also be used to send errors to a bug tracking program. We use this to start investigating an issue before the customer calls. Being proactive makes customers very happy!

In another WinForm/ WPF application I worked on if the exception made it this far, we logged the exception, notified the user, and then automatically restarted the app because we could not guarantee the application data was not corrupted.

Rule #3 – The DLL Layer

In DLL assemblies, where all reusable code should reside, **only** use **try/ catch** when the code can deal with a specific exception. This can be used to clean up things like database connections, file handles, or do a retry.

Defensive Programming

If an exception is thrown that is not handled, it should be allowed to bubble up to the application layer. This is so they can be logged, notify the user, and change program flow.

Never catch the following **Exception** types in DLL's, they do not give enough information to the calling code.

- **System.Exception**
- **System.ApplicationException**
- **System.SystemException**

```
try
{
    adminSqlConnection.Open();
}
catch (SqlException ex)
{
    adminSqlConnection.Close();
    throw new ActivationException("Unable to open a database
                                   connection. Does user have
                                   permission?", ex);
}
```

When throwing an **Exception**, always make sure to include the original **Exception** as the inner **Exception** (the **ex** in the code above), otherwise the stack trace will be lost which is very important for logging to make it easier to track down the issue.

Logging Exceptions

It is very important to log *every* exception to be reviewed by the development team. Exceptions should only be logged by the application layer to the project, not DLL's. *Never, ever DLL's.*

The simple answer to that is it would be tightly coupling a logging system to a DLL. If a different team at your company wants to use one of your DLL's and they do not use the same logging system as your team, then they are out of luck. This might cause additional work to remove or incorporate their logging system. So, just don't architect it that way in the first place. The only exception to this rule in .NET 5 would be to pass in the **ILogger** interface to classes including using dependency injection, the preferred method in ASP.NET.

Do not roll your own logging framework! Microsoft .NET has been around long enough that there many available, most for free. Make sure you pick a framework that also supports logging events such as performance information, report clicks, etc.

I also recommend choosing a logging framework that sends entries to the cloud such as Azure Application Insights. These frameworks make it easy to view and

Defensive Programming

query logs as well as setting up alerts. Make sure these frameworks support caching just in case it cannot be sent to the cloud or the program and/ or computer goes down.

The More Information the Better

Make sure your logging framework logs as much information as possible for the development team... the more, the better. Here is an example from a project I worked on.

```
Order.Processor.App|Error 1|FirstChanceException event raised in
Order.Processor.App.exe: Could not load file or
assembly...||||10|2017-12-27T00:37:33.0104314Z|77430049930|
```

Can you fix the issue with this information? I could not! This tells me nothing other than the time it happened. At this point, they should not even log. They are just hurting performance for no reason.

Below is the minimal information that the dotNetTips.Utility.Logger framework records. This is an example of the XML file output.

```
<LogEntry>
  <Id>da19f3af-67d7-4063-8d09-22163cad3293</Id>
  <EventId>0</EventId>
  <TimeStamp>2016-06-03T17:23:02.5394768Z</TimeStamp>
  <Severity>Error</Severity>
  <Category>Exception</Category>
  <User>dmccarter</User>
  <Message>The directory is not empty.</Message>
  <ErrorMessages>
    <Message> Exception Information Details:
      Exception Type: System.IO.IOException
      Message: The directory is not empty.
      TargetSite: Void WinIOError(Int32,
      System.String)
      Source: mscorlib HResult: -2147024751
      StackTrace Information Details: at
      System.IO.__Error.WinIOError(
      Int32 errorCode, String maybeFullPath)
      at System.IO.Directory.DeleteHelper(
      String fullPath, String userPath, Boolean
      recursive, Boolean
      throwOnTopLevelDirectoryNotFound) at
      System.IO.Directory.Delete(
      String fullPath, String userPath,
      Boolean recursive, Boolean checkHost)at
      dotNetTips.DotNetFileCleaner.MainModule
      .DeleteFolders()
    </Message>
```

Defensive Programming

```xml
    </ErrorMessages>
    <Information>
      <MachineName>DEV-VM</MachineName>
      <Source>dotNetTips.DotNetFileCleaner</Source>
    </Information>
    <Info>
      <Application.MappedMemory>92,098,560
                        </Application.MappedMemory>
      <ApplicationDomain.Name>DefaultDomain
                        </ApplicationDomain.Name>
      <Computer.Culture>en-US</Computer.Culture>
      <Computer.FreePhysicalMemory>3,307,802,624
                        </Computer.FreePhysicalMemory>
      <Computer.FreeVirtualMemory>140,736,813,912,064
                        </Computer.FreeVirtualMemory>
      <Computer.TotalPhysicalMemory>7,515,721,728
                        </Computer.TotalPhysicalMemory>
      <Computer.TotalVirtualMemory>140,737,488,224,256
                        </Computer.TotalVirtualMemory>
      <Exception.CallingAssembly>mscorlib.dll
                        </Exception.CallingAssembly>
      <Exception.CallingMethod>WinIOError
                        </Exception.CallingMethod>
      <Exception.CallingType>System.IO.__Error
                        </Exception.CallingType>
      <InfoItem>Error deleting directory:
            C:\Users\davidm\AppData\Local
            \Temp\ALM.
      </InfoItem>
      <Process.Id>7400</Process.Id>
      <Process.Name>C:\Users\davidm\AppData\Local
        \Apps\2.0\HCB1KECJ.CRM\L4H9VZ2K.932\
        0c9da9dfc_07e0.0001_e58c333f9e18183a\
        dotNetTips.DotNetFileCleaner.exe</Process.Name>
      <Thread.Id>6960</Thread.Id>
      <Thread.Name>UNKOWN</Thread.Name>
      <User.Domain>NW-WIN99-VS-2015</User.Domain>
      <User.Interactive>True</User.Interactive>
    </Info>
</LogEntry>
```

I have not found any logging frameworks that logs this much information! At one company I worked at, my development manager stated that this logging system *saved countless hours* on tracking down issues.

Defensive Programming

How to Catch *All* Exceptions

I also recommend using **AppDomain.FirstChanceException** event to be notified of exceptions fired anywhere in the application domain. This event fires for ALL exceptions (referenced assemblies too) BEFORE going to the **catch** block. For a detailed explanation and example, check out "256 Seconds with dotNetDave", Episode 2: http://bit.ly/256SecondsE2.

Logging in .NET 5

Logging in .NET 5 has completely changed (from the .NET Framework) and includes no **TraceListeners**. Also, it is not easy to access globally in your app. So, I added code to my open-source project to make this easier.

First, add **Microsoft.Extensions.Logging** package from NuGet. Then, install one of the appropriate packages for the output:

- **Microsoft.Extensions.Logging.ApplicationInsights**
- **Microsoft.Extensions.Logging.AzureAppServices**
- **Microsoft.Extensions.Logging.Console**
- **Microsoft.Extensions.Logging.Debug**
- **Microsoft.Extensions.Logging.EventLog**
- **Microsoft.Extensions.Logging.TraceSource for TraceListeners**

Here is an example of how to set up global logging in ASP.NET with the **AppLogging** class.

```
public void Configure(IApplicationBuilder app,
                      IHostingEnvironment env,
                      ILoggerFactory loggerFactory)
{
    if (env.IsDevelopment())
    {
        app.UseDeveloperExceptionPage();
    }

    AppLogging.CreateLogger<Program>(loggerFactory);
    AppLogging.LoggerFactory.AddDebug();
    AppLogging.LoggerFactory.AddProvider(new
    ConsoleLoggerProvider((text, logLevel) => logLevel >=
       LogLevel.Information, true));

    AppLogging.Logger.LogInformation($"App started at
       {DateTime.UtcNow}.");

    app.UseMvc();
```

Defensive Programming

```
}
```

Here is how you log (example in the code above too).

```
AppLogging.Logger.LogError(0, ex, $"Error deleting file:
                           {tempFile.FullName}");
```

More Information on Defensive Programming

Here is morning information on defensive programming that I recommend for attendees to my conference session on this subject.

- 256 Seconds with dotNetDave Episode 2 for details and example: https://bit.ly/256SecondsE2
- Defensive Coding in C# on Pluralsight.com, Author: Deborah Kurata
- Defensive Programming Articles on dotNetTips.com: https://bit.ly/DefensiveProgramming
- dotNetDave Explains... Object-Oriented Programming: https://bit.ly/dotNetOOP
- My Workflow Before I Submit Code Changes: https://bit.ly/CheckInWorkFlow
- The Ten Commandments of Egoless Programming: https://bit.ly/Egoless

Application Design

Proper application architecture for any project is *extremely* important. I cannot stress this enough! The number of times that I sat in a meeting with management and they expected me to go back to my desk and start coding right away is staggering. This even still happens to me and I am dotNetDave! In 2019, I was expected to deliver a solution after only a single two-hour meeting and no documented

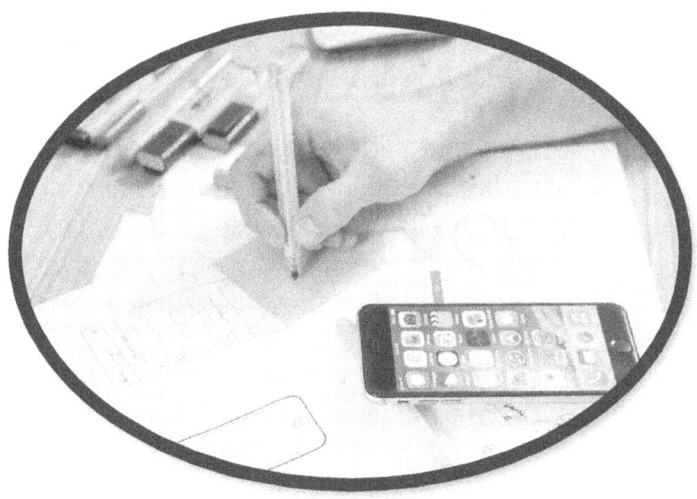

requirements! I have learned in my over 28 years of experience that this way of thinking by management never works. The more time that your team spends on architecture will pay off for the lifetime of the project and in the end, will be a huge cost saving!

I am going to state something that might create some hate mail...

I would like to also state that if you spend most of your time in meetings, you are also doing it wrong! I have also seen some development processes like Agile be abused and used as an excuse to not spend time documenting and architecting. This is just wrong on so many levels.

Application Design

N-Tier Architecture

Very early in my programming career, I learned how to architect projects using N-Tier architecture, also called multitier architecture, and I still use it in everything I design. Wikipedia defines it as:

> In software engineering, multitier architecture (often referred to as n-tier architecture) or multilayered architecture is a client-server architecture in which presentation, application processing, and data management functions are physically separated. The most widespread use of multitier architecture is the three-tier architecture.

> N-tier application architecture provides a model by which developers can create flexible and reusable applications. By segregating an application into tiers, developers acquire the option of modifying or adding a specific layer, instead of reworking the entire application. A three-tier architecture is typically composed of a presentation tier, a domain logic tier, and a data storage tier.

This is not an architecture book, but I wanted to show you the basics of how *I* approach designing projects, to jumpstart your team's project architecture. Below is the N-Tier diagram I show in my conference sessions and I even taught it to my beginner students at the University of California, San Diego in the United States on the first day of each class.

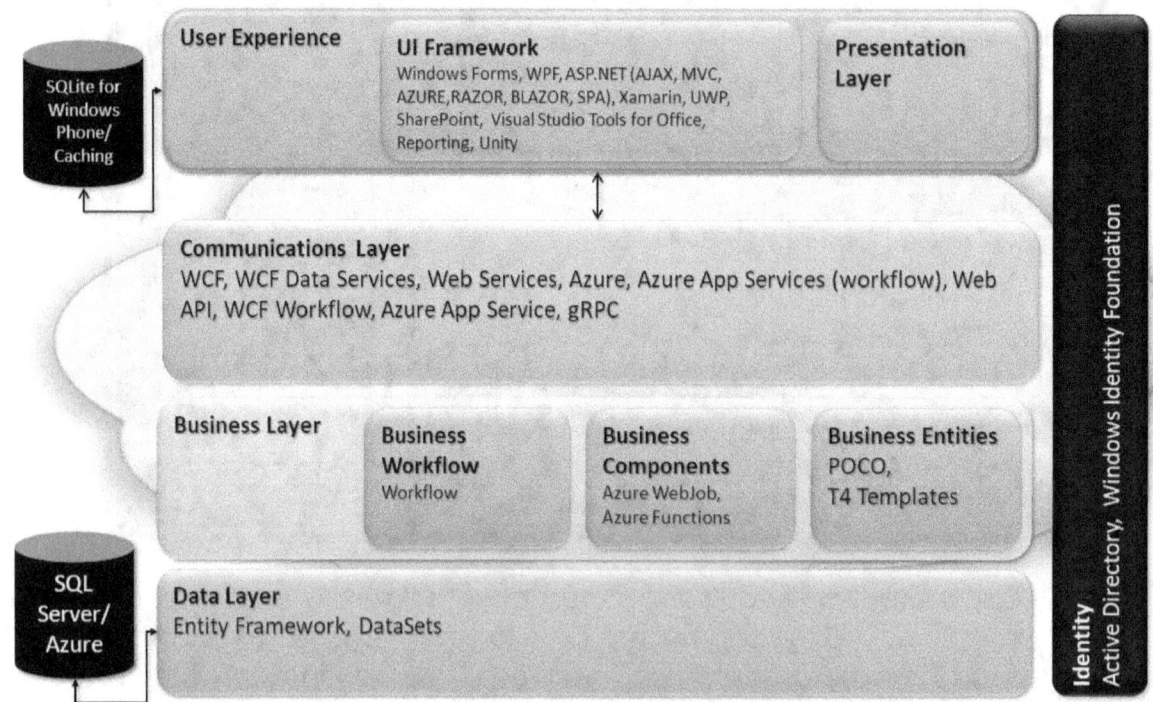

N-Tier/ Multitier Architecture Diagram

Here is a description of how I architect each layer.

Application Design

Data Layer

The first and most important is the data layer. Every app uses data in some manner and most of that is kept in databases like SQL Server, SQL Azure, Azure Cosmos DB, and even in files. Think of the data layer as the foundation of a building. Without a strong foundation that building will have huge issues in the future and will fall sooner than later. The same goes for *your* data layer.

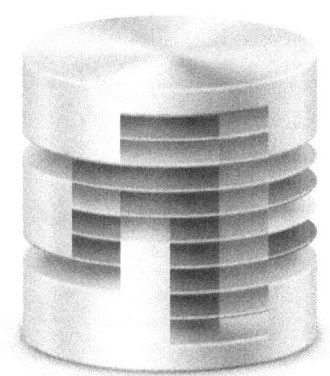

At one company I worked at, towards the end of my time there, I was in a major meeting with managers and vice presidents. They were talking about all the features that needed to be added to the product to the next release to increase annual revenue. Towards the end of the meeting, I was getting frustrated and I finally raised my hand and said, "The features you want will either be impossible or take so long that our competitor will release them before us, and we will lose customers if you don't break down and re-architect the database." They all looked at me with facial expressions like they have never heard this before until my boss said, "Dave has been telling you this for four years, why don't you listen to him?" Not long after that, they laid off all the high-level software engineers in my department, including me. Guess what happened? They lost customers and that product has not done well ever since. If they only listened!

I have also learned during my career that software developers **should not** design the database! One time when I said this at a conference, an attendee asked me "Why not?". My reply to him was "Do you want DBA's writing applications?". Everyone in the room yelled "NO!" and I said "Exactly!". Unless you are a genius, you cannot be an expert at both.

Application Design

Business Layer

Above the database layer is the business layer. This layer can include many features. Let us go over the major ones shown in the diagram.

Business Entities

An important part of the business layer is the business entities or "models". The reason I feel it is important is to allow these entities to be reused throughout all the other layers, which includes the data layer.

Most of the projects I work on (before I get there), typically put the entities used by the database layer in that layer. This is *not* the correct way to do it. These entities *must* be put in their assembly as shown in the dotNetTips.App.Ads.Entities.dll example in the Windows App Example section. The main reason for this is code reuse! Some projects will duplicate the entities in the data layer, in other layers, which is not the way to do it and *will* cause a maintenance nightmare.

If the entities are put in the data layer, then you would have to include the code to access the database in all the other layers. This is not ideal and could even be a security issue. In most projects, the only layer that should access the data layer is the communications layer and other services like Azure WebJobs, Azure Functions, and workflow.

These entities can include POCO (Plain Old CLR Objects), Entity Framework Code First entities, **DataSets**, and even auto-generated entities using T4 Templates or another class generator. I tend to put *only* these entities in the assembly, no other common code is used by the other layers.

Another reason this should be done is for data validation. As I describe in detail in the Class Design chapter, all data must be validated when being set in entities like these. If you follow this architecture, then all the other layers will be using the same validation code, even in client applications.

I have been separating the data entities from the data context (data access) for a long time. I even did it with the early version of Entity Framework before Code First classes were introduced. If you are using a different ORM (Object Relational Mapping) framework, make sure it allows this type of separation.

You can see a complete example of how to properly architect business entities by going to Appendix E.

Application Design

Business Components

The business layer is usually where I put non-communications layer services such as Azure WebJobs, Azure Functions, Windows Service or any other data related processing. If one of these services, such as an Azure Function exposed as an HTTP trigger, then these could also be part of the communications layer. But typically, these services are not exposed to the outside world.

Business Workflow

Coding workflow to process data is difficult without the use of a workflow framework. .NET Framework does have one project type for this, but unfortunately, .NET 5 does not. It is too bad since this can significantly reduce the complexity of coding workflow yourself.

There are third-party products that can be used, but since I have not used one in a long time, I cannot make a recommendation. Since Azure Durable Functions can help you in the workflow, I would put that in this layer.

Communications Layer

Most applications need to connect to backend services to receive and send data and that is where the communications layer comes in. These services are usually public but can also include services that communicate only within your own domain.

> **Communications Layer**
> WCF, WCF Data Services, Web Services, Azure, Web API, Azure App Service, gRPC

At the beginning of .NET, we had Web Services. After that, WCF (Windows Communications Foundation) was added in 2006. With the latest release of .NET, we have many more services including Azure App Service, gRPC, Web API (what I use the most) and many more. It seems like there is a new framework coming out all the time. It is hard to keep up with them, but the .NET team usually embraces them quickly.

The use of the identity layer is a big part of the communications layer to ensure that only users and apps with the correct security permissions can access these services.

In this layer, it is important to decrease the load on these services and servers by implementing caching, which I do not see used very much. Cache data as much as possible, including common data (like a list of countries or states) and user

Application Design

credentials to allow the services to respond to more requests per second. Server proxies can make this easy to set up for web services.

Also, try to make sure that applications calling these services perform chunky, not chatty calls. The biggest performance issue in modern-day apps is the **internet**! Something that I state a lot in my conference sessions is that applications should not go across the wire (the internet or local network) until you must and batch calls as much as possible.

> At one company I worked at, I wrote their first API (using Entity Framework and WCF Data Services) to expose data to their partners. One of the things I built into the process when onboarding new partners, was a code review of their applications that would be using the API (no matter what language the code was written in), which was usually done by me. The reason was that I wanted to make sure they were practicing chunky calls to the API. I had to reject most of the first few versions of the partner code due to them not coding this correctly.

I even wrote into the API logging, data, and reporting that would help me detect if they were doing chatty calls after their application went live. If I saw that they were not doing what we wanted, then I could, with just a click of a button, immediately disconnect their access to the API, after a few warnings of course.

Many of these services include batching features, so make sure they are being used since it affects the number of calls per second that they can handle. This *does* affect the performance and the *cost* of these services.

User Experience (UX)

We are finally at the user experience layer (also known as UX), which is the part of the project the users will interact with.

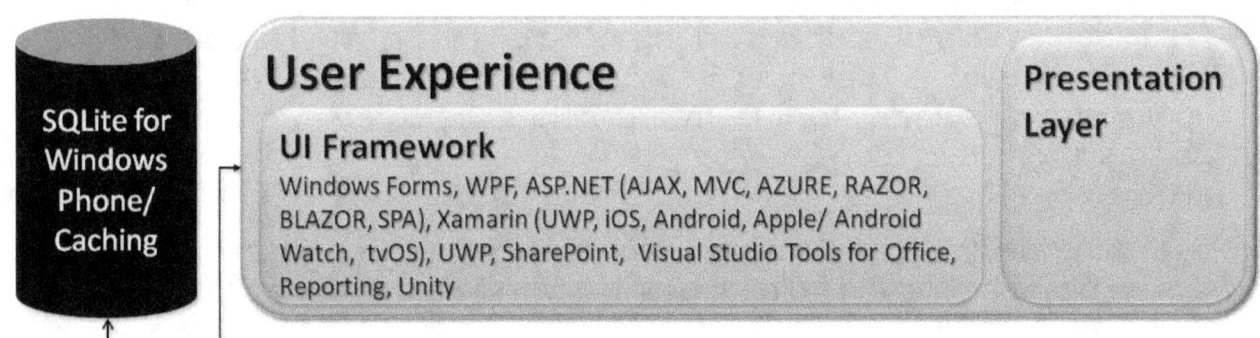

Application Design

This layer can include frameworks such as Windows Forms, WPF (Windows Presentation Foundation), ASP.NET web sites, Unity (for games), mobile apps (using Xamarin), VSTS (Visual Studio Tools for Office), reporting with frameworks such as SQL Server Reporting Services and much more.

Again, the identity layer is very important for this layer so only authorized users have access to the application.

Even when architecting the UX layer, consider putting forms, controls, etc. into re-usable assemblies. When I architected my free app for developers, I put most of the forms and controls into the dotNetTips.Dev.UI DLL. Everything that I thought could be reused in other apps I write in the future, I put into this assembly. As you can see in the graphic to the right, I wrote that assembly in VB.NET. The reason is that I believe that writing UX code is much easier and faster than writing it in C#. This assembly could be considered part of the presentation layer.

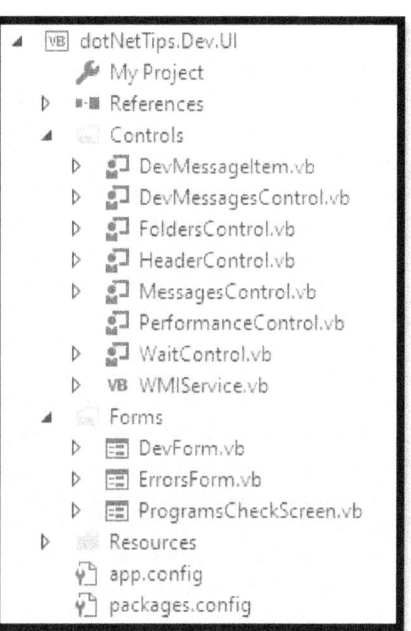

Presentation Layer

This layer should contain components for the user interface and manage user interaction. If you can write this layer in .NET Standard, then it could be used in all the operating systems that it supports.

Consider putting the following into this layer:

- **Caching**: Very important for the UX that I will discuss in the next section.
- **Composition**: This includes the creation of view and presentation layout.
- **Exception Management**: Since exceptions should only be logged or emailed in the UX layer, the handling of exceptions should be coded here including any global exception handling.
- **Input**: This can include controls and forms that the users use to input data. Include any localization code here so new locations and languages can be easing coded using resources. At a minimum, all text, and images that the user sees should be localized.
- **Layout**: Use this to create a common look and feel for your apps. Cascading Style Sheets (CSS) for websites and Model-View-Presenter (MVP) should be coded here.
- **Navigation**: Code that allows your users to navigate screens, wizards, or web pages should be coded here.

Take some time to architect this layer and always keep in mind how these features could be used in other apps in the future. If you do, you will save a lot of time and cost.

Application Design

Client-Side Caching

In today's mobile world, applications should be architected for "occasionally connected" by caching data on the client-side. The reason is that you CANNOT rely on the internet/ network being available or having timeouts due to slow connections or backend services being down.

Your users should be able to work when there is no connection or spotty connections to the backend data. I have been warning developers about this in classes and conference sessions for over ten years. Several years ago, mobile apps I used, such as Facebook or Twitter while in an airplane or even at a doctor's office, could not add a post so that it could be uploaded when the connection got better, but now they do. So why not add this capability right from the beginning architecture for the application? I can guarantee that adding this feature later will take a lot of time and money. It did take Facebook and Twitter a long time (years) to add this feature.

Working on the "perceived" speed of the app is *very* important. The table below shows you why.

Application Delay	User Perception
0-100 milliseconds	Instant
100-300 milliseconds	Small perceptible delay
300-1000 milliseconds	Machine is working
👎 1,000+ milliseconds	Mental context switch
👎 10,000+ milliseconds	Task is abandoned

From this table, apps should strive for a delay of 1 second or less. Anything above that could upset your users and they just might look for a better, faster app which means your company loses money. This is even important for web sites. I do not know about you, but if I wait 1-3 seconds for a page to load, I usually abandon the page and I might not ever visit that site again.

Application Design

Over 10 years ago, Microsoft came out with the Microsoft Sync Framework that made it much easier to sync data from ADO.NET, file systems and news feeds. I know for a fact that Microsoft used it for some of their services. If you think about all the complexities of syncing data, there is a lot of orchestration that needs to happen. For example, if John updates a data record on his computer,

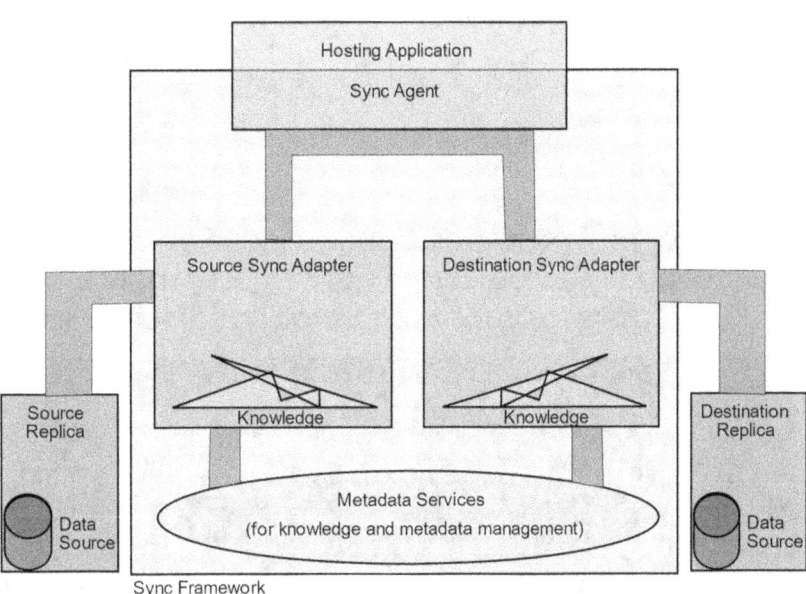
Sync Framework

and at the same time, Jane updates the same data record on her computer, when the data reaches the backend, which of those updates makes it into the database? Does the last one in wins, or do you allow the users to choose?

I believe that most apps are not architected this way, due to this complexity. Unfortunately, Microsoft has abandoned this framework and they have not provided a replacement. As I stated earlier, depending on the app, users should be able to do a minimal amount of work when there is not a connection to the backend. For example, for a very long time, Microsoft Outlook has been able to do this. Except for the syncing of data to the backend, almost everything works in Outlook when there is not a connection. I can read and send emails, create, or modify appointments, and much more. It even has a **Work Offline** feature! Your apps should strive to do the same as Outlook, it is a great example that most of us use every day.

Ever since .NET 2, ASP.NET has had caching built-in, even on proxy servers and in the browser. Sometime later they did make the memory caching available to all .NET apps. This helps but does not replace the Sync Framework.

Caching data for short timeframes such as one minute or even 5 seconds can speed up performance. If you want to improve the perceived speed of your app, consider caching the following data.

- Common app data that does not change often like a list of counties, states, etc.
- Time-limited authentication keys.

Using the **Lazy<T>** type can help too since it can be set up to only load data when it is requested.

Application Design

I hope that the information in this section will get your team to think about caching before writing a single line of code! I would love to hear about your real-world solutions.

Identity

Most every project needs identity (security) to only allow authorized users into the application or service. Many apps (mostly mobile and websites) also use this to track their users to usually sell a product or serve-up advertisements.

> **Identity**
>
> Active Directory, Windows Identity Foundation, Custom DB, 3rd Party Solutions (includes Office 365, Facebook, Google, Twitter)

There are many ways to implement identity in your project. These can include Active Directory (been around for a long time) to 3rd party solutions and services such as Office 365, Facebook, Google, Twitter, and OKTA, just to name a few. I would like to stress that identity needs to be architected in the project from the very beginning. Worrying about it at the end of the project will most certainly delay the project.

Most projects need to implement one or more different ways to secure it. This depends on the project. Make sure the appropriate security level is used since we hear in the news, almost daily, about companies being hacked or someone's laptop was stolen that is full of sensitive information. Heck, even security cameras like Ring from Amazon are being hacked. So even IoT projects need to be secure on the software and hardware level.

Next, I will show more examples of N-Tier Architecture that I have done in a few of my projects.

N-Tier Architecture & Code Reuse

Recently an intern on the team I am currently working on asked me to review the code from a new solution he has been tasked to complete. About a week or so later, I received the following from him via chat,

> "On the project I sent you, I don't understand what you mean by using a separate, reusable DLL. I've been trying to read about it, but I'm still not super sure."

My short reply to him via chat was,

Application Design

> "Generally, model classes are used in multiple projects. For the reusability of those models, they should be in their own separate DLL (C# project). Not only is this good reuse, but it also makes it much easier to unit test."

In *all* my code conference sessions, I preach the importance of coding for reuse, right from the beginning of the project. I recommend that 90% or more of any application code should be in reusable assemblies (DLL's), for many reasons that I will discuss. The only code in the actual app should be just enough to deal with the user and/or data coming to and from the backend API. Not every developer will agree with this way of coding, but it has saved me a lot of time and produces more stable, reliable code, and in the long run, saving the company money!

Do Not Listen to Your Boss!

One of the things I have been saying for a long time when thinking about the future of the project is "Don't listen to your boss!". Why?

> Well, as usual, I learn the hard way. One time back in the 90's my boss assigned to me, a web project to code (in the ASP and Visual Interdev days). I asked him "Will this always be a web project?". He answered in the affirmative. So, I wrote the website.
> At some point later, he came to me with an urgent need to support another app type than a web site. I told him; it will take a while because I would have to copy most of that website code out to a DLL (Visual Basic), so the code can be used for two different apps.

Application Design

This was not the answer he was looking for. If I just did not listen to him and architect it correctly from the beginning, supporting a different app would be trivial.

Ever since that day, I stopped listening to my bosses, when it comes to the future of the project and always architect with code reuse in mind... **always**!

Practice What You Preach Dave!

Since that day, I *always* put most of my code in re-usable assemblies, even my apps, and even in testing/ benchmarking apps. Don't believe me? Let me prove it to you.

Windows App Example

I have had an app for developers out for a while now called the dotNetTips.Utility Dev App (I hope you will check it out). Currently, the app has two main features. I could have just put all the code in the EXE... but I did not, as you will see.

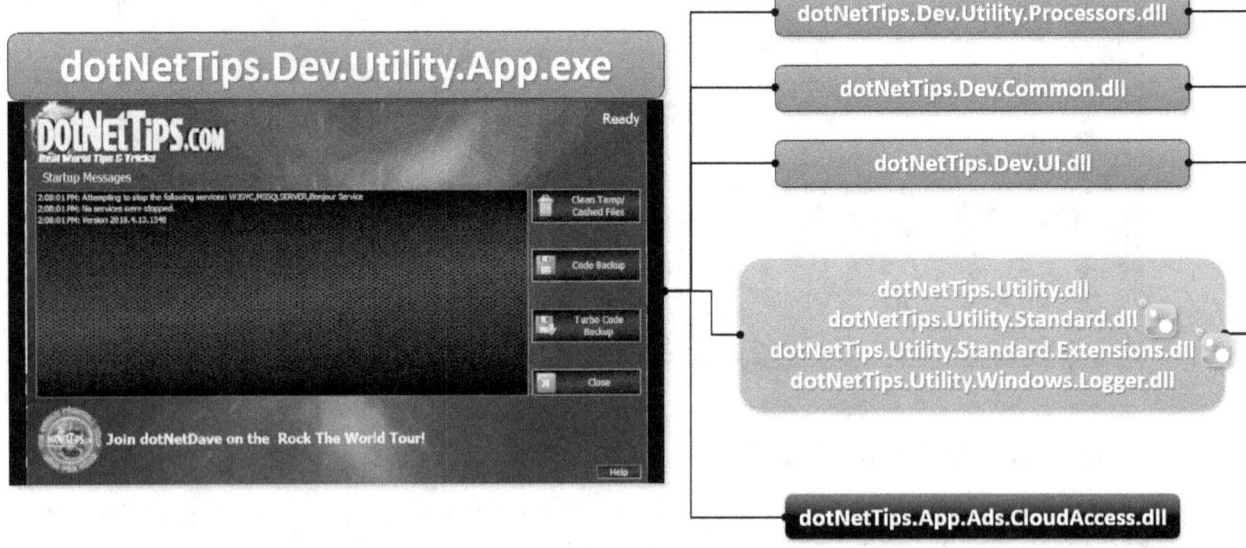

This shows how I separated the code into the different assemblies including the ones (in the green box) that are part of my open-source assemblies (the first two available on NuGet). I will give a brief description of what is contained in each.

1. **dotNetTips.Dev.Utility.App.exe (Clr C#)**
   This is the Windows Forms app that is distributed via ClickOnce. There is very little code in the app. Just enough to load/save data and show messages in the app (multi-threaded).

2. **dotNetTips.Dev.Utility.Processors.dll (Clr C#)**
   This assembly does the heavy lifting for the app. Currently; the app has two features. The first is to seek and destroy temp and cached files created by

Application Design

Visual Studio and SQL Server. The other is to scan your computer for source code and quickly back it up to OneDrive by default. Much of the processing code for each feature is in this assembly which includes sending status update messages to the app.

3. **dotNetTips.Dev.Utility.Common.dll (Clr C#)**
   This assembly has the common code used by the other assemblies in the solution. Some of the common code is configuration, the message type used to show information to the user in the app, a type used for queueing, and more.

4. **dotNetTips.Dev.UI.dll (Clr VB.NET)**
   This contains the custom controls and forms used in the app. Some of these include the control used to show messages to the user, header control, performance control, error form, and more.

5. **dotNetTips.App.Ads.CloudAccess.dll (.NET Core C#)**
   If a user clicks on an advertisement in the app (located at the bottom of the app), then this assembly sends that information directly to a queue in Azure. This assembly is part of a completely different solution that I will describe next.

Cloud App Example

I learned N-Tier Architecture (also called Multitier Architecture) a very long time ago and use it for any app/solution I am architecting. I use it in the example above, and this shows how I use it for cloud projects. This example shows my cloud app, all hosted in Azure. I am showing this because it shows what happens to the data sent from the user clicks for ads from the dotNetTips.Utility Dev App.

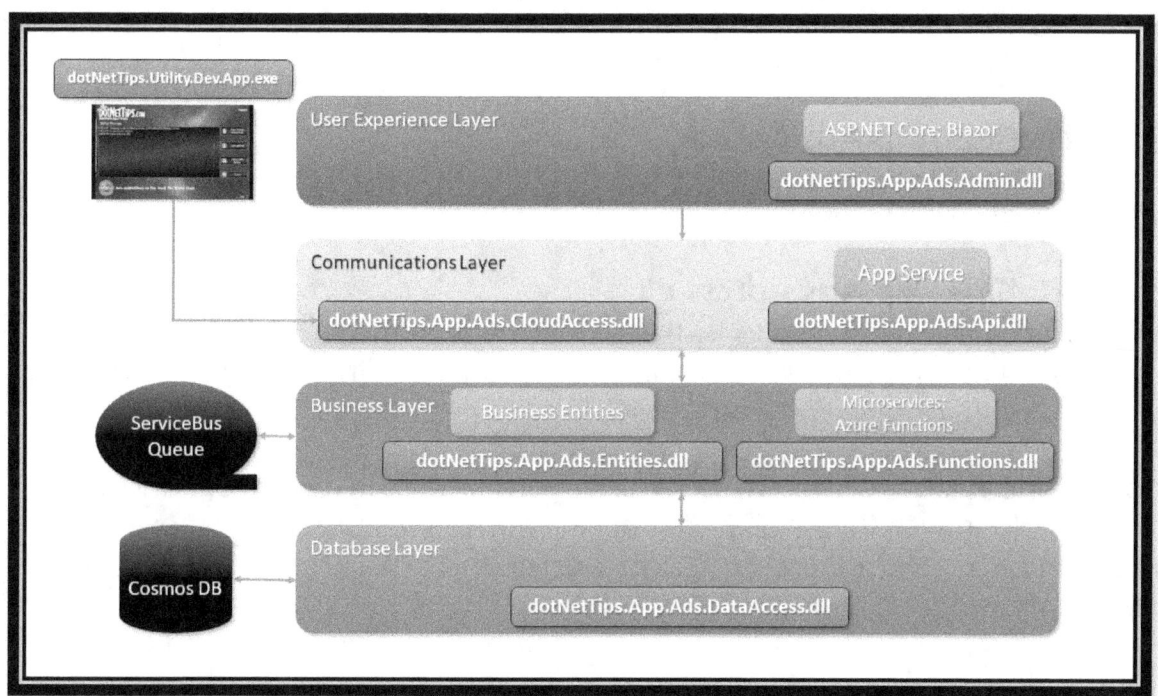

Application Design

As you can see, the ad click data is sent to an Azure ServiceBus Queue via the communications layer to the business layer then to the data layer, and saved to Cosmos DB. All these assemblies are written in C# using .NET Core. Here are the major responsibilities of each assembly.

1. **dotNetTips.App.Ads.DataAccess.dll**
   In the data layer, the code in this assembly is just to deal with retrieving and saving data to the database along with any custom methods I write to access the data. ***That is it***! Think about it like this, the only thing this layer should call is the actual database assemblies, such as the ones for SQL Server, Oracle, Cosmos DB, etc.

2. **dotNetTips.App.Ads.Entities.dll**
   This is where all the custom data entities used in the other layers should be. You can put other non-database classes there too. I know someone reading this will say, "Why not just put them in the data access assembly?". Easy, if you do that, you would have put that assembly on every layer that needs those models, including the client (users) machine. At this point, you have broken N-Tier architecture and will create larger deployments. It could also be a security risk.

3. **dotNetTips.App.Ads.Functions.dll**
   This is the assembly that contains my Azure Functions that is called when the user ad click data hits the ServiceBus Queue and saves it to Cosmos DB.

4. **dotNetTips.App.Ads.CloudAccess.dll**
   Currently, this assembly contains the code that sends the user ad click data to the ServiceBus Queue. I plan to add more to this assembly and release it as an open-source project in the future.

5. **dotNetTips.App.Ads.Api.dll**
   This is the ASP.NET website that is the API (using WebApi) that serves as the communications layer.

6. **dotNetTips.App.Ads.Admin.dll**
   This is the ASP.NET website that I use to maintain the ad data that is used by the dotNetTips.Utility Dev App. It is all written using the new Blazor framework that was released in November 2019.

Of course, the assemblies for these two solutions use .NET Framework and Core assemblies along with third-party assemblies (from DevExpress). For more information about this solution, you can read all the articles I have written by going to my website.

Application Design

The Benefits of Reuse

There are many benefits of code reuse. I will go over the major ones and why they are important.

Unit Testable

Unit testing is very important to validate the code and something I never have seen done very much. Most of the projects I work on as a contractor either have no unit tests or very few. Once, while I was at Microsoft, someone from the team that created IntelliTests (does not work in .NET 5) told me that teams should strive for 75% code coverage. I think this is a good goal. It is very important to do unit testing before sending it over to the quality assurance team. Tell your boss that this **is** a cost-saving!

If you follow what I say in my writing and are practicing good Object-Oriented Programming techniques, then unless a type and its methods are used by another assembly (except for MCV controllers and related types), they should be marked as internal, so they are *not* exported. This is a proper OOP design and can speed up performance. If you do this, then it is difficult to unit test them. Putting the code in re-usable DLL's fixes this issue since you will have to make key types and methods public, so they **are** exported.

There are more ways to test your code and app with integration, end-to-end, and visual testing. So, do not forget that before deployment too.

Easier to Maintain

Ever since my beginner programming days, I have seen code copied from one class to another. I still see it today! Once the same block of code is copied this way, then a major maintenance issue is instantly created! If there is a bug in the code or

Application Design

a change needs to be made, then you must do it in 2 or more places. Talk about wasting time and money!

Making reusable assemblies can fix this problem. There is a feature in Visual Studio that will show you where all the duplicate code is. Easy! If any code like this is found, just put it in a separate assembly. The way I approach coding now is that most of the code I write, will be reused, somewhere at some time in the future. So, I just do it right from the beginning, when writing new code.

Easier to Share

If most of the code is in reusable assemblies, then it is easier to share with others on your team, department, or another department. It is then very easy to make NuGet packages to share them too! It is very easy to do this with .NET 5 projects via Visual Studio. These packages can be shared within your company or on NuGet.org.

Easier to Update

Architecting solutions this way also makes updating easier. If a bug is fixed or some other non-breaking change is made, then only that assembly needs to be updated or downloaded. For example, if your boss walks into your office one day (this happened to me) and says that they have decided that the company will not use SQL Server anymore and now must use Oracle, then it is very easy to make this change without affecting the other layers.

If architected correctly, most of the rest of the app will not have to be updated at all! Talk about time and cost savings! In that example, it took me only about a day to change that project to use Oracle, including testing. I did not even need to modify the app (ASP.NET) except for the connection string in the config file.

If you get a kickback from your boss about this architecture, remind them that **this is a cost and time savings**! Maybe not now, but it will be in the future. *I guarantee it!*

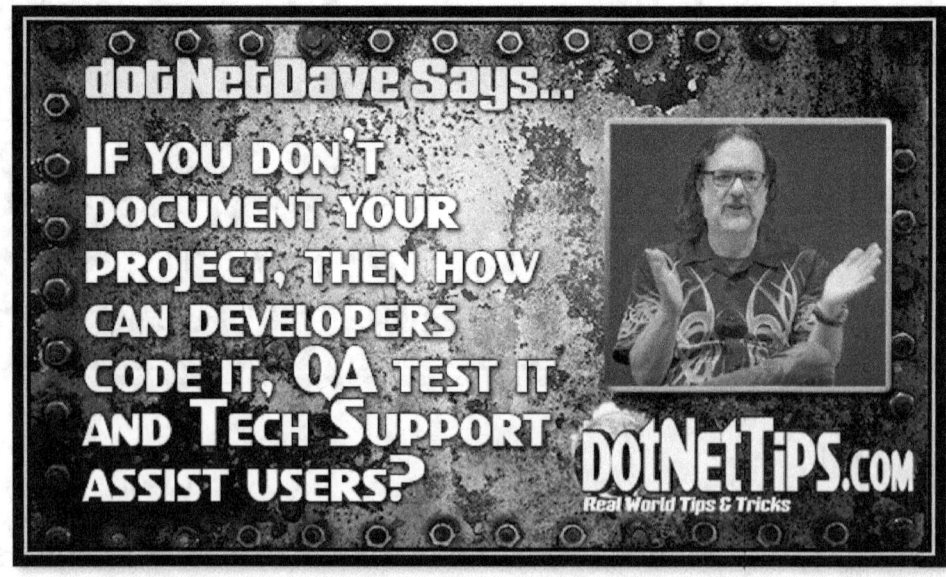

Word Choice

Avoid using class names that duplicate .NET namespaces. For example, do not use any of the following names as a class name: **System**, **Collections**, **Forms,** or **UI**. See the Class Library for a list of .NET namespaces. Also, avoid using identifiers that conflict with the keywords in this chapter. It is easy to see the .NET namespaces by using the Object Browser in Visual Studio.

Keywords

Keywords are predefined, reserved identifiers that have special meanings to the compiler. They cannot be used as identifiers in your program unless they include **@** as a prefix. For example, **@if** is a valid identifier but it is not because **if** is a keyword.

The first table in this topic lists keywords that are reserved identifiers in any part of a program. The second table in this topic lists the contextual keywords.

abstract	as	base	bool
break	byte	case	catch
char	checked	class	const
continue	decimal	default	delegate
do	double	else	enum
event	explicit	extern	false
finally	fixed	float	for
foreach	goto	if	implicit
in	int	interface	internal
is	lock	long	namespace
new	null	object	operator

Word Choice

out	override	params	private
protected	public	readonly	ref
return	sbyte	sealed	short
sizeof	stackalloc	static	string
struct	switch	this	throw
true	try	typeof	uint
ulong	unchecked	unsafe	ushort
using	using static	virtual	void
volatile	while		

Contextual Keywords

A contextual keyword is used to provide a specific meaning in the code, but it is not a reserved word in C#. Some contextual keywords, such as partial and where have special meanings in two or more contexts.

add	alias	ascending
async	await	by
descending	dynamic	equals
from	get	global
group	into	join
let	nameof	on
orderby	partial (type)	partial (method)
remove	select	set
unmanaged (generic type constraint)	value	var
when (filter condition)	where (generic type constraint)	where (query clause)
yield		

Capitalization Summary

When writing code, it is important to use a consistent capitalization standard when naming everything from classes to source files.

Type	Case	Notes
Class / Struct	PascalCasing	`AppDomain`
Enum type	Pascal Casing	`ErrorLevel`
Enum values	Pascal Casing	`FatalError`
Events	Pascal Casing	`ValueChanged`
Exception class	Pascal Casing	`WebException` Always ends with Exception
Interface	Pascal Casing	`IDisposable` Starts with `I`
Methods	Pascal Casing	`ToString`
Namespace	Pascal Casing	`System.Drawing`
Parameters	Camel Casing	`firstName`
Property	Pascal Casing	`BackColor`
Constants	Pascal Casting	`DefaultMinCharacter`
Read-only static field	Pascal Casing	`RedValue`

Capitalization Summary

Type	Case	Notes
Source Files*	Pascal Casing	▲ 🔒 📁 IO ▷ 🔒 C# DirectoryHelper.cs ▷ 🔒 C# DriveHelper.cs ▷ 🔒 C# FileHelper.cs ▷ 🔒 C# FileProcessor.cs ▷ 🔒 C# FileProgressEventArgs.cs ▷ 🔒 C# FileProgressState.cs ▷ 🔒 C# PathHelperc.cs ▷ 🔒 C# SpecialFolder.cs

As mentioned earlier in this book, use abbreviations sparingly.

Source Control

Since all developers need to deal with source control systems. Here are rules that I have come up with over the years to make the pain of dealing with them easier and so I do not break the build! I have yet to use a source control system that is easy to use and did not wipe out the new code I was working on.

Committing Code to Source Control Workflow

This is the workflow I use and recommend before any commit. Of course, you should be committing your code locally often to prevent code loss.

#1 - Document Classes and Methods

At a minimum, all the public and protected classes and methods need to be documented to make it easier for the developers to use your assembly. To make this easier, you can use the *FREE* Visual Studio extension GhostDoc from Submain.com. If you use proper naming standards, then writing this documentation is very quick and easy! These comments can also be easily converted to help files and websites. These comments will also show up in IntelliSense!

#2 - Run StyleCop

StyleCop is a free NuGet package for Visual Studio that was originally written by Microsoft and they have used it ever since the first version of .NET to ensure their classes all look consistent and look like it is all written by the same person. You should do the same in all your projects, *especially* if you have contractors on your team. For more detailed information about StyleCop, go to the Analyzing Code for Issues section in the Project Setup chapter.

#3 - Run Analyze in Visual Studio

To make sure my code is free from issues, I run Analyze in Visual Studio. If it finds anything then I fix them and start these steps over.

Source Control

#4 - Run Unit Tests

Now that all the possible code issues are fixed, run all the unit tests for the solution. If anything fails, fix it, and go back to setup #1.

#5 - Commit Code

After fixing or suppressing violations (only by a manager, code review, etc.), then commit the changed code into the code repository your company/ team uses. If the project is not set up for a continual build, then what I recommend and do, is call up a fellow developer and have them get the latest source and build the project. This will hopefully find any issues with missing files or files that were modified but for some reason did not make it into the commit of the code. In my experience I see this happen often from every code repository I have used. You *never* want to be the "one" that breaks the build.

This is my *minimum* workflow I do every time, and this keeps QA from bugging me and gives me more time to work on features!

Rules for Committing Code

I have been using source control programs for a very long time. I believe the first one was Visual Source Safe (don't laugh, it was a painful experience). Early in my career, I have learned many good practices that I still use to this day. If you are a .NET developer, before you commit code, you should follow my workflow that is discussed in the Committing Code to Source Control Workflow section. Developers that use other languages should still follow these rules, just the tools might be different.

Source Control

#1 Code in Source Control Is Golden

Do you like breaking the build or upset others in your team? I recently contracted with a company that the not so experienced developers, would break the build daily, sometimes for many hours. This caused many, many hours of lost work and delays in production releases.

With this *golden* rule, **never** commit code that:

- ⊗ Is not completed and ready for QA testing
- ⊗ Does not build
- ⊗ Does not pass **ALL** unit tests

I know that this should make sense to most developers, but I need to mention it since many do not. Thankfully, most modern-day repositories allow you to commit changes without pushing them to the repository until it passes the rules above.

#2 Do Not Commit Binaries That Can Be Built

Some companies have a policy that puts common assemblies (DLL's) into source control. If you own the source, this should **never** be done. These assemblies should be built during the build process. There are several reasons why this policy can be an issue:

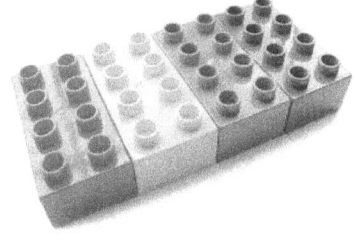

- Versioning can be the biggest issue. Project references always work better, especially for code that is changing often during the feature or bug that is being worked on.
- Is the common assembly folder in source control locked down so that only assemblies that have gone through the official QA and release process? I have never seen this done at companies. Usually, it is wide open to anyone who can commit the source. So, if someone makes a change, puts the assembly in the common folder it could break the code that others are working on.

The only DLLs that could be checked into source control are from third-party companies like GrapeCity, DevExpress, etc. I am not a huge fan of this either since these DLL's can be installed on the developers' machine and the build machine. If the third-party DLL offers a NuGet package, then there is no reason to check them into source control.

Source Control

If you want to share assemblies with other teams at your company, the best way would be to make NuGet packages and then host them on NuGet.org. Do not want to put them in the "cloud"? No problem, a NuGet server can be hosted locally at your company. Creating NuGet packages with Visual Studio and .NET 5 is super easy (just one checkbox click).

#3 Do Not Commit User, Temp, or Other Files Not Used for the Build

Many files should never be committed to source control. These are mostly user-based files, temp files, and more. What are they? The easiest way to find out is to look at the git ignore file for Visual Studio. Some of the common files to not commit are:

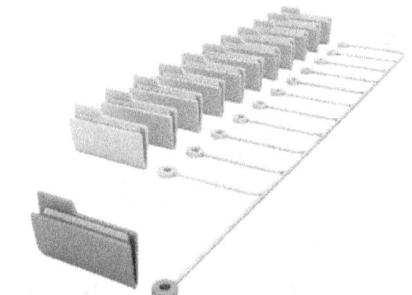

1. *.suo
2. *.user
3. *.vscc
4. *.userprefs
5. bin or obj folders

Some source control programs are good at this like Azure DevOps or GitHub and some are very bad at it like Perforce and PVCS.

#4 Backup, Backup and Backup Some More

Far too many source control problems like Perforce, PVCS, and even GitHub like to "clobber" your changes (wipe them out). I do not know how many hundreds of hours over the years I have seen wasted by this. So, to help with this issue, I created a backup app that auto-detects where all the source is on your machine and quickly backs it up. The latest version even has a "turbo" mode that only backs up changed files. See Appendix C for more information on this utility.

I always run my backup program before I get the latest from source control. I also do it at the end of the day. I hate losing work and this app has helped me recover any files that might have been clobbered.

Source Control

#5 After You Commit Major Code Changes

If you have not pushed any changes to the source control server in a while or have had made a major breaking change, make sure everything builds properly by following these steps. This needs to be done since you do not want to tell QA *"everything works on my machine"*!

1. Close Visual Studio, then rename your root source folder on your machine. For example, I change my "src" folder to "src.bak". This is so that we can get a clean version of the source in item #3.
2. If any projects use NuGet packages, remove the packages folder. This is usually right under your root source folder. I use a PowerShell script do make this easy (also removes bin and obj folders):

```
cd <source folder>:
Get-ChildItem .\ -include bin,obj,packages -Recurse | foreach ($_)
{ remove-item $_.fullname -Force -Recurse }
```

3. Go to your source control program or add-in and force a fetch of all the source code.
4. Fire up the solution you were working on and build it. If there are errors, fix them and then start this process over.

If you follow these 5 simple steps, your fellow team members will thank you! At one company I worked at, if someone broke the build, they would have to display a troll doll on their desk until the next person broke the build. In the past, in the Microsoft Office team, if a developer broke the build, they would have to stay late to babysit (monitor) the nightly build process! I guarantee this will help your team just like it does the teams I work for.

Database Naming Standard

Let us face it, in most companies that developers work for, end up doing database work. I do not agree with this since I think the DBA or BIA should handle database programming and we should stick to what we do best... coding. Would you want a DBA to write code or even a user interface? I think not. With that said, here are database naming standards for programmers. DBA's might not agree with how database developers name databases; stored procedures, etc. but we need something.

Stored Procedure Naming Standard

With every new version of SQL Server, standards have changed a bit and have become more like the .NET standards. You can see this in how Microsoft names their stored procedures in their newer programs.

NAMING CONVENTION

```
TableNameOrBusinessProcess_PredominantAction_<project, application, or logical segment>
```

I do not like underscores, but since these could get long, it might be good to make them easier to read. Also, prefixes are out in 2005 and above. They are only used by the system stored procedures to be backward compatible.

Predominant Actions:

- Select – returns multiple rows
- Get – Returns 1 row
- Update
- Delete
- Insert
- Extract
- Import
- Save – Combines insert/update

Database Naming Standard

Of course, we can add more to these if you want. Here are a few examples:

```
ClientLicense_Get
RentalCar_Save
RentalCar_Delete
Vendors_Select
```

As you can see with "RentalCar", if you put the action after the table name or business process, it is *much* easier to find everything you can do with Rental Cars.

Project, Application, or Logical Segment

This is optional; separating the stored procedures by one of these areas can be helpful by just adding this to the end of the stored procedure. Here is an example:

```
ClientLicense_Get_ClientAppliation
ClientLicense_Get_ServerAppliation
```

Also, as you can see, for the first two segments, follow normal Pascal casing.

Development with Visual Studio

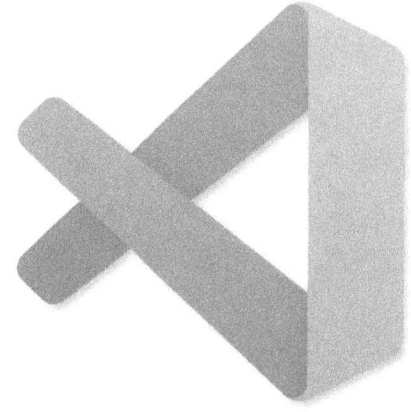

Visual Studio is an awesome IDE that makes it easy to develop .NET projects and I enjoy using it. I cannot imagine a better tool out there. There are a lot of great features in Visual Studio along with some issues. This chapter will focus on both. You can follow along with the issues and needed features that I have submitted to the Visual Studio team: https://bit.ly/VS2019Issues

Fixing NuGet Hell Issues

In the 9th episode of 256 Seconds with dotNetDave, I show how to help NuGet hell issues in Visual Studio. If you have issues building because of NuGet package errors, in this episode I show how to use a PowerShell script on how to fix it! This script could also help with DLL issues too. You can view this video by going to https://bit.ly/256SecondsE9

Many, many times (almost weekly), suddenly the build starts breaking for no apparent reason. This is usually due to multiple versions of a DLL or NuGet package in the debug or release build folder. There could be another reason too. The best way I fixed it is with the PowerShell script below.

First, the script deletes all bin, obj, and packages for a given folder (c:\src in the script below). Then it also deletes all the NuGet packages from your **.nuget** folder. This will force fresh copies of the NuGet packages that your solution is using.

PowerShell Script

Before running this script, close all instances of Visual Studio.

```
cd c:\src

Get-ChildItem .\ -include bin,obj,packages -Recurse | foreach ($_)
{ remove-item $_.fullname -Force -Recurse -Verbose }

cd C:
cd C:\Users\[user name]\.nuget\

Get-ChildItem .\ -include packages -Recurse | foreach ($_) {
remove-item $_.fullname -Force -Recurse -Verbose }
```

I have another script that is for deleting the bin, obj, packages folders from the current folder and its subfolders. I save it to a **.ps1** file and put it in the root folder of all my solutions.

Development with Visual Studio

```
Get-ChildItem .\ -include bin,obj,packages -Recurse | foreach ($_)
{ remove-item $_.fullname -Force -Recurse -Verbose }
```

Code Quality is a Feature, Not an Afterthought

I must admit something... I must admit that I get more and more frustrated with the lack of code quality in projects I work on as a contractor. Some are okay, but most are very far from it. What frustrates me more is that most of this poor-quality code I analyze is written or supervised by senior software engineers. Since I do not work permanently at a company anymore, I cannot make sure

that *code quality is a feature, not an afterthought*. By the time a company gets in trouble and hires me to work on their codebase, it is almost too late to implement code quality since it usually means major changes to the code and architecture.

> *As an example, recently I was hired for a contract about 1 ½ months before user acceptance testing started on the first version of three projects. These projects are not even in production yet and they already have over 4,200 code violations (one every 4 lines of code), including hundreds of violations from StyleCop. These three projects also needed major architectural changes so that the code can be reusable and unit-testable, something I discuss a lot in my conference sessions. This is an example of when it is almost too late to hire me. I fear most of the work I did in the first 1 ½ months will never make it into the main branch (it did not).*
>
> *On a contract a few years ago, their codebase had over 50,000 issues (not including StyleCop). I worked on it for about a year... just fixing their code issues. I did not even add one feature in that year! As with many contract jobs, they ran out of funding at the end of their fiscal year, so I moved on to another contract. About six months later they hired me back and in those six months, they introduced over 10,000 new code issues!*

Now, do you understand why I get frustrated? I have been writing and speaking about code quality for a very long time. I drill code quality into my student's heads in *all* the classes I teach. **All** my code sessions at conferences are wrapped around code quality.

Code Quality is a Feature, Not an Afterthought

Management Does Not Care, So You Have To

Let us face it, management at most companies only care about two things. The first is features, features and more features. Adding features is the easiest way to sell more product. The second thing they care about is adding those features at the lowest cost possible. Due to these two things, management *does not care about code quality* which always includes proper architecture, since to them, it is not a feature. They can only see what features cost *now* with no worry about how much it will cost the company in the *future* if code quality is not a feature from the very beginning. Especially when it comes to fixing bugs, which is not a feature either.

> *At one company I worked at, towards the end of my time there, I was in a major meeting with managers and vice presidents. They were talking about all the features that needed to be added to the product to sell more product. Towards the end of the meeting, I was getting frustrated and I finally raised my hand and said, "The features you want will either be impossible or take so long that our competitor will release them before us, and we will lose customers if you don't break down and re-architect the database." They all looked at me with expressions like they have never heard this before until my boss said, "Dave has been telling you this for four years, why don't you listen to him?" Not long after that, they laid off all the high-level software engineers in my department, including me. Guess what happened? They lost customers and have not done well ever since.*

So, it is up to *you*, the *coder*, to care about code quality or it will not happen. Why should you care? You will be the one that will have to maintain the code, add features, and fix bugs. If your projects are a pile of spaghetti code, then you will be just putting a band-aid over band-aid on top of it until it finally falls down and you have to start all over again, hopefully, right this time. It will be worse if the database is poorly architected as I discussed in the example above. So why not do it right in the first place?

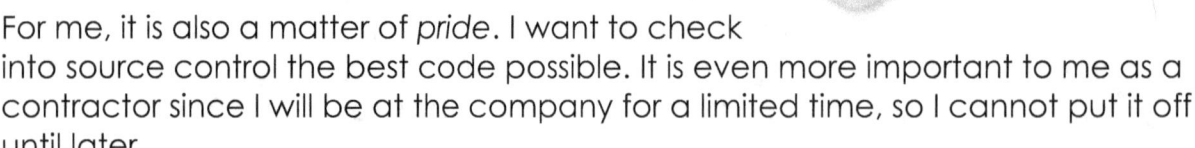

For me, it is also a matter of *pride*. I want to check into source control the best code possible. It is even more important to me as a contractor since I will be at the company for a limited time, so I cannot put it off until later.

Learning Code Quality

To learn code quality, it must be important to *you*. *You* must care about it and once you have been doing it as long as I have, it just becomes second nature. So

Code Quality is a Feature, Not an Afterthought

much so that these days, it is very painful for me to work on projects that code quality is not a feature and I am forced to use bad practices. Now that I think of it, maybe I should charge companies a higher hourly rate depending on the state of their code!

I was lucky in my beginner days to be mentored by great senior software engineers and learned best practices, most of which I still use today. Good code quality practices never go out of style, you just keep learning even better practices. So, if you can find a great team to work with, then that will be one of the best ways to learn good code quality practices. In the interview, you should ask them how they implement code quality (let me know what they say).

Books

Books are a good way to learn too. I always suggest getting books that can be used for many, many years like Clean Code by Robert C. Martin or Refactoring by Martin Fowler. Depending on the programming language you use, get the best book on object-oriented programming you can find. Also, books on design-patterns are a must too. When you learn the things in these books, you can use that knowledge for your entire programming career. I am a *very* big proponent of object-oriented programming that was first used back in the 1950s before I was even born! If you are a .NET developer, then my other books can help too.

Community Events

Community driven conferences, like Code Camp's, are a good place to learn since they are run by software developers just like you, so they know the importance of code quality. The bigger paid conference is usually not a good place to learn since they are driven by profit. I have previously written about this in my article titled *Soft Skills – As Important If Not More Important Than Technical Skills at Conferences* on dotNetTips.com.

Another great place to learn is local community events like User Groups, Meetups, and even your local C# Corner Chapter. Most of these types of groups will have multiple events each month, again driven by software engineers from your area. Most of these events are free, so why not take advantage of them? One of the reasons I can see the whole picture when it comes to architecting applications is because I founded a user group here in San Diego, California, and ran it for 20 years.

Online Training

Online videos could be a good way too. But I am not aware of very many on the subscription-based sites, like Pluralsight, except for the one titled Defensive Coding in C# by Deborah Kurata. There are free sites out there too like Channel 9 and my video site: http://bit.ly/dotNetDaveOnDemand.

Code Quality is a Feature, Not an Afterthought

Websites

There are tons of websites out there such as Coding Best Practices on C# Corner and the Code Quality category on my site. All the code on my site follows good code quality unless I am showing a bad code example. *I make sure of this.* So, follow sites that show all the examples using normal coding standards and code quality patterns. You can also check out Microsoft Patterns and Practices, which is now on GitHub (not sure why since it is harder to use). I am not aware of any blog site that just focuses on code quality. If you find one, please let me know!

Tools Help Find Issues & Help You Learn

Visual Studio extensions and other tools can help you find and fix issues with your code. Code analysis is a very important part of coding and there are hundreds of rules that these tools use. Not only should you run these tools before you commit any code to source control you have been working on, but they also should be part of the build process, so the state of the code can be easily seen. This is even more important if you hire contractors!

I have written about my workflow before I check in code in the article My Workflow Before I Submit Code Changes. In this article, I write in detail about the three tools I use. I use StyleCop (free) from Microsoft, then Analyze in Visual Studio. Other extensions that I use include Code Cracker, GhostDoc (for documenting code), Productivity Power Tools 2017/2019, StopOnFirstBuildError just to name a few.

Another tool that all developers need is a good refactoring tool. I use CodeRush from DevExpress. Jet Brains also has a refactoring tool called ReSharper. The refactoring that is built into Visual Studio, does not have enough features, so I suggest getting one of these two tools.

One great side-effect for most of these tools is that they teach you good coding practices! Once you fix the same issue over and over, eventually you will just code it correctly. This is one of the reasons why I know what I know when it comes to code quality. When you are trying to justify the cost of any of these tools, remember to tell your boss that you will become a better developer. **They are worth every penny!**

I hope I encouraged you to make code quality a feature of all code that you write. Make sure you bring it up in any planning meetings you attend. I also gave you some suggestions on how to learn good coding practices that include using tools for Visual Studio.

What Can Be Done to Make Code Quality Better?

Since 2014, all my conference sessions have been wrapped around code quality. It has always been very important to me and I try to include a lot of that concept in this book. Since that time, I have asked developers to participate in an online survey to see how they implement coding standards and enforce them. The last question I ask is "What can be done to make code quality better?". I have lots of ideas on how to make it better, but I want to know what other developers think. I hope you will participate in this survey by going to http://bit.ly/CodingStandards2020.

This chapter features those answers along with my comments. I do hope that the Visual Studio and .NET teams at Microsoft will read this chapter so that they can make it easier to implement good code quality and standards. Let us get started.

1. Unit Test Integration

> *"Always need to test the latest features with unit testing integration. Proper code commenting."*

I agree with this. I would add that **all** features need to have unit testing integration. The .NET Framework does help with this by using the IntelliTests feature in Visual Studio makes it easy to add encapsulation tests (the first pillar of Object-Oriented Programming) by running the code and tries to break it the code paths. When I was working with the PM of this team, he told me that teams should strive for 75% code coverage. I agree with this and would add that all public and protected methods need to have at a minimum encapsulation unit tests. Unfortunately, the Visual Studio team did not make IntelliTests available in .NET Core. I hope they do, but I have not heard that they are. So, .NET 5 developers are back to doing it all manually, which makes it very hard to reach that 75% goal and is why most code I see as part of my job have no unit tests or very little.

What Can Be Done to Make Code Quality Better?

These days, I see no code commenting or very little. Code these days should be "self-documenting" which does help but **does not** remove the need for commenting the code from the developer who wrote it. Of course, keeping these comments up to date is also important.

2. Training & Team Meetings

"Better standards, better training, team meetings/training on coding standards."

This suggestion is very important to make sure everyone on your team, including contractors, are on the same page. This kind of meeting needs to happen often. In the team I currently work in, I am the one that teaches coding standards in our weekly meeting and everyone on the team has a copy of this book.

3. Code Review

"Code isn't looked at by another party enough. Even when it is, egos are huge in the development community. People think that "attacks" on their code might as well be attacks on their skills or personality. Developers need to let that go."

Let's face it, we all have egos, some bigger than others. So, when someone attacks code we wrote, it is very tough to not take it personally. We could have spent days, weeks, or even months on the code and when someone points out all the issues, it can feel very defeating. What makes it worse is the way developers point out the issues or attacks them. Many developers use this to make themselves look superior or prove their worth in the team. These types of developers just attack and attack with no real solutions or helpful criticism. This just makes people shut down and stop listening or even worse, find a new job. Now the team has lost a valuable resource.

I am not aware that the proper way of reviewing code, so it does not attack the developer who wrote it is taught in any class. I certainly did not learn it in any class or workshop that I took.

If you are the one reviewing the code, make sure to do it in a calm and collected manner in the same way that *you* would want your code reviewed. Give helpful examples, point the developer to resources that can help, etc. The more you can help, the better the developer will be. We are all here to train each other, no matter what level you are at. If you are the reviewee, also stay calm, listen, and ask lots of questions on the parts that you do not understand.

What Can Be Done to Make Code Quality Better?

4. Code Analytics

> *"Do not allow code check-in if the standard check fails. Strict coding editor to follow standards. Regular coaching and mentoring. Code review and sharing the improvement plans."*

I like the idea in the first sentence of this suggestion. Since the code quality I see on most projects I analyze is pretty bad, wouldn't it be great that if out of the box, source control programs like GitHub, would not allow code to be pushed to the repository until these checks were done? I am not aware that any source control program does this. I checked GitHub actions and did not see anything.

For Microsoft .NET repositories, it should be **very easy** to enable and configure running Microsoft's StyleCop and Analyze before the code is added to the repository. I would also like the ability to run third-party analyzers. I will keep my fingers crosses (I hope the GitHub team reads this chapter).

5. Develop a Culture of Quality

> *"Engage developers and develop a culture of quality."*

I try very hard to do this in the teams that I work for and I do this in my conference sessions, and I did it when I taught at a local university. But that's me. I rarely seen this fostered in teams since code quality is not considered a feature. I have already written the Code Quality Is A Feature, Not an Afterthought chapter. Most managers do not care about code quality, only features since that is what sells more products. It is our responsibility as developers to push back and make sure this happens since we will have to fix bugs and add features.

6. Caring About Our Craft

> *"Ensure you have a team of developers who care about their craft and who care about the product they are developing. There is an intangible yet distinct difference between a developer punching the clock yet adhering to team coding standards; and a developer who truly cares about the work he/she is doing, and funnels that care and concern into creating the best solution he/she can."*

This important idea, and to me should be done during the interview process. I do talk about this more in my book titled Rock Your Career: Surviving the Technical Interview. In **every** interview I perform, I ask questions to try to assess this quality in developers. If a developer that does not care about their craft is hired into a team,

What Can Be Done to Make Code Quality Better?

it is very difficult to remove them, sometimes impossible if the team works for the government. So, it must be done as part of the interview process. The typical team these days is between 2–5 developers (based on my survey). Even one developer on the team who is there to "punch the clock", can hamper the entire team and delay the project. I know that in America we have a shortage of developers, but that is not an **excuse** to hire developers who will not fit in the team and company.

7. Keep Learning & Evolving

"Learn, learn, and learn more, never stop learning. Keep evolving. Practice by refactoring your code."

If this quote does not apply to you, you might be in the wrong profession. I talk a lot about this in my conference sessions and my books. Our world changes **every day**! If you want to keep up, you must be learning **all the time**. This is one of the reasons I love being a software engineer. There is no way to know everything, so the opportunity to learn is endless. It is the same reason I love playing guitar… I cannot learn every song.

At the same time, this can be and is very stressful. I had one professor call it "techno-stress". I have never forgotten that term and I suffer from it 110%! Since I am an "older developer", this gets harder as I age. I must limit what I want to learn and sometimes it might take me longer. This is just a part of aging. Back when I was starting in this world, programming was a lot less complex.

The more software is around, the more complex it gets. This is one of the reasons I suggest to beginner students or developers is to first focus on the "stack" you are most interested in. For example, if you are interested in mobile apps, become proficient on that stack, and tackle another one later. If you try to learn all the stacks right from the get-go, you will get very frustrated and might want to find a different profession.

It is also important that during the interview process that the interviewer asks questions to try to learn if they are hiring a developer who likes to learn and wants to evolve. I do it in **every** interview that I perform. For example, one of the last questions I **always ask** is "How do you keep up with technology?". If the interviewee does not have a really good answer, off the top of their head, I will not want to hire them. I look at it like this… I am a teacher, trainer, and conference speaker, I can teach anything, but **only** if the person is willing to learn. I will **always hire** someone with less experience over someone who is more experienced but is unwilling to learn (I have been burned by this early in my career).

8. No One Is Perfect

"Some of the old school programmers think they code perfectly."

What Can Be Done to Make Code Quality Better?

This gets back to the egos discussed earlier. The more developers learn and grow in their profession, the more perfect they think they become. Hopefully, *part* of this is true, I hope they do get better. It is their attitude that might get in the way. I have worked on teams where a developer has a senior position (mostly due to the time they spent at the company), but they have never grown from their beginner days.

I hope my readers do not think that I think I code perfectly… I do not (no one does). I *freely* admit that since I am *always* willing to learn. I am sure in my articles and books and even when I speak at a conference, I might sound like that, but I am not perfect, and neither is my code. I just have a lot of care and passion to make it as good as I can, especially since I only take contracting jobs. I am there for a limited time and I want to leave behind the best code I can that is *easy* to understand.

9. Teach Students Standards & Architecture

> *"Teaching kids from the start when they are learning in school, that standards and comments are critical and if you can't follow acceptable standards, don't apply. I see students naming their variables so stupid, and they should get a grade based not only if the code works, but in general… standards are practiced."*

Since I taught programming classes at the University of California, San Diego for almost 18 years, teaching my students good coding standards and architecture right from the beginning was very important to me. In *all* my classes, I made this book required, even in beginner classes. Sure, I made around $2 per book, but that was not the reason I did it. I wanted to make sure they would be hirable once they completed the program. Especially if they were being interviewed by me (which did happen). Also, in all my classes, since I taught them coding standards and good architecture practices, I did grade them on it.

Once, while I was speaking in St. Louis, Missouri, one of the attendees told me that they teach coding standards in college there. I was very surprised but very happy that it was being done.

Another college here in San Diego, California asked me to be on their computer science advisory board. At the first meeting, I told them that everyone I interviewed that went through their program I could not hire. I thought that this would be my last meeting. But at least one of the directors there seemed receptive and talked to me at length about my thoughts. I came up with a new program that all seniors

What Can Be Done to Make Code Quality Better?

would have to go through before getting a degree, to help them be more hirable. They were about to implement my new program when they lost interest in the board and it was dissolved. This is very unfortunate for the students that continue to go through their degree programs.

I do believe this should be taught in any computer science degree or program, but I do not see it happening. If you went through a program that *did* teach coding standards and code quality, I would like to hear your story. Also, if you are going through a program that does not teach this, I am more than willing to help *any* school get this added to their program.

10. Coding Standards = Secure, Robust & Maintainable Code

> "The coding standard should be predefined in terms of both technical as well as non-technical such as business test cases. We should use standard coding in a way such that it would result in secure, robust & more maintainable. Comments & documentation both should be used as well as early discussions between developers, managers & users on paper help to make our software code more standard. We should be very careful to add or remove even the small changes, features on the live system after deployment as several small changes in a hurry without documentation leads to serious issues. We should never write everything on a single page as some developers write CSS, HTML, and server-side scripts all on a single page. Using third-party control and can reference after careful inspection i.e., version and support. The code should be written as per business requirements. Browsers & devices should be kept in mind where the software will run."

This comment, to me, sums up this chapter. I would like to add that the entire team, including management, *must* make code quality important, right at the beginning and throughout the life of the project. In my experience, most developers are on-board with this, but management is not since it is not a feature that can be sold to customers. It seems now that everyday companies are being hacked, data is being stolen, important services and sites are going down, and more. This is only going to get worse. So, it is important to build in code quality for all software, even if users are unaware of it.

Definitions

This chapter discusses many of the definitions used in this book.

Capitalization Styles Defined

Pascal case

The first letter in the identifier and the first letter of each subsequent concatenated word are capitalized.

EXAMPLE

```
BackColor
DataSet
```

Camel case

The first letter of an identifier is lowercase, and the first letter of each subsequent concatenated word is capitalized.

EXAMPLE

```
numberOfDays
isValid
```

Uppercase

All letters in the identifier are capitalized.

EXAMPLE

```
ID
PI
```

Hungarian Type Notation Defined

Hungarian Notation is any of a variety of standards for organizing a computer program by selecting a schema for naming your variables so that their type is readily available to someone familiar with the notation. It is, in fact, a commenting technique.

Definitions

EXAMPLE

```
strFirstName
iNumberOfDays
```

There are different opinions about using this kind of type of notation in programming nowadays. Some say that it is useful, and it should be used everywhere to enhance the clarity of your code. Others say it just obfuscates your code because it has no real advantage in modern programming environments.

If you have to Hungarian Notation in .NET, use it wisely, meaning, only use Hungarian Notation for private or local variables, which are only accessible and interesting to the programmer of the class.

Do not use it with public variables, properties, or parameters in methods, because they are exposed to the outside world. Someone who uses your classes and accesses properties of your class is not interested in type but just wants to use them.

Appendix A - Coding Standards Survey

Since 2014 I have been conducting a coding standard survey to see how other teams are implementing coding standards at their company. Below are the results of this survey. I hope you will participate by going to http://bit.ly/CodingStandards2020

#1: How Many Developers Are in Your Team?

Lately, most of the development teams I work in are small, usually 2-5. In one recent contract, there were only two developers, no database developers, and no QA. I am curious about what the average is.

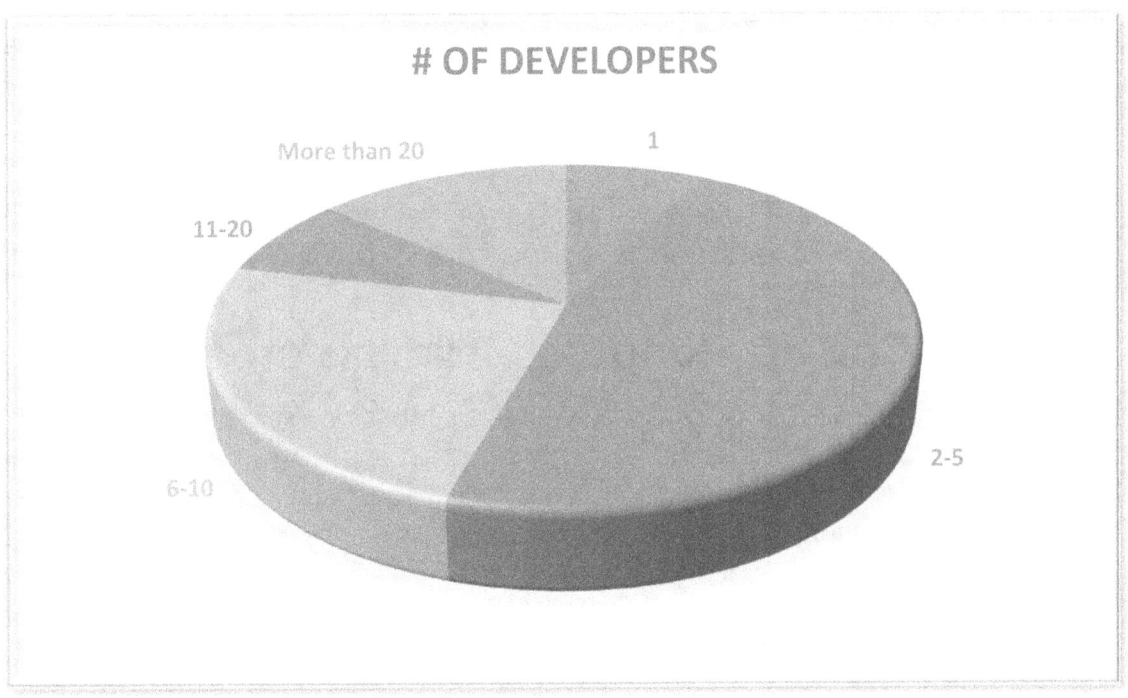

As you can see below, most teams are between 2-5. This is my experience in the teams I work in.

#2: Does Your Team Use Documented Coding Standards?

In my experience, when I go to work at a company, the vast majority do not use or have documented coding standards. After I start, I get them to practice and enforce coding standards with the basis of those standards being this book. At my last full-time job, every developer in the department got a copy of my book, even if they worked in a different country!

Appendix A - Coding Standards Survey

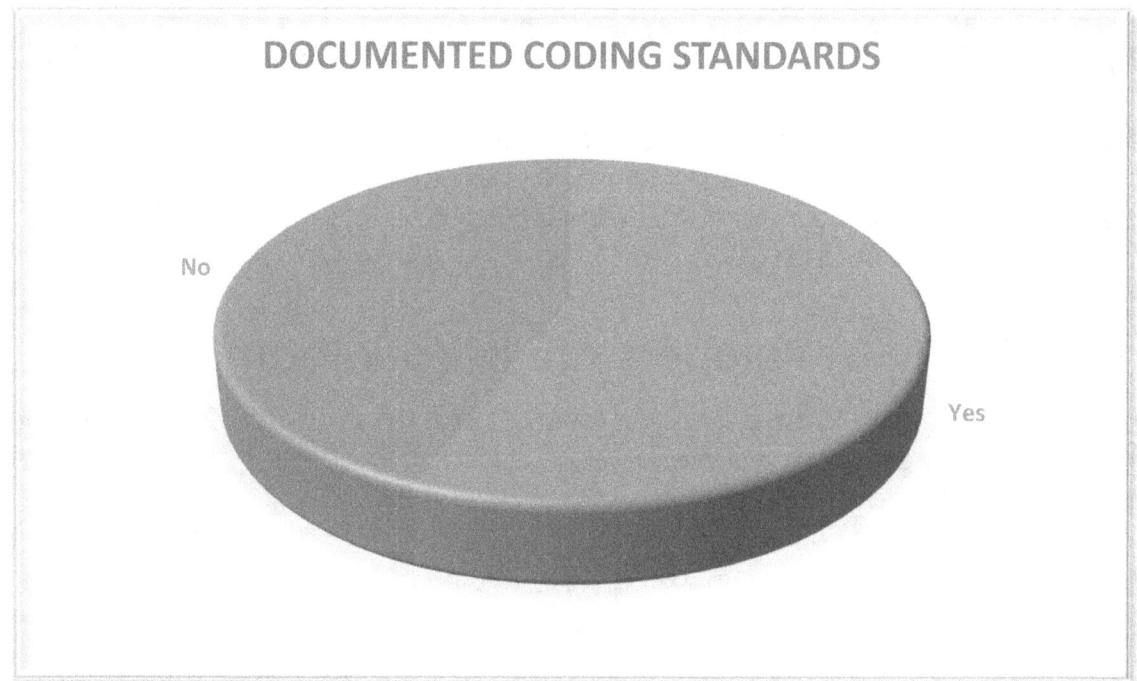

What worries me about this result is the number of developers who do not use documented standards. Any team (more than 1) must have them documented!

#3: How Are Coding Standards Administered?

Once a team has coding standards in place, they must be enforced. If a programmer has done standards in the past, it is hard for them to change to a new one. Even more important is making sure they are followed by contractors since their time in the team is limited. The most important is to make sure they are followed by beginners, so they learn right from the get-go.

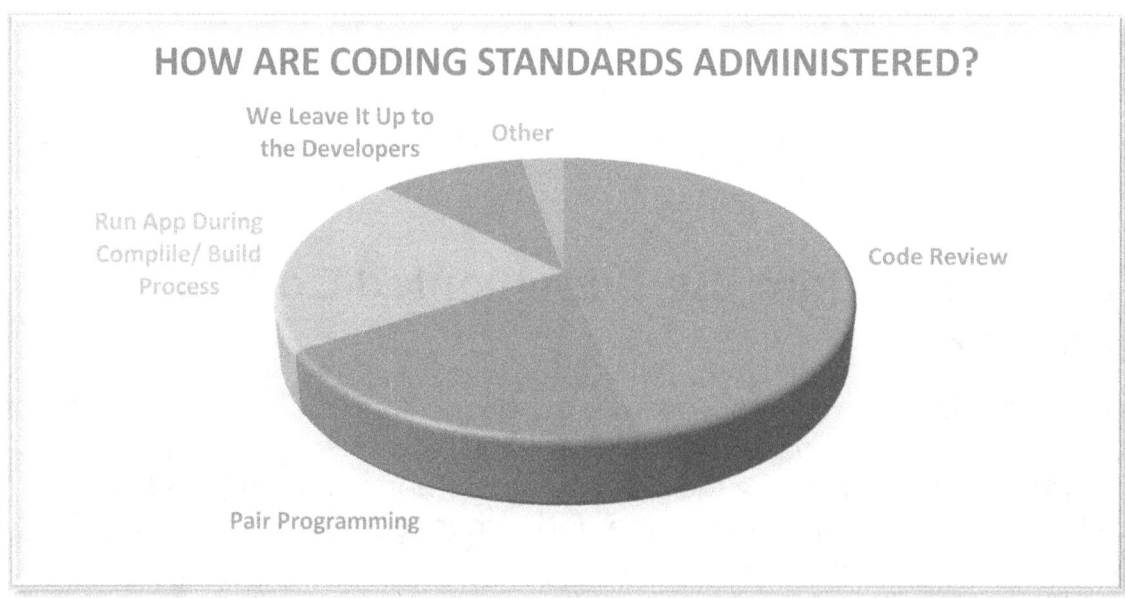

Appendix A - Coding Standards Survey

Code review is the most popular, but as we all know, when deadlines are looming this is usually cut from the schedule. So, it must be combined with running a code analysis tool during the build process and not release to QA until the minimum number of violations (hopefully that number is zero) is reached.

What tools should you use? The one I use is Visual Studio Analyze.

#4: What Does Your Team Use as Coding Standards Documentation?

It is very important to document your team coding standards and as you can see below, the Microsoft Framework Design Guidelines (online) is used the most. Of course, I wish this book was number one, but I hope that company's use it as the basis for their standards. No matter what the standards are, make sure they are easily accessible by developers either in print or online.

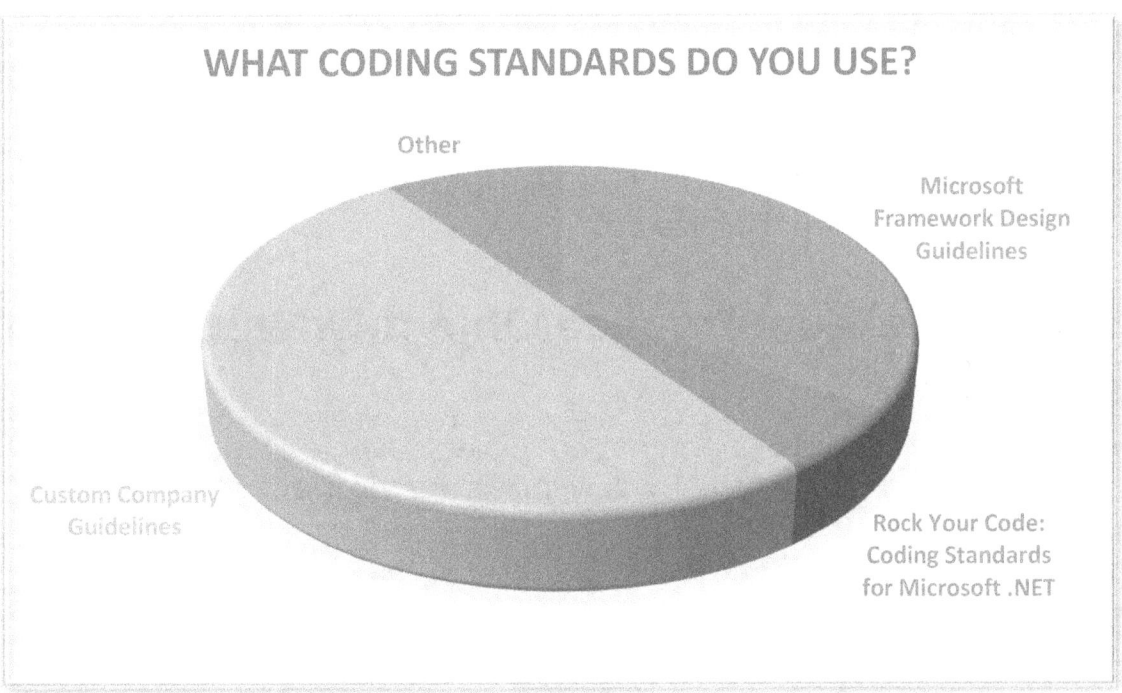

Developers, make sure you follow the standards and do not deviate from them unless you get them officially changed. What is good for the company is good for you!

#5: Where Did You Learn Coding Standards?

For the developers who do follow coding standards, I was curious where they learned how. One time when I was speaking in St. Louis, one of the attendees told me that they learned at college. I was very surprised by that. I have never seen it taught in class unless I was teaching it. I even made this book required to take the class, even beginner classes since I wanted to start them off right!

Appendix A - Coding Standards Survey

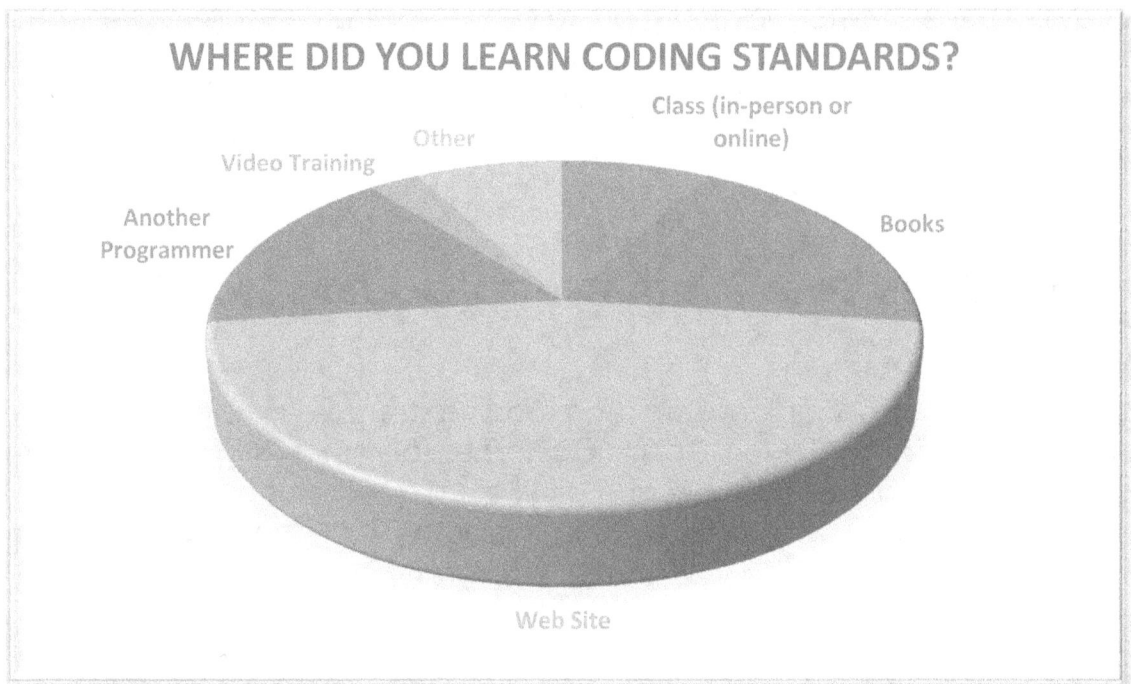

No one in the survey indicated that they learn coding standards from video training sites such as Pluralsight or Channel 9. I tried to do coding standards training on Pluralsight, but they were not interested.

#6: Does Your Team Practice Object-Oriented Programming

Since I have included a new chapter about Object-Oriented Programming in this book, I was curious about how many developers use this practice.

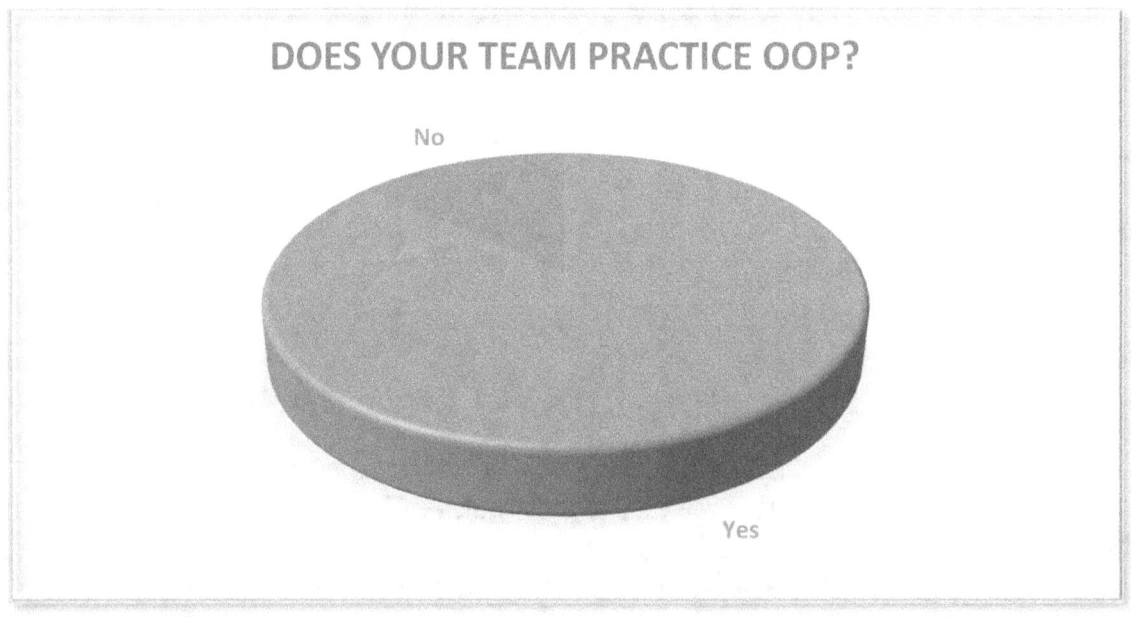

Appendix A - Coding Standards Survey

I am curious about the developers who do not use OOP. What they use instead? In the past 10 years, I have not worked on a single codebase that implemented OOP properly, unless I architected it.

#7: Does Your Company Provide Any Applications to Make It Easier to Abide by The Coding Standards?

To boost developer productivity, any team needs to provide good quality Visual Studio add-ins and applications to help make coding standards easier. This will also lead to better code quality and happier users.

Analyze in Visual Studio is the winner. I do use it along with CodeRush and StyleCop.

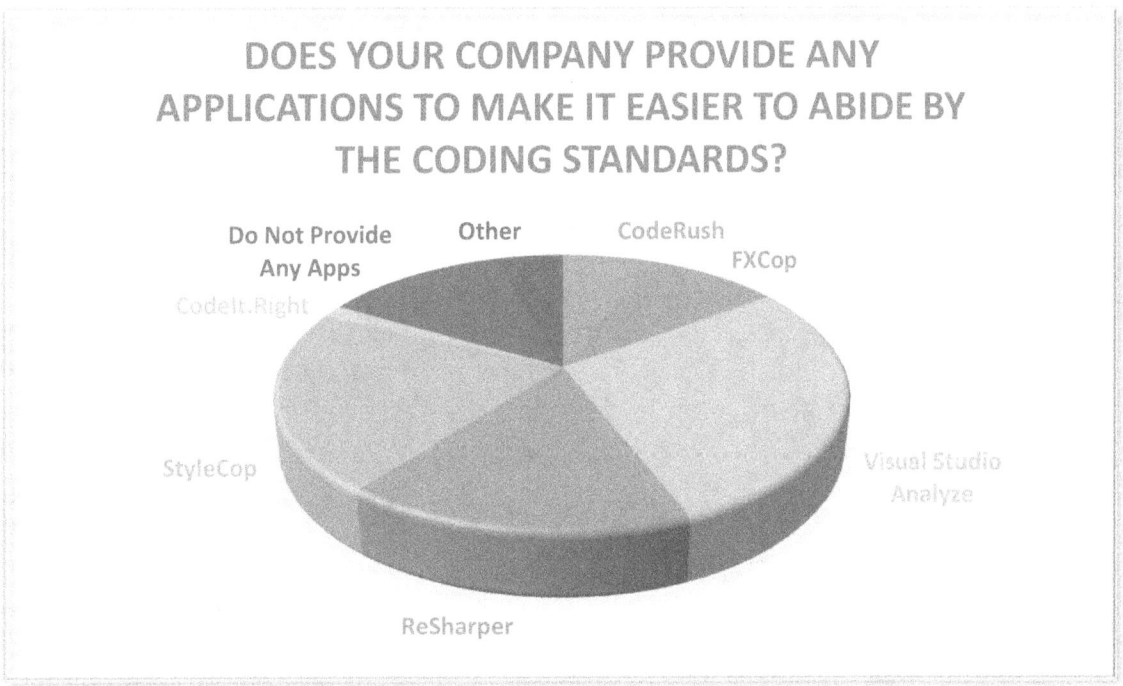

What worries me the most about these results is that 7% of companies do not provide any tools at all. This blows my mind. Most of the companies I have worked for do not provide any tools. Since I do have these tools (since I am a Microsoft MVP) regardless of what the company provides, I am usually the only developer in the team properly refactoring code, analyzing code, etc.

#8: If You Took Over Someone's Code, How Painful Was That Experience?

When I ask this question in my conference sessions, I usually see 90% of hands go up indicating that the experience was painful. The next question I ask is what the first thing is you want to do after taking over someone else's code and the usually the answer is... **rewrite it**!

Appendix A - Coding Standards Survey

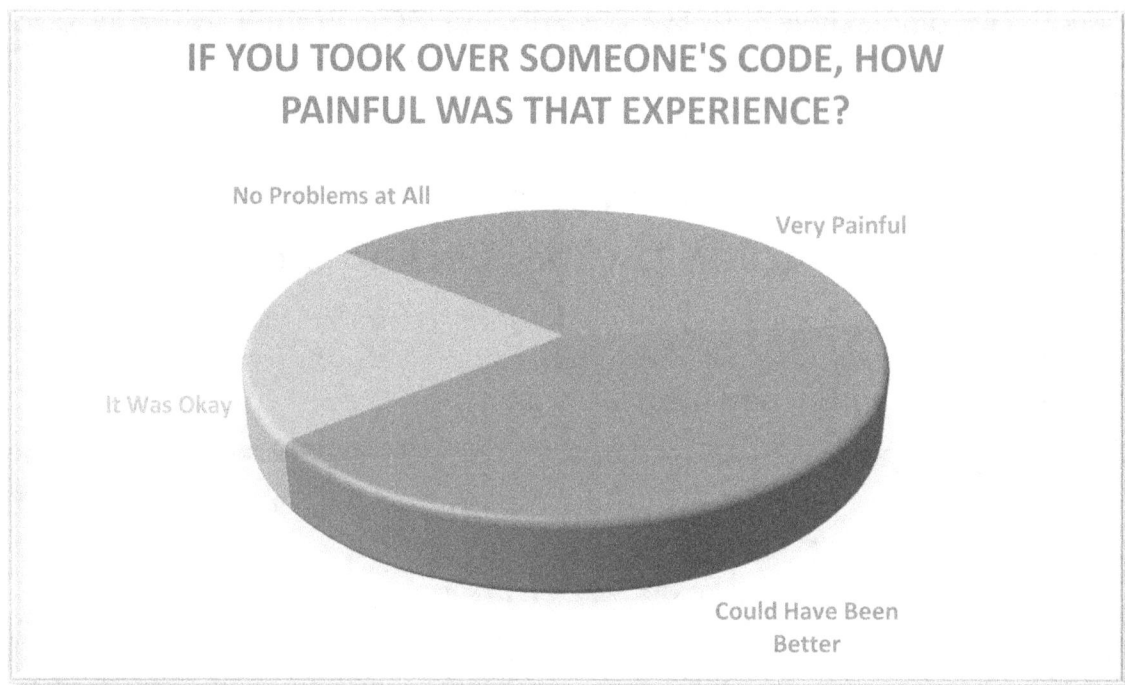

I would venture to guess that most companies would not allow code to be re-written since it takes away from writing new features. The first time I had to take over someone else's code I did not ask my boss, I just did it during downtime after the first release of our product. Therefore, it is very important to always implement and follow great coding standards. This book is the first step in that direction.

#9: Do You Believe Coding Standards Are Important to Produce Stable Code?

I would hope that all developers feel coding standards are important, but only 91% feel this way. Until this reaches 100%, I will keep releasing new editions of this book and giving my Röck Yoür Cöde: Coding Standards for Microsoft .NET conference session.

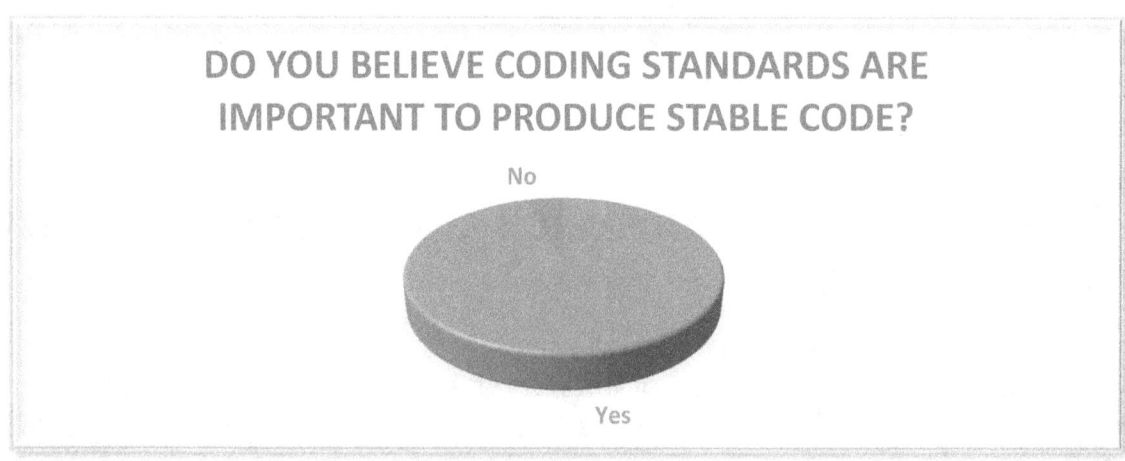

Appendix A - Coding Standards Survey

It is also very important for teams to foster coding standards education for their developers.

Other Comments

Here are some other comments from the survey.

- Consistent code reviews and pair programming.
- Follow a standard of practice for clean code and good unit testing and integration testing case scenarios.
- Follow consistent design patterns where they are appropriate. Frequent peer reviews (e.g., on every change request).
- Gated build should reject the code if standards are not met.
- Make sure that the development team is using and agreeing to use the same coding standards documentation. Senior developers should be doing code review and sharing knowledge as to why some code needs to be replaced.
- More analyzers (or easier to make rules for them)
- Peer review, code review & help of automated tools.
- Regular peer reviews, training, company-sponsored round tables.
- Self-documenting code, which I have not seen where I have worked.
- Smarter code analyzers and auto-corrections, easier way to create your own code standard rules.
- The ability to not using stupid variable names within functions.
- To reflect upon the code that you are writing and ask, "could this line/method/class be clearer/more efficient?" - continually. The SOLID principles - and all the other standards that exist - should be a tool in the mind of the reflective coder to help them judge what they have just written. These standards should not become yet another ideology - to be followed blindly to excess.
- Total team buy-in of standards simple standards.

Thanks to all that have taken this survey and providing input. I hope you will participate by going to http://bit.ly/CodingStandards2020

Appendix B - dotNetTips.Utility

For a while now, I have made available the common code that I have been writing ever since .NET was released as my open-source project titled "dotNetTips.Utility". It was originally available on CodePlex. The latest version for .NET 4.x and .NET Core 3.x is on GitHub. There are tons of helper methods that will make your .NET coding life easier.

Spargine

In early 2021, I will be releasing my open-source code for .NET under a new name called Spargine! This release represents a clean break from the .NET Framework and .NET Core and only supports .NET 5 and above. There are already lots of new code that I think you will find useful. Make sure to subscribe to dotNetTips.com for notifications.

Download Source

.NET 5 source: https://github.com/RealDotNetDave/dotNetTips.Spargine

.NET Core source: https://github.com/RealDotNetDave/dotNetTips.Utility.Core

NuGet

All the .NET Core/ Standard versions of these assemblies are also available via NuGet: https://www.nuget.org/profiles/davidmccarter. The .NET 5 version of these packages will be released sometime in 2021.

Appendix B - dotNetTips.Utility

davidmccarter

dotNetTips.Utility.Standard.Extensions by: davidmccarter
6,532 total downloads · last updated a month ago · Latest version: 2020.11.19.1
David McCarter dotNetDave dotNetTips.com
Common .NET Standard Code Extensions

dotNetTips.Utility.Standard by: davidmccarter
6,169 total downloads · last updated a month ago · Latest version: 2020.11.19.1
David McCarter dotNetDave dotNetTips.com
Common .NET Standard Code

dotNetTips.Utility.Standard.Tester by: davidmccarter
1,448 total downloads · last updated a month ago · Latest version: 2020.11.19.1
David McCarter dotNetDave dotNetTips.com
Common .NET Standard code for use in unit tests and benchmarking.

dotNetTips.Utility.Core.Windows by: davidmccarter
797 total downloads · last updated a month ago · Latest version: 2020.11.19.1
David McCarter dotNetDave dotNetTips.com
Common .NET Core Code for Windows

dotNetTips.Utility.Standard.Common by: davidmccarter
674 total downloads · last updated a month ago · Latest version: 2020.11.19.1
Common .NET Standard Code

5 Packages

15,620 Total downloads of packages

Bulletproof Disposable Types

Whenever I perform a code review on .NET projects, hands down, the number one issue is developers not calling **.Dispose()** on disposable objects. Ever since .NET was released, I have been preaching how important this is. If not done properly, it is most likely to create virtual memory leak issues that will eventually cause the application to stop and freeze the server or user's computer. This can also cause performance issues.

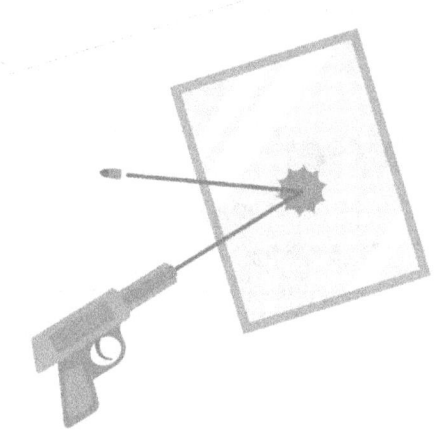

Recently, after doing a review on a company code base, I had a meeting with the development manager. I asked him "Do you have any backend servers that you need to re-boot regularly?". He said "YES"! I told him "I know *exactly* what the issues are!". The issue is most of their code, if not all of it, did not call **.Dispose()** of any disposable object. It took me about three months to fix them all!

How do you know if all your code is calling **.Dispose()** properly? Running a memory profiler will help with this.

Appendix B - dotNetTips.Utility

Making Dispose Easier

A while ago I wrote extension methods to make calling **.Dispose()** easier in my open-source assemblies. Just install the dotNetTips.Utility.Standard.Extensions package.

Disposing Local Variables

To dispose of a variable, I created the **TryDispose()** extension method. Here is an example of how to use it:

```
disposableObject.TryDispose();
```

TryDispose() checks to make sure the object is not null and then calls **.Dispose()**. If the code uses a "**using**" code block, then it calls **.Dispose()** for you and it would not need to use this method.

Disposing Fields

TryDispose() is great for a variable but how about a type that has disposable fields? I created a method for that too called **.DisposeFields()**. Here it is in action using the proper **IDisposable** pattern:

```
protected bool disposed;

public virtual void Dispose()
{
   Dispose(true);

   GC.SuppressFinalize(this);
}

protected virtual void Dispose(bool disposing)
{
   if (this.disposed)
   {
      return;
   }

   if (disposing)
   {
      this.DisposeFields();
   }

   this.disposed = true;
}
```

DisposeFields() looks at all the fields in the object and if any of them implement **IDisposable** then **.Dispose()** is called. The cool thing about this method is that it

Appendix B - dotNetTips.Utility

prevents another developer from adding a new **IDisposable** field and not add it to the **.Dispose()** call. I call this *"Future Proofing"*.

Disposing Collections

I have been using these two extension methods for a long time. But recently, I found that a client of mine is putting disposable objects into a collection. I've never used a collection like that, so I wrote a method for that too called **.DisposeCollection()** that works with **IEnumerable**, **IEnumerable<T>** and **IDictionary<TKey, TValue>**. **DisposeFields()** will check to see if the object supports **IEnumerable**, if it does, then it also calls **.DisposeCollection()**.

Making Sure There Are Not Any Virtual Memory Leaks

One downside to using code analyzers to find **IDisposable** issues is that I have yet to find one that finds everything. The way I know to find every issue is to use a memory profiler. The ONLY way to find them all is to run the code preferably on a near to production setup.

The memory profiler I use is called .NET Memory Profiler from SciTech Software AB. I have tried all the major profilers out there and this one works the best, even in .NET 5. It helps me to drill down to where the possible memory leak is and even see the data it contains. Be warned… tracking down issues in a profiler can take a while due to all the false positives. There are more things that this memory profiler can find so I recommend checking it out before your project goes to production. See Appendix D for more information.

Calculating Total Size of Files in a Directory

The **DirectoryInfo** type in .NET does not have a method to return the total size of the files underneath that directory, so I added an extension method called **GetSize()**. I need this for some upcoming changes I need to do to my free app for .NET developers. Here is how to use it.

```
var directory = new DirectoryInfo(Environment.GetFolderPath(
                        Environment.SpecialFolder.Cookies));

var result = directory.GetSize(searchPattern: "*.cookie",
                        searchOPtion:
SearchOption.AllDirectories);
```

Checking that the User is an Administrator

In my free app for software engineers, I check to see if the user is running the app using admin rights, I use **App.IsUserAdministrator()**. In this app, I warn the user

Appendix B - dotNetTips.Utility

that the app will work better running under admin rights. Here is how I do that in the app.

```
if (App.IsUserAdministrator() == false)
{
    this.WriteUserMessage(new DevMessage { Message =
                        Resources.UserMessageCouldNotRunAsAdmin,
                        Type = MessageType.Important });
}
```

Checking to See if the Current Process is Already Running

Since C# apps do not have an easy way to prevent two instances of the same app from running (like VB.NET projects do) I needed that check for my free app for software engineers. So, I use **App.IsRunning()**. In my app, if the app is already running, I just shut down the app that is loading by using **App.Kill()**.

Based on my benchmark testing, **App.IsRunning()** has a performance mean of 377,618.047 ns.

Checking to See if a Process is Running

In my free app for software engineers, when the app starts, I check to see if Visual Studio is running and if it is, I warn the user that they should close it before using the app. I use the **App.IsProcessRunning()** method as shown below.

```
App.IsProcessRunning("devenv");
```

Based on my benchmark testing, this method has a performance mean of 220,639.168 ns.

Copying a File Asynchronously

The File type in .NET does not support any async methods. So, I created **FileHelper.CopyFileAysnc()** that uses the async methods from **FileStream**. Here is an example on how to use it.

```
var result = await FileHelper.CopyFileAsync(file: fileToCopy,
                        destinationFolder: this._tempPath)
                        .ConfigureAwait(true);
```

CopyFileAysnc() returns the file size as a long.

Appendix B - dotNetTips.Utility

Custom App Settings for .NET

Awhile back (I think version2), the .NET team added a feature to non-web apps called Settings. I loved this feature since it made it easy to add *strongly typed* app settings. Ever since then, I have been recommending to developers in this book to use these settings over the string-based settings in the app.config that can cause errors and we all want to avoid those! They were easy to add in the project properties and even could configure the setting to be app-based (read-only) and updatable user settings.

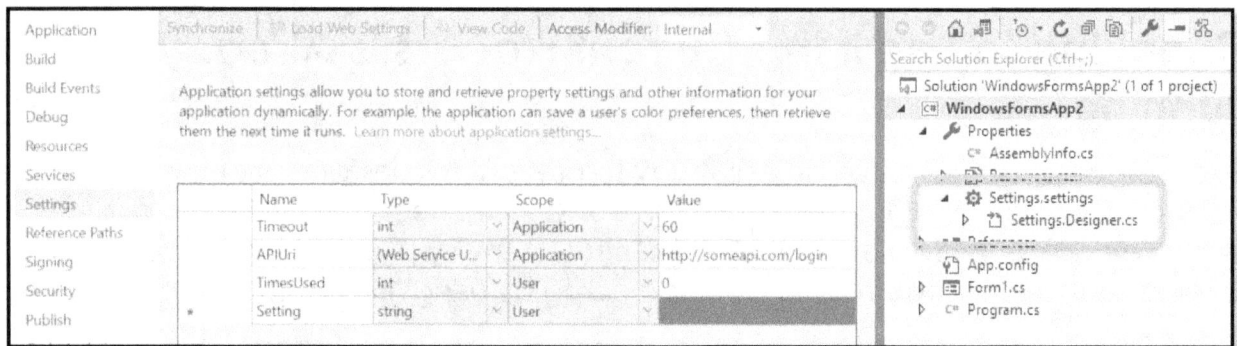

This designer created a class called **Settings** as shown below.

```
namespace WindowsFormsApp2.Properties {

    [global::System.Runtime.CompilerServices.CompilerGeneratedAttribute()]
    [global::System.CodeDom.Compiler.GeneratedCodeAttribute
      ("Microsoft.VisualStudio.Editors.SettingsDesigner.SettingsSingleFileGenerator", "16.8.1.0")]
    internal sealed partial class Settings : global::System.Configuration.ApplicationSettingsBase {

        private static Settings defaultInstance = ((Settings)
          (global::System.Configuration.ApplicationSettingsBase.Synchronized(new Settings())));

        public static Settings Default {
            get {
                return defaultInstance;
            }
        }

        [global::System.Configuration.ApplicationScopedSettingAttribute()]
        [global::System.Diagnostics.DebuggerNonUserCodeAttribute()]
        [global::System.Configuration.DefaultSettingValueAttribute("60")]
        public int Timeout {
            get {
                return ((int)(this["Timeout"]));
            }
        }
```

Since these settings are strongly typed, they were very easy to use in your code as shown below.

Appendix B - dotNetTips.Utility

```
[STAThread]
static void Main()
{
    Application.EnableVisualStyles();
    Application.SetCompatibleTextRenderingDefault(false);
    Settings.Default.TimesUsed += 1;
    Application.Run(new Form1());
}
```

Unfortunately, the .NET team did not move this feature to .NET 5 projects. I have asked the team to implement it in 2019, but as far as I can tell, they have not even considered it yet.

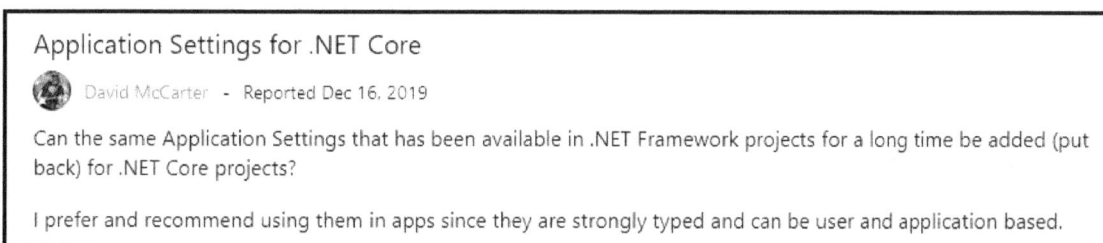

Introducing Config.cs

Since not every app will use settings in the cloud, when .NET Core 2 came out, I decided to create a class that *sort* of mimicked this feature minus the designer. The class in my open-source project is called **Config.cs**. This class uses any custom class that you choose to define your settings. It also includes load and save methods and automatically saves the file in the local application data folder for the app. For example, for my free app for developers, the settings are saved in **C:\Users\david\AppData\Local\dotNetTips.com\dotNetTips.Dev.Utility.App.config**. Currently, it serializes the data as XML. Here is a portion of the config file for this app.

Appendix B - dotNetTips.Utility

```xml
<DaysToKeepBackedUpFolders>7</DaysToKeepBackedUpFolders>
<FileBackupConfig>
  <BackupFolder>
    <Enabled>true</Enabled>
    <FilesOlderThanDays>0</FilesOlderThanDays>
    <FolderRetention>Keep</FolderRetention>
    <Path>C:\Users\david\OneDrive - dotNetTips.com\Backup</Path>
    <Recursive>false</Recursive>
    <SearchPattern>*.*</SearchPattern>
  </BackupFolder>
  <DaysToKeepBackedUpFolders>7</DaysToKeepBackedUpFolders>
  <FilesLifetimeInfo>
    <TotalFileSize>3435407579</TotalFileSize>
    <TotalFileCount>64525</TotalFileCount>
    <TotalPerformanceInMilliseconds>836658.82260000554</TotalPerformanceInMilliseconds>
  </FilesLifetimeInfo>
  <IgnoreFileTypes>
    <string>aps</string>
    <string>bak</string>
    <string>cache</string>
    <string>cachefile</string>
    <string>csdef</string>
    <string>dbmdl</string>
    <string>dll</string>
    <string>docstates</string>
    <string>dotCover</string>
    <string>gpState</string>
    <string>JustCode</string>
    <string>ncb</string>
    <string>nupkg</string>
    <string>opendb</string>
    <string>opensdf</string>
    <string>optpfx</string>
```

For this app, the custom settings type I created is called **DevConfig**. Here is what it looks like in the class designer.

Appendix B - dotNetTips.Utility

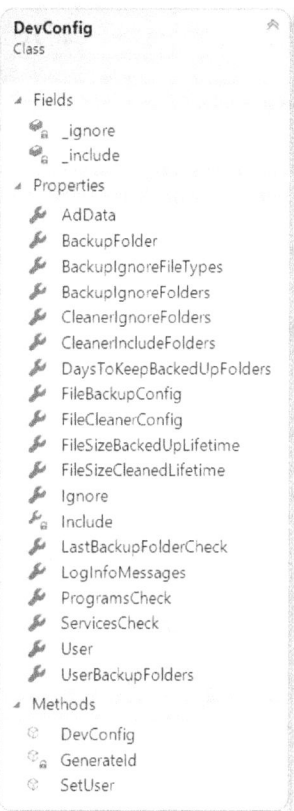

This is how the configuration type is used.

```
public class AppDevConfig : Config<DevConfig>
{
   public AppDevConfig()
   {}
}
```

Usage

To access the settings, just use the **Instance** property. Here is an example of updating a setting.

```
this._config.Instance.FileSizeBackedUpLifetime = 0;
```

I even store collections of data like this.

```
//Download graphics
foreach (var ad in this._config.Instance().AdData.Ads)
{
   // Code removed for brevity
}
```

In the future, I do plan to add the ability to save as JSON or XML. While I wait to see if the Visual Studio and .NET team will add back **Settings**, this solution works well for my apps and I hope it helps yours also.

Appendix B - dotNetTips.Utility

DateTime & DateTimeOffset Extensions

If you talk to any seasoned developer, they will usually say that dealing with dates and times is a real pain. While it has gotten better since .NET was first released, it could be better. For this article, I will be showing the extension methods that are in my open-source project, dotNetTips.Utility.Standard.Extensions for the **DateTime** and **DateTimeOffset** types. This project is also a NuGet package too. Most of the examples below work for both the **DateTime** and **DateTimeOffset** types. All the code examples are from the unit test project for the assembly.

Before I show you the code, I would like to say, "*Stop using DateTime!*". Any new code should use **DateTimeOffset** (as Microsoft recommends) so it can properly handle time zone information. **DateTimeOffset** can also be used with SQL Server. You should also strive to change older projects to use this new type too. Though that will be harder to implement. Make sure you have *plenty* of unit tests *before* changing to **DateTimeOffset**.

Looking for The Previous Day of the Week

If you want to find a previous day of the week, you can use the **GetLast()** extension method below with the **DayOfWeek** enumeration.

```
var result = DateTime.Now.GetLastDayOfWeek(DayOfWeek.Monday);
```

Output

Here is the result of the code above using the current date of Friday, 7/17/2020.

```
7/13/2020 11:24:46 AM
```

Looking for The Next Day of the Week

If you want to find the next day of the week, you can use the **GetNext()** extension method below with the **DayOfWeek** enumeration.

```
var result = DateTime.Now.GetNextDayOfWeek(DayOfWeek.Monday);
```

Output

Here is the result of the code above using the current date of Friday, 7/17/2020.

```
7/20/2020 11:24:46 AM
```

Looking for a Date that Intersects a Date Range

If you want to find if a date intersects a date range, you can use the **Intersects()** extension method below.

```
var now = DateTime.Now;
```

Appendix B - dotNetTips.Utility

```
var result = now.Intersects(endDate: now.AddDays(100),
                            intersectingStartDate: now.AddDays(1),
                            intersectingEndDate: now.AddDays(10));
```

Looking for a Date in a Date Range

If you want to find if a date is within a given date range, you can use the **IsInRange()** extension method below.

```
var now = DateTime.Now;
var result = now.IsInRange(beginningTime:
                            now.Subtract(new TimeSpan(1, 0, 0, 0)),
                           endTime: now.AddDays(10));
```

Converting a Date using Time Zone Offset

If you want to convert local time to UTC using the time zone offset number, you can use the **LocalTimeFromUtc()** extension method below.

```
var now = DateTime.Now;
var result = now.LocalTimeFromUtc(-5);
```

Output

Here is the result of the code above using the current date of Friday, 7/17/2020 11:55:24.

```
7/17/2020 1:55:24 PM
```

Looking for the Max Date

If you want to convert local time to UTC using the time zone offset number, you can use the **Max()** extension method below.

```
var now = DateTime.Now;
var result = now.Max(now.Subtract(new TimeSpan(1, 0, 0, 0)));
```

Looking the Day After a Weekday

If you want to get the next (specified) day of the week, you can use the **NextDayOfWeek()** extension method below with the **DayOfWeek** enumeration.

```
var now = DateTime.Now;
var result = now.NextDayOfWeek(DayOfWeek.Sunday);
```

Output

Here is the result of the code above using the current date of Saturday, 7/18/2020 08:28:16.

Appendix B - dotNetTips.Utility

```
7/19/2020 8:28:16 AM
```

Creating a Friendly Date String

If you want to get a friendly date string to show to users, you can use the **ToFriendlyDateString()** extension method below.

```
var result = DateTime.Now.ToFriendlyDateString();
```

Output

Here is the result of the code above.

```
Today @ 8:31:01 am
```

Downloading File from Web Asynchronously

If you need to download a file from the web asynchronously, then you can use **FileHelper.DownloadFileFromWebAsysc()** that will store it in a file location of your choice. Here is an example of how to use it.

```
var fileToDownload = @"https://dotnettips.com/dotnettips.png";

await FileHelper.DownloadFileFromWebAsync(new Uri(fileToDownload),
  Path.Combine(this._tempPath.FullName,
"dotNetTips.Com.logo.png"));
```

Ensuring a Host is Available

One of the things I mention in my Defensive Programming conference session is to periodically check to ensure that a host, such as www.google.com, is available before sending a request. If the host is unavailable, it can cause exceptions in the application. This also allows you to disable buttons in the click such as "Send" until the host is available again. I have been coding like this since the very early days of .NET.

I created a method called **NetworkHelper.IsHostAvailable()** to ping the host. Here is an example on how you can use it to check Google.

```
var result = NetworkHelper.IsHostAvailable("www.google.com",
timeout: 500);
var result = NetworkHelper.IsHostAvailable("8.8.4.4", timeout:
500);
```

In my unit test, using **IsHostAvaialble()** to check www.googe.com took around 70 milliseconds.

Appendix B - dotNetTips.Utility

String Extensions

Here are more string extensions that I have added in this release.

- **FromBase64()**: Converts a Base64 string to string.
- **Extract()**: Extracts a string from a beginning and end value.
- **ToTitleCase()**: Converts a string to title case (capitalize the first letter of each word).
- **Parse<T>()**: Parses a string to a type.
- **ToBase64()**: Converts a string to a Base64 string.
- **ComputeHash()**: Computes a hash from a string value. Formats supported are: HMAC, MACMD5, HMACSHA1, HMACSHA256, HMACSHA384, HMACSHA512, MD5, SHA1, SHA256, SHA384 and SHA512. Based on my benchmark testing, using SHA256 with this method has a performance mean of 11,159.774 ns.

Retrieving Application Executing Folder

If you need to retrieve the location of where the current executable is running from you can use **App.ExecutingFolder()**. This is an example of the result of my unit test project.

```
C:\\src\\GitHub\\dotNetTips.Utility.Core\\src\\Unit
Tests\\dotNetTips.Utility.Standard.Tests\\bin\\Debug\\netcoreapp3.1
```

Retrieving Application Information

To easily retrieve common application information, you can use **App.AppInfo()**. It is very simple to use.

```
var info = App.AppInfo;
```

Here is an example of the results from my unit tests.

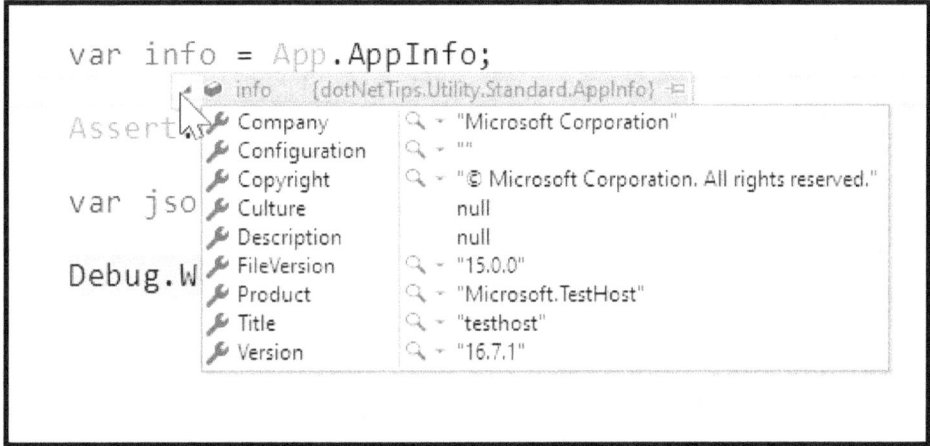

Appendix B - dotNetTips.Utility

Retrieving & Changing Culture

When .NET or you need to know the current culture and localization information to format data based on the users' location, that is all held in the **CultureInfo** type. To make retrieving this information you can use **App.CurrentCulture()** or **App.CurrentUICulture()**. Below is an example of just some of the information for **CurrentCulture**.

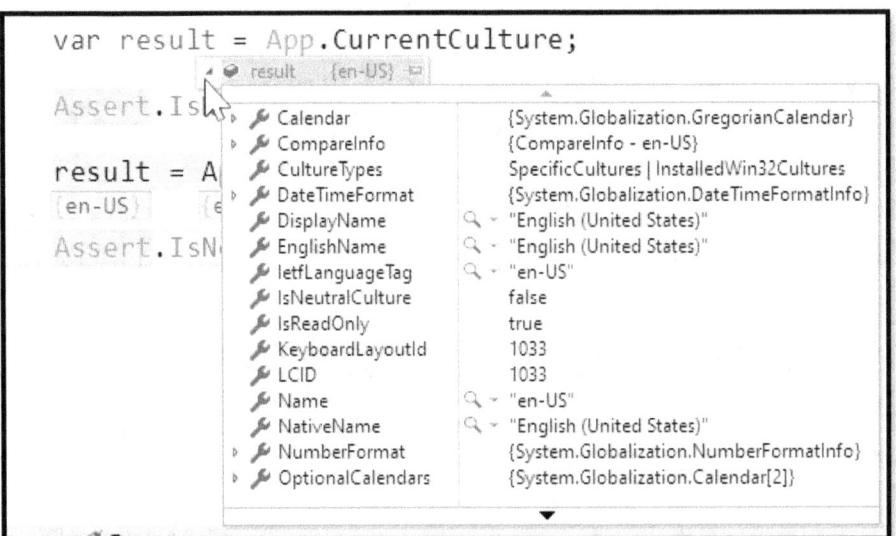

Once when working on a project, one of the requirements was that the user could on-the-fly change the culture that the current thread is running under. If you need to change the culture, you can do it using the methods below.

```
App.ChangeCulture("aa");
App.ChangeUICulture("af");
```

Retrieving Computer Information

For information that I use to log issues or information, I created a type called **ComputerInfo()** that returns common information. Here is just some of the information from my system.

```
ComputerCulture:eng,
ComputerUICulture:eng
FrameworkDescription:.NET Core 3.1.9
FrameworkVersion:{_Build:9,_Major:3,_Minor:1,_Revision:-1}
HasShutdownStarted:false,
IPAddress:123.456.7.8
Is64BitOperatingSystem:true
Is64BitProcess:true
IsUserInteractive:true
LogicalDrives:[C:\\]
MachineName:DESKTOP-ABCDEF,
```

```
OSDescription:Microsoft Windows 10.0.19041
OsMemoryPageSize:4096
PhysicalMemoryInUse:49057792
ProcessorCount:4,
SystemDirectory:C:\\WINDOWS\\system32,
UserDomainName:DESKTOP- AA2FHJ
UserName:david
```

Retrieving Environment Variables

The values in the Windows environment variables can be very useful to retrieve information about the user and system. You can use
App.GetEnviromentVariables() to retrieve this information. Below is an example of just some of the data from my system.

```
USERPROFILE:C:\Users\david
USERNAME:david
CommonProgramFiles:C:\Program Files\Common Files
USERDOMAIN:DESKTOP-ABCDEF
PROCESSOR_REVISION:8e09
ProgramFiles(x86):C:\Program Files (x86)
VisualStudioEdition:Microsoft Visual Studio Enterprise 2019
SystemDrive:C:
VSLS_SESSION_KEEPALIVE_INTERVAL:0
SESSIONNAME:Console
USERDOMAIN_ROAMINGPROFILE:DESKTOP-C22DAVET
CommonProgramFiles(x86):C:\Program Files (x86)\Common Files
ALLUSERSPROFILE:C:\ProgramData
HOMEDRIVE:C:
COMPUTERNAME:DESKTOP-ABCDEF
PUBLIC:C:\Users\Public
VSAPPIDNAME:devenv.exe
ProgramFiles:C:\Program Files
PROCESSOR_ARCHITECTURE:AMD64
windir:C:\WINDOWS
NUMBER_OF_PROCESSORS:4
ProgramData:C:\ProgramData
TMP:C:\Users\david\AppData\Local\Temp
TEMP:C:\Users\david\AppData\Local\Temp
VisualStudioDir:C:\Users\david\Documents\Visual Studio 2019
HOMEPATH:\Users\david
OS:Windows_NT
LOCALAPPDATA:C:\Users\david\AppData\Local
APPDATA:C:\Users\david\AppData\Roaming
VisualStudioVersion:16.0
SystemRoot:C:\WINDOWS
```

Appendix B - dotNetTips.Utility

```
PROCESSOR_IDENTIFIER:Intel64 Family 6 Model 142 Stepping 9,
GenuineIntel
```

Retrieving the .NET Framework Description

When you are logging information when an exception is thrown, it might be useful to log the .NET Framework description that the app is running under. To do this, you can use **App.FrameworkDescripion**. Here is an example of the output.

```
.NET Core 3.1.9
```

Using Common Control Characters

When creating or checking stings, there are a lot of common control characters that we use. To make using them easier, I created a static class called **ControlChars**. Here are its current values.

```
At = '@'
Back = '\b'
Backslash = '\\'
Colon = ':'
Comma = ','
Cr = '\r'
CR = '\r'
CRLF = "\r\n"
Dot = '.'
DoubleQuote = '"'
EndAngleBracket = '>'
EndComment = ')'
EndSquareBracket = ']'
FormFeed = '\f'
ForwardSlash = '/'
LF = '\n'
NewLine = "\r\n"
NullChar = '\0'
Quote = '\"'
SingleQuote = '\''
Space = ' '
StartAngleBracket = '<'
StartComment = '('
StartSquareBracket = '['
Tab = '\t'
Underscore = '_'
VerticalTab = '\v'
```

Since all these values are constants, it *could* improve performance.

Appendix B - dotNetTips.Utility

Temporary File Manager

Many apps, client and server-based, need to create temporary files to process data but far too many apps, even Visual Studio, do not clean up all the files they generated. So, to make creating these files easy and maintain those files, I created the TempFileManager type in the dotNetTips.Utility.Core.Windows NuGet package! I created this class a long time ago for a project written in the .NET Framework (Clr) and now I have moved it to .NET Core and made some enhancements. Below are examples of how to use it.

Creating a Temporary File

Creating a single temporary file is easy. Below is an example:

```
using (var tfm = new TempFileManager())
{
    var cachefile = tfm.CreateFile();

    //Process file code
}
```

TempFileManager implements **IDisposable** to ensure the files are deleted when not in use anymore. So, make sure to always use the using statement.

Creating Multiple Temporary Files

Creating multiple files at the same time is easy too.

```
using (var tfm = new TempFileManager())
{
    var result = tfm.CreateFiles(10);

    foreach (var file in result)
    {
        // Process file
    }
}
```

All the temporary files are creating in the **C:\Users\<current user>\AppData\Local\Temp** folder as shown below.

Appendix B - dotNetTips.Utility

Name	Date modified	Type	Size
tmpF78A.tmp	10/20/2020 11:11 AM	TMP File	0 KB
tmpF78B.tmp	10/20/2020 11:11 AM	TMP File	0 KB
tmpF78C.tmp	10/20/2020 11:11 AM	TMP File	0 KB
tmpF783.tmp	10/20/2020 11:11 AM	TMP File	0 KB
tmpF784.tmp	10/20/2020 11:11 AM	TMP File	0 KB
tmpF785.tmp	10/20/2020 11:11 AM	TMP File	0 KB
tmpF786.tmp	10/20/2020 11:11 AM	TMP File	0 KB
tmpF787.tmp	10/20/2020 11:11 AM	TMP File	0 KB
tmpF788.tmp	10/20/2020 11:11 AM	TMP File	0 KB
tmpF789.tmp	10/20/2020 11:11 AM	TMP File	0 KB

Other Useful Methods

Here are the other methods in the class.

- **DeleteAllFiles()**: Deletes the files being tracked and their names are removed from the list.
- **DeleteFile()**: Deletes a single file and removes it from the list.
- **FilesList()**: Returns a list of all the files being tracked.

If you find `TempFileManager` useful, please let me know if there is anything, I can add to make it more useful to you.

Deleting Files with Events

While working on the dotNetTips.Utility Dev App, I wanted to make the deletion of files even faster. While writing this utility I found and worked on speed issues, almost all relating to updating the user interface. So, to decouple the deleting from the UI, I decided to add a new feature to dotNetTips.Utility.Standard open-source code and NuGet package.

Processor Class

I added a new class in the **dotNetTips.Utility.Standard.IO** namespace called `FileProcessor`. The purpose of this class is to copy, move, and delete files while firing events that can be used to update the UI. Unlike other methods I have used in other frameworks if an exception occurs, it fires an event and keeps processing. First, I created the event:

```
public event EventHandler<FileProgressEventArgs> Processed;

protected virtual void OnProcessed(FileProgressEventArgs e) =>
                                Processed?.Invoke(this, e);
```

Appendix B - dotNetTips.Utility

Here is one of the methods in this class.

```csharp
public int DeleteFiles(IEnumerable<FileInfo> files)
{
   Encapsulation.TryValidateParam(files, nameof(files));

   var successCount = 0;

   List<FileInfo> list = files.ToList();

   for (int i = 0; i < list.Count; i++)
   {
      FileInfo tempFile = list[i];

      if (tempFile.Exists)
      {
         try
         {
            var psw = PerformanceStopwatch.StartNew();

            tempFile.Delete();

            var perf = psw.StopReset();

            successCount += 1;

            this.OnProcessed(new FileProgressEventArgs
            {
               Name = tempFile.FullName,
               Message = tempFile.Name,
               ProgressState = FileProgressState.Deleted,
               Size = tempFile.Length,
               SpeedInMilliseconds = perf.TotalMilliseconds
            });
         }
         catch (Exception ex) when (ex is IOException ||
                            ex is SecurityException ||
                            ex is UnauthorizedAccessException)
         {
            this.OnProcessed(new FileProgressEventArgs
            {
               Name = tempFile.FullName,
               ProgressState = FileProgressState.Error,
               Size = tempFile.Length,
               Message = ex.Message
            });
         }
      }
      else
```

```csharp
        {
            this.OnProcessed(new FileProgressEventArgs
            {
                Name = tempFile.FullName,
                ProgressState = FileProgressState.Error,
                Message = Resources.FileNotFound
            });
        }
    }

    return successCount;
}
```

This new class helped my utility go from deleting 1K files per second to up to around 2K per second!

Progressive Retry for Network Calls

In today's mobile world, many calls across the internet or network could fail for many different reasons. Some could be the service is busy, the network is slow, and many more. For these types of calls, it is advisable to retry the call if there is an error. The current code base I am working on connects to Salesforce to retrieve and update data. Salesforce is one of those backend services that could experience these types of issues.

To help with these types of network issues, I have added a new method to my open-source code called **ProgressiveRetry()**. This method will try the call a given number of times. If there is an error, it will wait for a given milliseconds that increases with each error. Below is the code for this call.

```csharp
/// <summary>
/// Progressive retry for a function call.
/// </summary>
/// <param name="operation">The operation to perform.</param>
/// <param name="retryCount">The retry count (default 3).</param>
/// <param name="retryWaitMilliseconds">Retry milliseconds</param>
/// <returns>System.Int32.</returns>
public static int ProgressiveRetry(Action operation,
    byte retryCount = 3, int retryWaitMilliseconds = 100)
{

    var attempts = 0;
    do
    {
      try
        {
            attempts++;
            operation();
```

Appendix B - dotNetTips.Utility

```
      return attempts;
    }
    catch (Exception ex)
    {
      if (attempts == retryCount)
      {
        throw;
      }
      Debug.WriteLine(ex.GetAllMessages());
      Task.Delay(retryWaitMilliseconds * attempts).Wait();
    }
  } while (true);
  }
}
```

Here is example code on how to use **ProgressiveRetry()**.

```
var result = false;
var count = ExecutionHelper.ProgressiveRetry(() =>
{
  result = NetworkHelper.IsHostAvailable("wordpress.com");
}, retryCount: 3, retryWaitMilliseconds: 225);
```

The next time you are coding calls across the network, I hope you will check out this method. It is available in the dotNetTips.Utility.Standard NuGet package.

IAsyncEnumerable Interface in .NET

The release of .NET Core 3 in September 2019 includes a brand new IAsyncEnumerable interface in the **System.Collections.Generic** namespace. The Microsoft documentation simply states:

> *Exposes an enumerator that provides asynchronous iteration over values of a specified type.*

This new interface sounded interesting, so I looked at the code in my open-source assembly to see if I could implement it somewhere. I chose the code for **LoadFiles()** in the **DirectoryHelper** class that loads files from a collection of directories. The code looks like this:

```
public static IEnumerable<FileInfo> LoadFiles(
                    IEnumerable<DirectoryInfo> directories,
                    string searchPattern,
                    SearchOption searchOption)
{
  var files = new List<FileInfo>();
```

Appendix B - dotNetTips.Utility

```
  foreach (var directory in directories.Where(dir=> dir.Exists)
                                .Select(dir=> dir))
  {
    files.AddRange(directory.EnumerateFiles(searchPattern,
                                  searchOption));
  }

  return files.AsEnumerable();
}
```

Using **LoadFiles()** is simple.

```
foreach (var file in DirectoryHelper.LoadFiles(searchFolders,
                            "*.*",
                            SearchOption.AllDirectories))
{
   // Process File
}
```

Since this method is a blocking one, with some changes, I turned **LoadFiles()** into a new method called **LoadFilesAsync()**. The code now looks like this:

```
public static async IAsyncEnumerable<IEnumerable<FileInfo>>
       LoadFilesAsync(IEnumerable<DirectoryInfo> directories,
       string searchPattern, SearchOption searchOption)
{
   var options = new EnumerationOptions() { IgnoreInaccessible
                                  = true };

   if (searchOption == SearchOption.AllDirectories)
   {
     options.RecurseSubdirectories = true;
   }

   var dirs = directories.Where(dir=> dir.Exists)
                    .Select(dir=> dir);

   foreach (var directory in dirs)
   {
     var files = await Task.Run(() =>
       directory.EnumerateFiles(searchPattern, options));
     yield return files;
   }
}
```

As you can see above, I changed the return type from:

```
IEnumerable<FileInfo>
```

Appendix B - dotNetTips.Utility

To:
```
async IAsyncEnumerable<IEnumerable<FileInfo>>
```

Then I wrapped the call to **directory.EnumerateFiles()** in a **Task.Run()**. After getting the files in each directory, I **yield** back the collection of files to the calling method. So, using **LoadFilesAsync()** is slightly different using the new **await foreach()** in .NET.

```
await foreach (var files in DirectoryHelper.LoadFilesAsync(
                            searchFolders, "*.*",
                            SearchOption.AllDirectories))
{
   foreach (var file in files)
   {
      // Process file
   }
}
```

Each time the files are returned from the call to **EnumerateFiles()** when it hits the **yield**, it returns that list to the calling code for processing. That way the calling code show above will be able to iterate over the list of files, while **LoadFilesAsync()** loads the next list of files. Now, let's test the performance.

Performance

I wanted to see if one of these methods were more performant than the other. Below are the results of my benchmark tests.

Method	Mean	Error	StdDev	Gen 0	Gen 1	Gen 2	Allocated
LoadFiles	228,264.0 us	1,553.20 us	1,452.86 us	0	0	0	4160376 B
LoadFilesAsync	114,063.0 us	443.55 us	414.89 us	200	0	0	3642381 B

As you can see, for the number of files tested with my benchmark, **LoadFilesAsync()** is faster and allocates less memory! Make sure to benchmark your code that implements **IAsyncEnumerable**.

Making Encapsulation Easy

Encapsulation is the first pillar of Object-Oriented Programming (OOP), yet most code that I see does not implement encapsulation correctly or not all. Like I say in many of my conference sessions *"If you do not implement encapsulation, you aren't doing OOP!"* I also say *"Bad data in, bad data out!"*.

Several years ago, Microsoft Labs came out with Code Contracts which made encapsulation easier, so I implemented it in all my projects and even did conference sessions about it. Unfortunately, the future of Code Contracts looks dim and it does not work in .NET Core. Since I moved a lot of the code I have been

Appendix B - dotNetTips.Utility

writing since .NET came out in my open-source project dotNetTips.Utility to .NET Standard & .NET Core, I wanted to try to mimic the encapsulation features of Code Contracts.

Introducing the dotNetTips.Utility.OOP Namespace

I created a new namespace in my open-source project called **OOP** in both my .NET Portable (Clr) project and .NET Standard (Core) project. The first class in this namespace is named **Encapsulation**. In this class, you will find overloaded methods called **TryValidateParam()**, designed to make encapsulation easier. Here one of the methods in this class.

```
public static void TryValidateParam<TException>(bool condition,
                string paramName = "", string message = "")
                where TException : ArgumentException, new()
{
   // Confirm proper Exception type
   var t = typeof(TException);

   if (t.Name == nameof(Exception))
   {
      throw new InvalidCastException(
              Resources.CannotBeOfTypeException,
              nameof(TException)));
   }

   var defaultMessage = Resources.ParameterIsInvalid;

   if (string.IsNullOrEmpty(message) == false)
   {
      defaultMessage = message;
   }

   if (condition == false)
   {
      var ex = Activator.CreateInstance(typeof(TException),
              paramName, defaultMessage).As<TException>();
      throw ex;
   }
}
```

There are a few things I would like to point out in this method. First, it prevents users from throwing the type **Exception**, which you should *never* do since it is not descriptive enough. The only **Exception** type that should be thrown when checking parameters is one derived from **ArgumentException**. The exceptions included in the .NET are:

- **ArgumentNullException**

- **ArgumentOutOfRangeException**

If one of these types does not meet your needs, then create your type by inheriting **ArgumentException**. I did this in dotNetTips.Utility with the **ArgumentInvalidException** and **ArgumentReadOnlyException**.

The overloaded methods in this class make it easy to check strings, collections, enums, GUIDs, and many more.

EXAMPLE

Here is an example of how to use **TryValidateParam**.

```
public static DateTime GetLastDay(this DateTime input,
                                  DayOfWeek dayOfWeek)
{
  Encapsulation.TryValidateParam(dayOfWeek, nameof(dayOfWeek));

  var daysToSubtract = input.DayOfWeek > dayOfWeek ?
                       input.DayOfWeek -
                       dayOfWeek : (7 - (int)dayOfWeek) +
                       (int)input.DayOfWeek;

  return input.AddDays(daysToSubtract * -1);
}
```

I hope you will implement this in your code too.

String Builder Extensions

Recently, I was looking at the source code for Entity Framework Core and found a few interesting extension methods for the **StringBuilder** class. So I moved the ones I liked to my open-source project called dotNetTips.Utility.Standard.Extensions and is part of the NuGet package too.

Appending Bytes

If you want to combine an array of byte values in **StringBuilder**, you can use the **AppendBytes()** extension method below.

```
var sb = new StringBuilder();
var byteArray = RandomData.GenerateByteArray(1);
sb.AppendBytes(byteArray);
```

Output

Here is the result of the above code.

```
0x644060FDE6231F9CFF37B93A73C70B3DA677512A3012AB766B2A07891A3F47EDB
1F0
```

Appendix B - dotNetTips.Utility

Appending Values

There are many times that values from a collection need to be combined into a delimited string. You can use the **AppendValues()** method as shown below.

```
var sb = new StringBuilder();
var values = RandomData.GenerateWords(5, 5, 7);
sb.AppendValues(",", values);
```

Output

Here is the result from the code above.

```
BgMes, oGsreY, kpcJ^, bAA]U, Jov`rE
```

This method is overloaded to accept the following types for the collection of strings: **IEnumerable<string>**, **IEnumerable<T>**.

Appending Values using an Action

If you want to combine values from a collection using a custom action that allows for more flexibility, then using **ApendValues()** as shown below will do the trick.

```
var sb = new StringBuilder();
var values =
RandomData.GenerateCoordinateCollection<Coordinate>(5);

sb.AppendValues(", ",values, (sb, coordinate) =>
{
    sb.Append(coordinate.X);
    sb.Append(ControlChars.Colon);
    sb.Append(coordinate.Y);
});
```

Output

Here is the result from the code above.

```
1598221432:-705467152, -616323156:-1857438448,
-1686969361:1572163353, -1328828514:-1887231033,
53532470:-120489468
```

I hope you will try these **StringBuilder** extension methods in your code. Just install the NuGet package and you are ready to go!

Testing Assembly

In 2019, while I was working on benchmark tests for my new book on code & app performance, I wanted to use "real-world" data types like a person or a coordinate along with methods for creating random words, email addresses, URLs, etc. After I

Appendix B - dotNetTips.Utility

worked on the code, I thought that most of it could be re-used by myself in other projects, so I moved it into an assembly. Then I thought others might like to use it so then I turned it into a NuGet package!

The new .NET Standard assembly and NuGet package are called dotNetTips.Utility.Standard.Tester. The main goal is to make it simple to create these real-world objects along with lots of other methods to created random data. Some of the methods include the use of fixed-length strings that I needed for the benchmark tests. I am even starting to use this assembly on projects where I work.

I will next describe some of the methods and objects I use the most.

Person Types

For the benchmark tests for my performance book, I created three **Person** types that reflect different ways that I see developers create classes. All of them implement from the **IPerson** interface that defines these properties:

```
Address1    Address2    BornOn
CellPhone   City        Country
Email       FirstName   HomePhone
Id          LastName    PostalCode
```

The three different types that implement **IPerson** are:

Person: This type represents how I see most model classes created for use in web API service calls or Entity Framework by implementing the properties in **IPerson** as auto-implemented properties.

PersonFixed: This type is implemented the same as **Person** and adds a property for **Age** and implements methods for the **IComparable<T>** and **IEquatable<T>** interfaces. It also overrides **GetHashCode()**, **ToString()** and **Equals()** and implements operators. It also uses the **DebuggerDisplay** attribute.

PersonProper: This type is implemented the same as **PersonFixed** and adds validation to all appropriate properties. It also uses the **Serializable**, **XmlRoot,** and **DataContract** attributes. The type represents how most data objects *should* be implemented (as mentioned throughout this book) and should usually be the one that you should use in your tests.

Along with those types, there is a **PersonCollection<>** that is used to return a collection of any of the types that implement **IPerson**.

Appendix B - dotNetTips.Utility

Coordinate Types

Also, for my benchmark tests, I created two structure types that implement the **ICoordinate** interface. The interface has only two properties, **X** and **Y**. The two different types that implement **ICoordinate** are:

Coordinate: This structure implements **X** and **Y** as auto-properties. It implements the **IEquatable<>** interface. It also overrides **ToString()**, **Equals()** and **GetHashCode()**. It implements operators (since structures do not by default have them) and uses the **Serializable** attribute.

CoordinateProper: This structure is implemented the same as **Coordinate** and implements the **IComparable** and **IComparable<>** interfaces. This structure should be used most often in your tests.

Random Data Methods

Using random data is very important if you are testing processing in your assemblies. I do not know how many times in the past I forgot to test the last name value that includes an apostrophe which can cause SQL Server inserts or updates to fail. Humans are not very good at coming up with random data, code can solve that.

I created the **RandomData** static type that helps with generating random data. There are many methods in this class, and I add new ones often, especially when working on a new edition of my books. The methods are listed below along with sample output (most from using **?** in the Immediate Window in Visual Studio).

Method	Output
GenerateCharacter()	82 'R'
GenerateCharacter(char minValue, char maxValue)	65 'A'
GenerateCoordinate<T>()	X: 178765551 Y: -2145952440
GenerateCoordinateCollection<T>(int count)	[0]: {2089369587--284215139} [1]: {244137335-1577361939}
GenerateDecimal(decimal minValue, decimal maxValue, int decimalPlaces)	95.15
GenerateDomainExtension()	.co.uk
GenerateEmailAddress()	fbxpfvtanqysqmuqfh@kiuvf.fr

GenerateFile(string fileName, int fileLength)	c:\\temp\\UnitTest.test
GenerateFiles(int count, int fileLength)	**Path:** "C:\\Users\\dotNetDave\\AppData\\Local\\Temp\\" **Files:** Count = 100 **Raw View:** ("C:\\Users\\david\\AppData\\Local\\Temp\\", {System.Collections.Generic.List<string>})
GenerateFiles(int count = 100, int fileLength, string fileExtension)	**Path:** "C:\\Users\\david\\AppData\\Local\\Temp\\" **Files:** Count = 100 **Raw View:** ("C:\\Users\\david\\AppData\\Local\\Temp\\", {System.Collections.Generic.List<string>})
GenerateFiles(string path, int count, int fileLength)	[0]: "c:\\temp\\dobybcyx.1j" [1]: "c:\\temp\\zo2ggwub.3ro"
GenerateInteger(int min, int max)	100
GenerateKey()	f7f0af78003d4ab194b5a4024d02112a
GenerateNumber(int length)	446085072052112
GeneratePerson<T>(int addressLength, int cityLength, int countryLength, int firstNameLength, int lastNameLength, int postalCodeLength	N/A
GeneratePersonCollection<T>	[0]:"eemdqrbmgtypqxgjijsjmp@fpdgwbswvg.fr" [1]:"roxmoiksscmrixp@wdfgjorfxydcw.de"

Appendix B - dotNetTips.Utility

GeneratePhoneNumberUSA()	284-424-2216
GenerateRandomFileName()	C:\\Users\\dotNetDave\\AppData\\Local\\Temp\\3nvoblq5.lz1
GenerateRandomFileName(string path)	c:\\temp\\0yiv4iiu.uuv
GenerateRandomFileName(int fileNameLength, string extension)	C:\\Users\\dotNetDave\\AppData\\Local\\Temp\\FOGWYNDRBM.dotnettips
GenerateRandomFileName(string path, int fileNameLength, string extension)	C:\\temp\\FFDHRBMDXP.dotnettips
GenerateRelativeUrl()	/ljsylu/rsglcurkiylqld/wejdbuainlgjofnv/uwbrjftyt/
GenerateTempFile(int fileLength)	C:\\Users\\dotNetDave\\AppData\\Local\\Temp\\klxpckpo.24h
GenerateUrl()	https://www.agngbgluhawxhnmoxvdogla.hdtmdjmiagwlx.com/r/ulhekwhqnicq/
GenerateUrlHostName()	https://www.ehvjnbhcpcivgiccugim.lfa.net
GenerateUrlHostnameNoProtocol()	www.wucqcapnybi.kejdwudpbstekhxic.co.uk
GenerateUrlHostnameNoSubdomain()	elqqcw.org.uk
GenerateUrlPart()	/rregyyjxpjiats
GenerateWord(int length)	mL_g[E_E_CsoJvjshI]CFjFKa
GenerateWord(int minLength, int maxLength)	oMOYxlFvqclVQK
GenerateWord(int length, char minCharacter, char maxCharacter)	LBEEUMHHHK
GenerateWord(int minLength, int maxLength, char minCharacter, char maxCharacter)	ACRNFTPAE

Appendix B - dotNetTips.Utility

All methods in **RandomData** have corresponding unit tests.

Usage Examples

To install the NuGet package, run the following from the Package Manager Console in Visual Studio:

Install-Package dotNetTips.Utility.Standard.Tester

This is an example of how I use this package in one of my benchmark projects.

```
[Benchmark]
public void TestSortDelegate()
{
  var collection =
      RandomData.GeneratePersonCollection<PersonProper>(100);

  collection.Sort(delegate (PersonProper p1, PersonProper p2)
  {
    return p1.LastName.CompareTo(p2.LastName);
  });

  base.Consumer.Consume(collection);
}
```

Here is how I use it in a unit test project.

```
[TestMethod]
public void AddItemsToCachTest()
{
  var cache = InMemoryCache.Instance;

  for (int count = 0; count < 100; count++)
  {
    cache.AddCacheItem<int>(key: RandomData.GenerateKey(),
            item: RandomData.GenerateInteger(count, 1000000);
  }

  Assert.IsTrue(cache.Count == 100);
}
```

I hope that you will check out the **dotNetTips.Utility.Standard.Tester** NuGet package for use in your testing projects. Need something added? I hope you will send me an email or contribute to the project on GitHub.

Appendix C - dotNetTips.com Apps

I have been creating apps for .NET developers. Apps are listed below including how to download them.

dotNetTips.Utility Dev App

With this free app, I combined my previous dev cleaner and dev backup apps into one with more features coming soon.

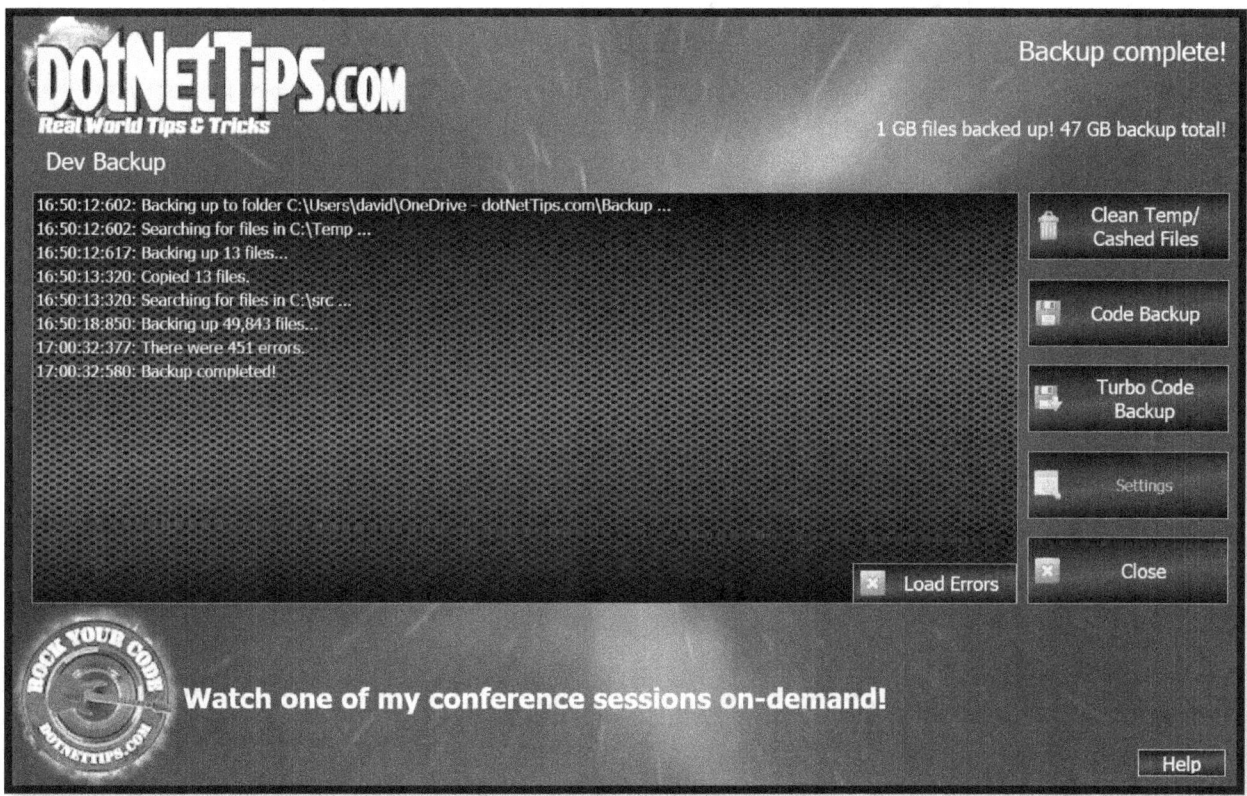

Clean Visual Studio & SQL Server Temp and Cached Files

This feature will quickly remove temporary and cached files created by Visual Studio and SQL Server. The reason I created this app is that from time-to-time Visual Studio builds will error for some unexplained reason, especially after getting new source from source control. It is because these temporary and cached files that are not removed by Visual Studio and can cause these types of issues. After just one day of coding, this app can find and delete thousands of files!

This feature will automatically detect where these files are and delete them if they are not in use and the user has proper permissions. To help remove some of these issues, the app will stop IIS, SQL Server, and other services before deleting files and then restart them after it's done.

Appendix C - dotNetTips.com Apps

Features

- Auto-detects temporary and cache folders created by Visual Studio and SQL Server
- Fast! Can delete up to 2K files per second!
- Starts and stops Windows services that could prevent files from being cleaned

I have gotten a few questions on why a Visual Studio developer needs this feature. Here is why… on June 21, 2016, suddenly, I was getting two hundred unit test failures after getting the latest files from source control. I ran this utility and ran the unit tests again. I then got zero failures.

Also, once I updated all NuGet packages in a solution and it would not build anymore. Ran this app and then it built fine!

Quickly Backup Source Code

This feature will quickly backup your Visual Studio code files. I use this feature to backup source files before retrieving source from source control (since some of these programs wipe out code changes) and at the end of the day.

When the first backup is triggered and then every 7 days (default), this feature will scan all your drives for source code. For every folder found, it will ask you if you want to add that folder to the backup process. There is even a "turbo backup" that will back up files with the archive flag set.

This feature will backup files to your OneDrive folder, so they will be in the cloud (location can be changed via the config file). By default, this feature will remove any backup folders older than 7 days.

To download, please go here: http://bit.ly/DevUtility

Appendix D - Third Party Products

Below are products that I use *every day* that I code that helps to produce rock-solid code.

I AM NOT BEING PAID TO PROMOTE THESE TOOLS IN THIS BOOK

GhostDoc

GhostDoc is a Visual Studio extension for developers who need to generate XML comments from source code using customizable templates, maintain clean and up-to-date documentation, produce help documentation in multiple formats, use intelligent source code spell checker in Visual Studio, and more.

I have been using GhostDoc from Submain.com to make it super easy to document my classes. If you use the coding standards in this book, then GhostDoc will write the documentation for you! You might have to tweak it a bit, but over 90% will be done for you.

Key Features

Here are some of the key features of GhostDoc.

- Automatic XML Comment Generation
- Customizable XMAL Comment Templates
- Documentation from the Build.
- Visual Comment Editor.
- Documentation in your preferred format
- Smart Spell Check
- Easy Code Documentation Maintenance
- Custom Help Content
- StyleCop Compliance

I use GhostDoc Enterprise. There is also a Pro version along with a **_FREE_** Community version. For more about GhostDoc, you can view my 256 Seconds With dotNetDave – My Workflow Before I Submit Code Changes video by going to https://bit.ly/CheckInWorkFlow.

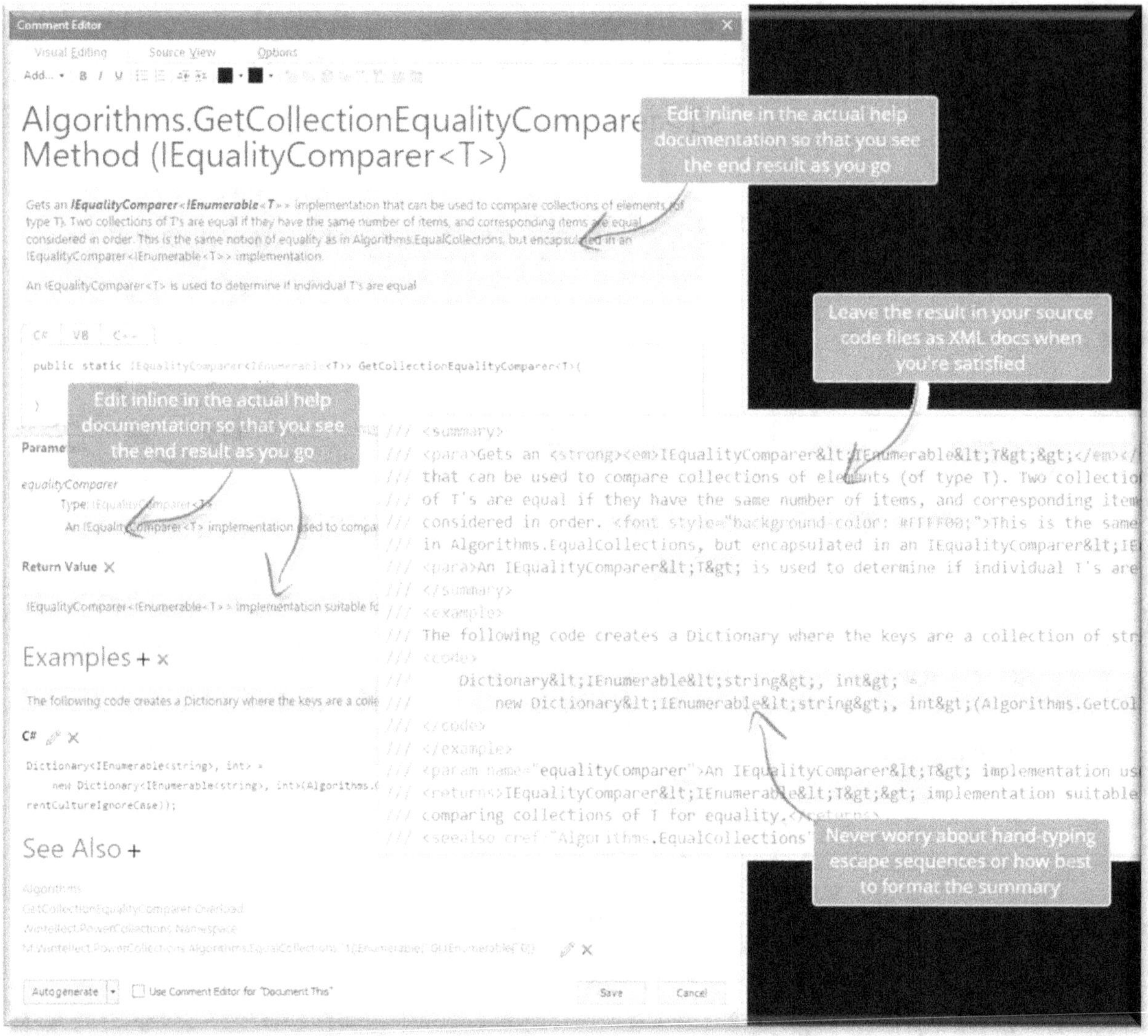

Appendix D - Third Party Products

CodeRush

After over 20 years, I have decided to start recognizing the third-party components and add-ins to Visual Studio that I use just about every day and swear by. The first is the only refactoring tool that I have used for Microsoft .NET called CodeRush for Visual Studio by Developer Express Inc. (DevExpress.com). I have tried others, including the very limited refactoring in Visual Studio, but I always come back to CodeRush.

Appendix D - Third Party Products

Code refactoring is a very important part of coding and is a skill of any professional developer. If you are new to code refactoring, here is the description of it from Wikipedia.

> In computer programming and software design, code refactoring is the process of restructuring existing computer code—changing the factoring—without changing its external behavior. Refactoring is intended to improve the design, structure, and/or implementation of the software (its non-functional attributes) while preserving its functionality. Potential advantages of refactoring may include improved code readability and reduced complexity; these can improve the source code's maintainability and create a simpler, cleaner, or more expressive internal architecture or object model to improve extensibility. Another potential goal for refactoring is improved performance; software engineers face an ongoing challenge to write programs that perform faster or use less memory.

Many of the teams I have worked for recently either do not do this or do not provide a tool like CodeRush for its developers. These tools will pay for themself after the first use! Another thing that most managers do not understand is that tools like this will teach their developers the correct way of producing better quality code! It's a win all around if you ask me!

Now, let us talk about CodeRush. I will now list the features I use the most. I would like to point out that CodeRush has always worked for both C# and VB.NET. It now includes support for Razor and XAML.

Code Refactoring

Well, this is the #1 feature of course. With usually just one mouse click you can refactor code with common patterns. Here are some of my favorites:

- Compress to/expand the null coalescing operation
- Compress to/ expand a ternary expression
- Convert to and from an auto-implemented property
- Convert to constant
- Convert to a property with a backing field
- Convert to string interpolation
- Extract interface
- Extract string to a resource (very important for globalization)
- ForEach to For/For to ForEach
- ForEach to Linq
- Import missing namespaces

Appendix D - Third Party Products

- Inline method
- Inline temp
- Introducing using statement (very important to prevent virtual memory leaks)
- Move type to file
- Remove redundant assignment
- Remove redundant type qualifier
- Remove type qualifier
- Rename type to match the file
- Simplify expression
- Use expression body

I'd like to point out that many of these refactorings can be done on an entire class at a time which saves a lot of time. Especially if you are refactoring an older codebase.

Other Features

Refactoring is not the only thing that CodeRush does. Here are just a few.

- Coding assistance
- Static code analysis
- Code style assistance
- Debugging assistance
- Unit testing assistance
- Decompiling tool

To get your very own FREE copy of CodeRush, go to the **Special Offer** section of the **Introduction** chapter.

.NET Memory Profiler

None of the code analysis tools mentioned in this chapter will find *every* issue when it comes to memory and performance issues. The only way to find the rest is by using a memory profiler tool on running code as near to the production machine setup as possible.

I have tried all the major tools on the market and the one that I like the best is .NET Memory Profiler from SciTech Software. This tool will profile any .NET process including ASP.NET, Windows Store App, remote processes and it supports .NET Core and .NET 5.

Appendix D - Third Party Products

When running a profile, you can view analysis gathering live with the view below.

After the profile is complete, an overview of the issues is shown.

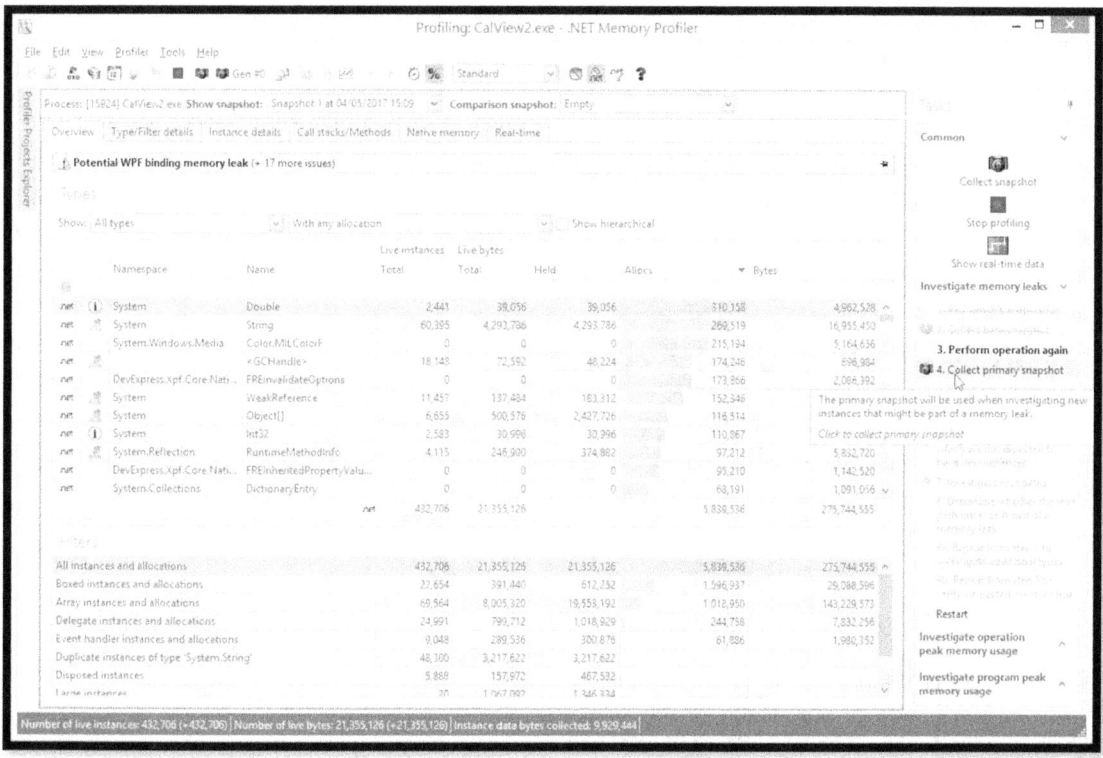

215

Appendix D - Third Party Products

Here is where the analysis begins. For most of the issues, it can be drilled into the Filter Details view.

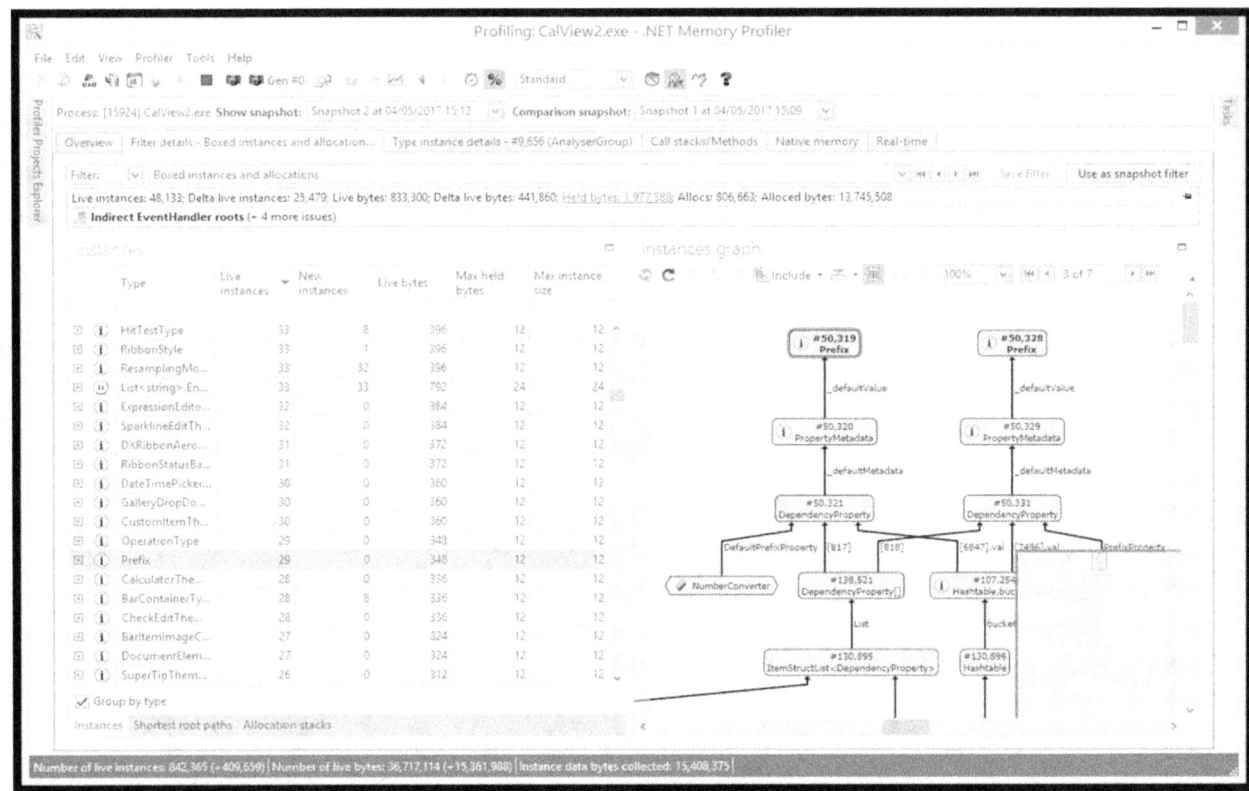

You can drill into where the issue started and even the values that the object is holding.

Allocate the Time for Analysis

I must warn you, the analysis of the memory profile can be *very* time-consuming. Make sure this is accounted for at this time in the schedule. Also, make sure that the team leader or someone that knows a lot about how memory and performance work in .NET does the analysis. I cannot stress enough how important this is *before* going into production.

My Favorite Visual Studio Extensions

I use many Visual Studio Extensions to help me to be a better, more productive developer. Here are some of my favorites.

- Automatic Versions 2.
- CodeMaid
- EditorConfig Language Service
- Power Commands for Visual Studio
- Productivity Power Tools 2017/2019

Appendix D - Third Party Products

- Tweaks
- Visual Studio IntelliCode

I hope you will try these extensions and let me know how you like them or if you have any others to recommend.

Appendix E - The Complete Person Type

Below is the complete **PersonProper** type that is featured in this book. It features the standards discussed in this book. Some of those features are:

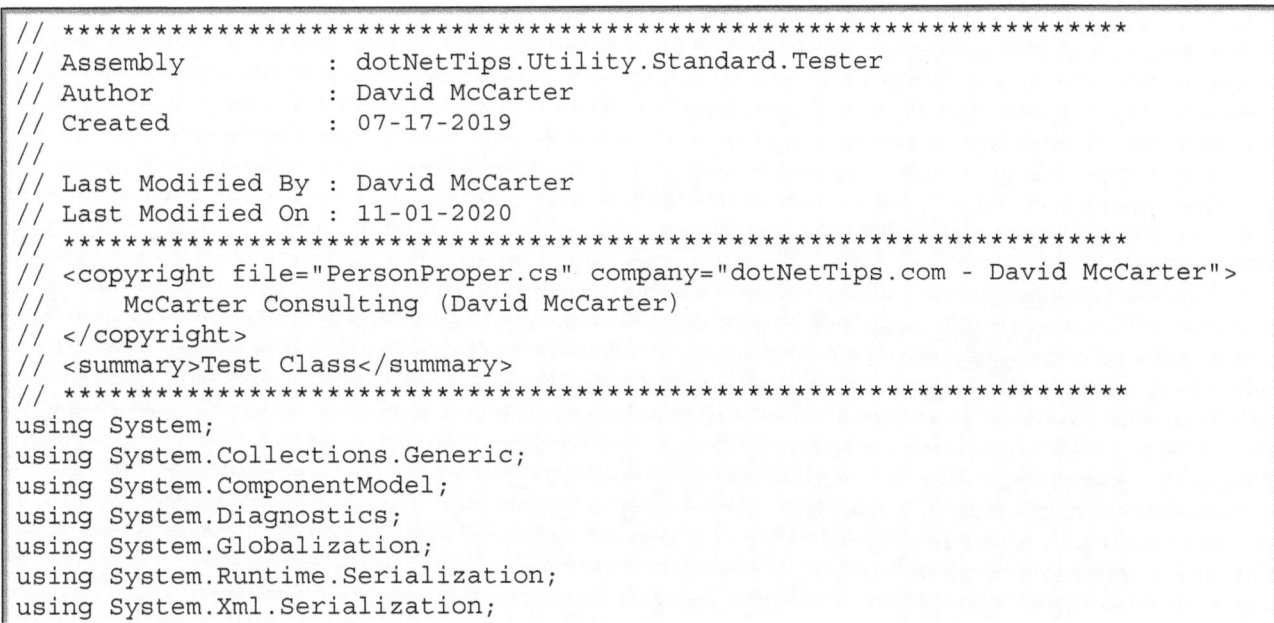

- Proper header required by StyleCop.
- Proper namespace sorting.
- Proper field, property, and method sorting.
- XML commenting for ALL fields, properties and methods required by StyleCop.
- Proper field, property, and method naming.
- Configuration for JSON and XML serialization.
- Properly setting data (not calling methods) in the constructor.
- Proper data validation.
- Properly implementing **IComparable** and **IComparable<T>**.
- Properly overriding **ToString()** and **GetHashCode()**.

This class is from the dotNetTips.Utility.Standard.Tester NuGet package.

```
// *******************************************************************
// Assembly         : dotNetTips.Utility.Standard.Tester
// Author           : David McCarter
// Created          : 07-17-2019
//
// Last Modified By : David McCarter
// Last Modified On : 11-01-2020
// *******************************************************************
// <copyright file="PersonProper.cs" company="dotNetTips.com - David McCarter">
//     McCarter Consulting (David McCarter)
// </copyright>
// <summary>Test Class</summary>
// *******************************************************************
using System;
using System.Collections.Generic;
using System.ComponentModel;
using System.Diagnostics;
using System.Globalization;
using System.Runtime.Serialization;
using System.Xml.Serialization;
```

Appendix E - The Complete Person Type

```csharp
using dotNetTips.Utility.Standard.Extensions;
using dotNetTips.Utility.Standard.OOP;
using dotNetTips.Utility.Standard.Tester.Properties;

namespace dotNetTips.Utility.Standard.Tester.Models
{
    /// <summary>
    /// Person class that implements interfaces and validates data.
    /// Implements the <see
cref="dotNetTips.Utility.Standard.Tester.Models.IPerson" />
    /// Implements the <see cref="System.IComparable" />
    /// </summary>
    /// <seealso cref="dotNetTips.Utility.Standard.Tester.Models.IPerson" />
    /// <seealso cref="System.IComparable" />
    [DebuggerDisplay("{Email}")]
    [Serializable]
    [XmlRoot(ElementName = "PersonProper", Namespace =
"http://dotNetTips.Utility.Standard.Tester.Models")]
    [DataContract(Name = "personProper", Namespace =
"http://dotNetTips.Utility.Standard.Tester.Models")]
    public sealed class PersonProper : IPerson, IDataModel<PersonProper,
string>, IPersonPlus
    {
        /// <summary>
        /// Address 1.
        /// </summary>
        [NonSerialized]
        private string _address1;

        /// <summary>
        /// Address 2.
        /// </summary>
        [NonSerialized]
        private string _address2;

        /// <summary>
        /// The born on date and time.
        /// </summary>
        [NonSerialized]
        private DateTimeOffset _bornOn;

        /// <summary>
        /// The cell phone number.
        /// </summary>
        [NonSerialized]
        private string _cellPhone;

        /// <summary>
        /// The city name.
        /// </summary>
        [NonSerialized]
        private string _city;

        /// <summary>
        /// The country name.
        /// </summary>
        [NonSerialized]
        private string _country = "USA";
```

Appendix E - The Complete Person Type

```csharp
/// <summary>
/// The email address.
/// </summary>
[NonSerialized]
private string _email;

/// <summary>
/// The first name.
/// </summary>
[NonSerialized]
private string _firstName;

/// <summary>
/// The home phone number.
/// </summary>
[NonSerialized]
private string _homePhone;

/// <summary>
/// The unique identifier.
/// </summary>
[NonSerialized]
private string _id;

/// <summary>
/// The last name.
/// </summary>
[NonSerialized]
private string _lastName;

/// <summary>
/// The postal code.
/// </summary>
[NonSerialized]
private string _postalCode;

/// <summary>
/// Initializes a new instance of <see cref="PersonFixed" />.
/// </summary>
[EditorBrowsable(EditorBrowsableState.Never)]
public PersonProper()
{
}

/// <summary>
/// Initializes a new instance of <see cref="PersonFixed" />.
/// </summary>
/// <param name="id">The unique identifier.</param>
/// <param name="email">The email address.</param>
public PersonProper(string id, string email)
{
    this.Id = id;
    this.Email = email;
}

/// <summary>
/// Gets or sets first address.
```

Appendix E - The Complete Person Type

```csharp
        /// </summary>
        /// <value>The address1.</value>
        /// <exception cref="ArgumentOutOfRangeException">Address1</exception>
        /// <exception cref="System.ArgumentOutOfRangeException">Address1 -
Address length is limited to 100 characters.</exception>
        [DataMember(Name = "address1")]
        [XmlElement]
        public string Address1
        {
            get
            {
                return this._address1;
            }

            set
            {
                if (this._address1 == value)
                {
                    return;
                }

                this._address1 = value.HasValue(0, 100) == false
                   ? throw new ArgumentOutOfRangeException(nameof(this.Address1),
                       Resources.AddressLengthIsLimitedTo100Characters) : value;
            }
        }

        /// <summary>
        /// Gets or sets second address.
        /// </summary>
        /// <value>The address2.</value>
        /// <exception cref="ArgumentOutOfRangeException">Address2</exception>
        /// <exception cref="System.ArgumentOutOfRangeException">Address2 -
Address length is limited to 100 characters.</exception>
        [DataMember(Name = "address2")]
        [XmlElement]
        public string Address2
        {
            get
            {
                return this._address2;
            }

            set
            {
                if (this._address2 == value)
                {
                    return;
                }

                this._address2 = value.HasValue(0, 100) == false
                   ? throw new ArgumentOutOfRangeException(nameof(this.Address2),
                       Resources.AddressLengthIsLimitedTo100Characters) : value;
            }
        }

        /// <summary>
        /// Gets the person's current age.
```

Appendix E - The Complete Person Type

```csharp
        /// </summary>
        /// <value>The age.</value>
        [IgnoreDataMember]
        public TimeSpan Age => this.CalculateAge();

        /// <summary>
        /// Gets or sets the born on date and time.
        /// </summary>
        /// <value>The born on.</value>
        /// <exception cref="ArgumentOutOfRangeException">BornOn</exception>
        /// <exception cref="System.ArgumentOutOfRangeException">BornOn - Person
BornOn cannot be in the future.</exception>
        [DataMember(Name = "bornOn")]
        [XmlElement]
        public DateTimeOffset BornOn
        {
            get
            {
                return this._bornOn;
            }

            set
            {
                if (this._bornOn == value)
                {
                    return;
                }

                this._bornOn = value.ToUniversalTime() > DateTimeOffset.UtcNow
                    ? throw new ArgumentOutOfRangeException(nameof(this.BornOn),
                      Resources.PersonBornOnCannotBeInTheFuture) : value;
            }
        }

        /// <summary>
        /// Gets or sets the cell phone number.
        /// </summary>
        /// <value>The cell phone.</value>
        /// <exception cref="ArgumentOutOfRangeException">CellPhone</exception>
        /// <exception cref="System.ArgumentOutOfRangeException">CellPhone -
Address length is limited to 50 characters.</exception>
        [DataMember(Name = "cellPhone")]
        [XmlElement]
        public string CellPhone
        {
            get
            {
                return this._cellPhone;
            }

            set
            {
                if (this._cellPhone == value)
                {
                    return;
                }

                this._cellPhone = value.HasValue(0, 50) == false
```

Appendix E - The Complete Person Type

```csharp
                ? throw new ArgumentOutOfRangeException(nameof(this.CellPhone),
                    Resources.PhoneNumberIsLimitedTo50Characters) : value;
            }
        }

        /// <summary>
        /// Gets or sets the city name.
        /// </summary>
        /// <value>The city.</value>
        /// <exception cref="ArgumentOutOfRangeException">City</exception>
        /// <exception cref="System.ArgumentOutOfRangeException">City - City length is limited to 100 characters.</exception>
        [DataMember(Name = "city")]
        [XmlElement]
        public string City
        {
            get
            {
                return this._city;
            }

            set
            {
                if (this._city == value)
                {
                    return;
                }

                this._city = value.HasValue(0, 100) == false
                   ? throw new ArgumentOutOfRangeException(nameof(this.City),
                       Resources.CityLengthIsLimitedTo100Characters) : value;
            }
        }

        /// <summary>
        /// Gets or sets the country.
        /// </summary>
        /// <value>The country.</value>
        /// <exception cref="ArgumentOutOfRangeException">Country</exception>
        /// <exception cref="System.ArgumentOutOfRangeException">Country - Country length is limited to 50 characters.</exception>
        [DataMember(Name = "country")]
        [XmlElement]
        public string Country
        {
            get
            {
                return this._country;
            }

            set
            {
                if (this._country == value)
                {
                    return;
                }

                this._country = value.HasValue(0, 50) == false
```

Appendix E - The Complete Person Type

```csharp
                    ? throw new ArgumentOutOfRangeException(nameof(this.Country),
                        Resources.CountryLengthIsLimitedTo50Characters) : value;
            }
        }

        /// <summary>
        /// Gets the email.
        /// </summary>
        /// <value>The email.</value>
        /// <exception cref="ArgumentOutOfRangeException">Email</exception>
        /// <exception cref="System.ArgumentOutOfRangeException">Email - Email
length is limited to 75 characters.</exception>
        [DataMember(Name = "email", IsRequired = true)]
        [XmlElement(IsNullable = false)]
        public string Email
        {
            get
            {
                return this._email;
            }

            set
            {
                if (this._email == value)
                {
                    return;
                }

                this._email = value.HasValue(0, 75) == false
                    ? throw new ArgumentOutOfRangeException(nameof(this.Email),
                        Resources.EmailLengthIsLimitedTo75Characters) : value;
            }
        }

        /// <summary>
        /// Gets or sets the first name.
        /// </summary>
        /// <value>The first name.</value>
        /// <exception cref="ArgumentOutOfRangeException">FirstName</exception>
        /// <exception cref="System.ArgumentOutOfRangeException">Email - First
name length is limited to 50 characters.</exception>
        [DataMember(Name = "firstName")]
        [XmlElement]
        public string FirstName
        {
            get
            {
                return this._firstName;
            }
            set
            {
                if (this._firstName == value)
                {
                    return;
                }

                this._firstName = value.HasValue(0, 50) == false
                    ? throw new ArgumentOutOfRangeException(nameof(this.FirstName),
```

Appendix E - The Complete Person Type

```csharp
                    Resources.FirstNameLengthIsLimitedTo50Characters) : value;
            }
        }

        /// <summary>
        /// Gets or sets the home phone.
        /// </summary>
        /// <value>The home phone.</value>
        /// <exception cref="ArgumentOutOfRangeException">HomePhone</exception>
        /// <exception cref="System.ArgumentOutOfRangeException">HomePhone - Home phone length is limited to 50 characters.</exception>
        [DataMember(Name = "homePhone")]
        [XmlElement]
        public string HomePhone
        {
            get
            {
                return this._homePhone;
            }
            set
            {
                if (this._homePhone == value)
                {
                    return;
                }

                this._homePhone = value.HasValue(0, 50) == false
                  ? throw new ArgumentOutOfRangeException(nameof(this.HomePhone),
                    Resources.PhoneNumberIsLimitedTo50Characters) : value;
            }
        }

        /// <summary>
        /// Gets the identifier.
        /// </summary>
        /// <value>The identifier.</value>
        /// <exception cref="ArgumentOutOfRangeException">Id</exception>
        /// <exception cref="System.ArgumentOutOfRangeException">Id - Id length is limited to 256 characters.</exception>
        [DataMember(Name = "id", IsRequired = true)]
        [XmlElement(IsNullable = false)]
        public string Id
        {
            get
            {
            return this._id;
            }
            set
            {
                if (this._id == value)
                {
                    return;
                }

                this._id = value.HasValue(1, 50) == false
                   ? throw new ArgumentOutOfRangeException(nameof(this.Id),
                     Resources.IdLengthIsLimitedTo50Characters) : value;
            }
```

Appendix E - The Complete Person Type

```csharp
        }

        /// <summary>
        /// Gets or sets the last name.
        /// </summary>
        /// <value>The last name.</value>
        /// <exception cref="ArgumentOutOfRangeException">LastName</exception>
        /// <exception cref="System.ArgumentOutOfRangeException">LastName - Last name length is limited to 50 characters.</exception>
        [DataMember(Name = "lastName")]
        [XmlElement]
        public string LastName
        {
            get
            {
                return this._lastName;
            }
            set
            {
                if (this._lastName == value)
                {
                    return;
                }

                this._lastName = value.HasValue(0, 50) == false
                   ? throw new ArgumentOutOfRangeException(nameof(this.LastName),
                       Resources.LastNameLengthIsLimitedTo50Characters) : value;
            }
        }

        /// <summary>
        /// Gets or sets the postal code.
        /// </summary>
        /// <value>The postal code.</value>
        /// <exception cref="ArgumentOutOfRangeException">PostalCode</exception>
        /// <exception cref="System.ArgumentOutOfRangeException">PostalCode - Postal code length is limited to 20 characters.</exception>
        [DataMember(Name = "postalCode")]
        [XmlElement]
        public string PostalCode
        {
            get
            {
                return this._postalCode;
            }
            set
            {
                if (this._postalCode == value)
                {
                    return;
                }

                this._postalCode = value.HasValue(0, 15) == false
                   ? throw new ArgumentOutOfRangeException(nameof(this.PostalCode),
                       Resources.PostalCodeLengthIsLimitedTo15Characters) : value;
            }
        }
```

Appendix E - The Complete Person Type

```csharp
/// <summary>
/// Implements the &gt;= operator.
/// </summary>
/// <param name="left">The left.</param>
/// <param name="right">The right.</param>
/// <returns>The result of the operator.</returns>
public static bool operator >=(PersonProper left, PersonProper right)
        => left is null ? right is null : left.CompareTo(right) >= 0;

/// <summary>
/// Implements the &gt; operator.
/// </summary>
/// <param name="left">The left.</param>
/// <param name="right">The right.</param>
/// <returns>The result of the operator.</returns>
public static bool operator >(PersonProper left, PersonProper right)
        => left is object && left.CompareTo(right) > 0;

/// <summary>
/// Implements the == operator.
/// </summary>
/// <param name="left">The left.</param>
/// <param name="right">The right.</param>
/// <returns>The result of the operator.</returns>
public static bool operator ==(PersonProper left, PersonProper right)
{
    if (left is null)
    {
        return right is null;
    }

    return left.Equals(right);
}

/// <summary>
/// Implements the &lt;= operator.
/// </summary>
/// <param name="left">The left.</param>
/// <param name="right">The right.</param>
/// <returns>The result of the operator.</returns>
public static bool operator <=(PersonProper left, PersonProper right)
        => left is null || left.CompareTo(right) <= 0;

/// <summary>
/// Implements the &lt; operator.
/// </summary>
/// <param name="left">The left.</param>
/// <param name="right">The right.</param>
/// <returns>The result of the operator.</returns>
public static bool operator <(PersonProper left, PersonProper right)
        => left is null ? right is object : left.CompareTo(right) < 0;

/// <summary>
/// Implements the != operator.
/// </summary>
/// <param name="left">The left.</param>
/// <param name="right">The right.</param>
/// <returns>The result of the operator.</returns>
```

Appendix E - The Complete Person Type

```csharp
public static bool operator !=(PersonProper left, PersonProper right)
    => !( left == right );

/// <summary>
/// Compares to.
/// </summary>
/// <param name="other">The other.</param>
/// <returns>System.Int32.</returns>
public int CompareTo(PersonProper other)
{
    if (other == null)
    {
        return 1;
    }

    var result = string.Compare(this._address1, other._address1,
                        StringComparison.OrdinalIgnoreCase);
    if (result != 0)
    {
        return result;
    }

    result = string.Compare(this._address2, other._address2,
                        StringComparison.OrdinalIgnoreCase);
    if (result != 0)
    {
        return result;
    }

    result = this._bornOn.CompareTo(other._bornOn);
    if (result != 0)
    {
        return result;
    }

    result = string.Compare(this._cellPhone, other._cellPhone,
                        StringComparison.OrdinalIgnoreCase);
    if (result != 0)
    {
        return result;
    }

    result = string.Compare(this._city, other._city,
                        StringComparison.OrdinalIgnoreCase);
    if (result != 0)
    {
        return result;
    }

    result = string.Compare(this._country, other._country,
                        StringComparison.OrdinalIgnoreCase);
    if (result != 0)
    {
        return result;
    }

    result = string.Compare(this._email, other._email,
                        StringComparison.OrdinalIgnoreCase);
```

Appendix E - The Complete Person Type

```csharp
            if (result != 0)
            {
                return result;
            }

            result = string.Compare(this._firstName, other._firstName,
                            StringComparison.OrdinalIgnoreCase);
            if (result != 0)
            {
                return result;
            }

            result = string.Compare(this._homePhone, other._homePhone,
                            StringComparison.OrdinalIgnoreCase);
            if (result != 0)
            {
                return result;
            }

            result = string.Compare(this._id, other._id,
                            StringComparison.OrdinalIgnoreCase);
            if (result != 0)
            {
                return result;
            }

            result = string.Compare(this._lastName, other._lastName,
                            StringComparison.OrdinalIgnoreCase);
            if (result != 0)
            {
                return result;
            }

            result = string.Compare(this._postalCode, other._postalCode,
                            StringComparison.OrdinalIgnoreCase);
            if (result != 0)
            {
                return result;
            }

            return result;
        }

        /// <summary>
        /// Determines whether the specified <see cref="System.Object" /> is equal to this instance.
        /// </summary>
        /// <param name="obj">The object to compare with the current object.</param>
        /// <returns><c>true</c> if the specified <see cref="System.Object" /> is equal to this instance; otherwise, <c>false</c>.</returns>
        /// <exception cref="NotImplementedException"></exception>
        public override bool Equals(object obj)
        {
            if (ReferenceEquals(this, obj))
            {
                return true;
            }
```

Appendix E - The Complete Person Type

```csharp
            return false;
        }

        /// <summary>
        /// Equals the specified other.
        /// </summary>
        /// <param name="other">The other.</param>
        /// <returns><c>true</c> if XXXX, <c>false</c> otherwise.</returns>
        /// <exception cref="NotImplementedException"></exception>
        public bool Equals(PersonProper other)
        {
            if (other == null)
            {
                return false;
            }

            return ReferenceEquals(this, other);
        }


        /// <summary>
        /// Returns the hash code for this instance based on id.
        /// </summary>
        /// <returns>A hash code for this instance, suitable for use in hashing algorithms and data structures like a hash table.</returns>
        public override int GetHashCode()
        {
            //TODO: CHANGE TO HashCode.Combine(Email, Id)
            var hashCode = -1058553241;
            hashCode = hashCode * -1521134295 +
               EqualityComparer<string>.Default.GetHashCode(this.Id);
            return hashCode;
        }

        /// <summary>
        /// Returns a <see cref="System.String" /> of the users id.
        /// </summary>
        /// <returns>A <see cref="System.String" /> of the users id.</returns>
        public override string ToString()
                => this.Id.ToString(CultureInfo.CurrentCulture);

        /// <summary>
        /// Calculates the person's current age.
        /// </summary>
        /// <returns>TimeSpan.</returns>
        private TimeSpan CalculateAge()
                => DateTimeOffset.UtcNow.Subtract(this.BornOn);

    }
}
```

Appendix F – Programming Acronyms & Terms

Acronyms are used a lot in software engineering. So much that I cannot remember them all, so I created this appendix to help. This appendix contains common acronyms and terms used in Microsoft .NET and software in general.

Name	Acronym	Description
Abstract Class		In programming languages, an abstract class is a generic class (or type of object) used as a basis for creating specific objects that conform to its protocol, or the set of operations it supports. Abstract classes are not instantiated directly.
Access Control List	ACL	An access-control list (ACL), with respect to a computer file system, is a list of permissions attached to an object. An ACL specifies which users or system processes are granted access to objects, as well as what operations are allowed on given objects. Each entry in a typical ACL specifies a subject and an operation.
Active		Pertaining to an entity such as the device, program, file, record, or portion of the screen that is currently operational or subject to command operations.
Active Directory	AD	Active Directory is a directory service developed by Microsoft for Windows domain networks. It is included in most Windows Server operating systems as a set of processes and services. Initially, Active Directory was only in charge of centralized domain

Appendix F – Programming Acronyms & Terms

Name	Acronym	Description
		management. However, Active Directory became an umbrella title for a broad range of directory-based identity-related services.
Active Directory Services Interface	ADSI	Active Directory Service Interfaces is a set of COM interfaces used to access the features of directory services from different network providers. ADSI is used in a distributed computing environment to present a single set of directory service interfaces for managing network resources. Administrators and developers can use ADSI services to enumerate and manage the resources in a directory service, no matter which network environment contains the resource.
Active Server Pages	ASP	Is Microsoft's first server-side script engine for dynamically generated web pages. Was first released in 1996.
Active Server Pages for Microsoft .NET	ASP.NET	Is an open-source, server-side web-application framework designed for web development to produce dynamic web pages. It was developed by Microsoft to allow programmers to build dynamic web sites, applications, and services. Was first released in 2002.
Active Template Library	ATL	The Active Template Library is a set of template-based C++ classes that let you create small, fast Component Object Model (COM) objects. It has special support for key COM features, including stock implementations, dual interfaces, standard COM enumerator

Appendix F – Programming Acronyms & Terms

Name	Acronym	Description
		interfaces, connection points, tear-off interfaces, and ActiveX controls.
ActiveX		A set of technologies that allows software components to interact with one another in a networked environment, regardless of the language in which the components were created.
ActiveX Data Objects for Microsoft .NET.	ADO.NET	Is a data access technology from the Microsoft .NET Framework that provides communication between relational and non-relational systems through a common set of components. ADO.NET is a set of computer software components that programmers can use to access data and data services from a database. It is a part of the base class library that is included with the Microsoft .NET Framework. It is used by programmers to access and modify data stored in relational database systems, though it can also access data in non-relational data sources.
ActiveX Data Objects for Visual Basic.	ADO	In computing, Microsoft's ActiveX Data Objects comprises a set of Component Object Model (COM) objects for accessing data sources. A part of MDAC (Microsoft Data Access Components), it provides a middleware layer between programming languages and OLE DB (a means of accessing data stores, whether databases or not, in a uniform manner). ADO allows a developer to write programs that access data without knowing how the database is implemented; developers must be aware of the

Appendix F – Programming Acronyms & Terms

Name	Acronym	Description
		database for connection only. No knowledge of SQL is required to access a database when using ADO, although one can use ADO to execute SQL commands directly (with the disadvantage of introducing a dependency upon the type of database used).
Amazon Web Services	AWS	Amazon Web Services is a subsidiary of Amazon that provides on-demand cloud computing platforms and APIs to individuals, companies, and governments, on a metered pay-as-you-go basis. In aggregate, these cloud computing web services provide a set of primitive abstract technical infrastructure and distributed computing building blocks and tools.
API Management		Hybrid, multi-cloud management platform for APIs across all environments in Azure.
Application Gateway		Secure, scalable, and highly available web front ends in Azure.
Application Insights		Application Insights, a feature of Azure Monitor, is an extensible Application Performance Management (APM) service for developers and DevOps professionals. Use it to monitor your live applications. It will automatically detect performance anomalies and includes powerful analytics tools to help you diagnose issues and to understand what users do with your app. It is designed to help you continuously improve performance and usability. It works for apps on a

Appendix F – Programming Acronyms & Terms

Name	Acronym	Description
		wide variety of platforms including .NET, Node.js, Java, and Python hosted on-premises, hybrid, or any public cloud. It integrates with your DevOps process and has connection points to a variety of development tools. It can monitor and analyze telemetry from mobile apps by integrating with Visual Studio App Center.
Application Programming Interface	API	A set of routines that an application uses to request and carry out lower-level services performed by a computer's or device's operating system. These routines usually carry out maintenance tasks such as managing files and displaying information.
ASP.NET Web Services Source File	ASMX	Defines Web services called by an Active Server Page (.ASP file); automatically compiled by ASP.NET when a request to the service is made; can be accessed over the Internet or from a local network.
Asynchronous JavaScript and XML	AJAX	Is a set of web development techniques using many web technologies on the client-side to create asynchronous web applications. With Ajax, web applications can send and retrieve data from a server asynchronously (in the background) without interfering with the display and behavior of the existing page. By decoupling the data interchange layer from the presentation layer, Ajax allows web pages and, by extension, web applications, to change content dynamically without the need to reload the

Appendix F – Programming Acronyms & Terms

Name	Acronym	Description
		entire page. In practice, modern implementations utilize JSON instead of XML.
Atom Publishing Protocol	AtomPub	The name Atom applies to a pair of related Web standards. The Atom Syndication Format is an XML language used for web feeds, while the Atom Publishing Protocol is a simple HTTP-based protocol for creating and updating web resources. Web feeds allow software programs to check for updates published on a website.
Atom Syndication Format	ATOM	Atom applies to a pair of related Web standards. The Atom Syndication Format is an XML language used for web feeds, while the Atom Publishing Protocol (AtomPub or APP) is a simple HTTP-based protocol for creating and updating web resources.
Authentication Service	AS	Is a component of Windows Server operating systems that provides centralized user authentication, authorization, and accounting.
Authorization	Auth	The process of granting a person, computer process, or device access to certain information, services, or functionality. Authorization is derived from the identity of the person, computer process, or device requesting access, which is verified through authentication.
Azure Data Explorer	ADE	Azure Data Explorer is a fast, fully managed data analytics service for real-time analysis of large volumes of data streaming from applications, websites, IoT devices,

Appendix F – Programming Acronyms & Terms

Name	Acronym	Description
		and more. You can use Azure Data Explorer to collect, store, and analyze diverse data to improve products, enhance customer experiences, monitor devices, and boost operations.
Azure DevTest Labs		Azure DevTest Labs provides developers and testers a self-service sandbox environment to quickly create Dev/Test environments while minimizing waste and controlling costs.
Azure Event Hubs	AEH	A big data streaming platform and event ingestion service. It can receive and process millions of events per second. Data sent to an event hub can be transformed and stored by using any real-time analytics provider or batching/storage adapters.
Azure Front Door	AFD	Enables scaling and protection for many popular Microsoft services, including Office 365, Bing, Xbox, LinkedIn, and Microsoft Teams.
Azure Function	AF	Allows developers to take action by connecting to data sources or messaging solutions thus making it easy to process and react to events. Developers can leverage Azure Functions to build HTTP-based API endpoints accessible by a wide range of applications, mobile, and IoT devices.
Azure HD Insight		Easily runs popular open-source frameworks—including Apache Hadoop, Spark, and Kafka—using Azure HDInsight, cost-effective, enterprise-grade service for open-

Appendix F – Programming Acronyms & Terms

Name	Acronym	Description
		source analytics. Effortlessly process massive amounts of data and get all the benefits of the broad open-source ecosystem with the global scale of Azure.
Azure Media Services	AMS	Cloud-based media workflow platform to index, package, protect, and stream video at scale
Azure Relay		The Azure Relay service enables you to securely expose services that run in your corporate network to the public cloud. You can do so without opening a port on your firewall or making intrusive changes to your corporate network infrastructure.
Azure Security Center	ASC	Is a unified infrastructure security management system that strengthens the security posture of your data centers and provides advanced threat protection across your hybrid workloads in the cloud - whether they are in Azure or not - as well as on-premises.
Azure Stream Analytics	ASA	Easy-to-use, a real-time analytics service that is designed for mission-critical workloads. Build an end-to-end serverless streaming pipeline with just a few clicks. Uses SQL—easily extensible with custom code and built-in machine learning capabilities for more advanced scenarios. Runs the most demanding workloads with the confidence of a financially backed SLA.
Azure Stream Analytics Job		Azure Stream Analytics is a real-time analytics and complex event-processing engine that is designed

Appendix F – Programming Acronyms & Terms

Name	Acronym	Description
		to analyze and process high volumes of fast streaming data from multiple sources simultaneously. Patterns and relationships can be identified in information extracted from many input sources including devices, sensors, clickstreams, social media feeds, and applications. These patterns can be used to trigger actions and initiate workflows such as creating alerts, feeding information to a reporting tool, or storing transformed data for later use. Also, Stream Analytics is available on Azure IoT Edge runtime, enabling to process data on IoT devices.
Azure Synapse Analytics	ASA	Is a limitless analytics service that brings together enterprise data warehousing and Big Data analytics. It gives you the freedom to query data on your terms, using either serverless or provisioned resources—at scale. Azure Synapse brings these two worlds together with a unified experience to ingest, prepare, manage, and serve data for immediate BI and machine learning needs.
Base Class Library (part of FCL)	BCL	Is a simple runtime library for modern programming languages. It serves as the Standard for the runtime library for the language C# as well as one of the CLI Standard Libraries.
Basic Input Output System	BIOS	BIOS (basic input/output system) is the program a computer's microprocessor uses to start the computer system after it is powered on. It also manages data flow

Appendix F – Programming Acronyms & Terms

Name	Acronym	Description
		between the computer's operating system (OS) and attached devices, such as the hard disk, video adapter, keyboard, mouse, and printer.
BIN	bin	A handling unit for storing and transferring items.
Binary Application Markup Language	BMAL	Is a file format of Microsoft that is generated by compiling XAML files.
Blockchain		By design, a blockchain is resistant to modification of the data. It is "an open, distributed ledger that can record transactions between two parties efficiently and in a verifiable and permanent way". For use as a distributed ledger, a blockchain is typically managed by a peer-to-peer network collectively adhering to a protocol for inter-node communication and validating new blocks. Once recorded, the data in any given block cannot be altered retroactively without the alteration of all subsequent blocks, which requires consensus of the network majority. Although blockchain records are not unalterable, blockchains may be considered secure by design and exemplify a distributed computing system with high Byzantine fault tolerance. Decentralized consensus has therefore been claimed with a blockchain
Browser Capabilities Component	MSWC	The ASP Browser Capabilities component creates a BrowserType object that determines the type, capabilities, and version number of a visitor's browser. When a browser

Appendix F – Programming Acronyms & Terms

Name	Acronym	Description
		connects to a server, a User-Agent header is also sent to the server. This header contains information about the browser.
Buffer		An area of memory reserved for temporarily holding data before that data is used by a receiving device or application. Buffering protects against the interruption of data flow.
Bug		A bug is a general term used to denote an unexpected error or defect in hardware or software, which causes it to malfunction. Even though bugs are often considered to be insignificant computer glitches, there have been instances where bugs have caused life-threatening conditions and led to major financial losses. This makes it imperative to invest in the process of finding bugs before programs are rolled out for their application.
Build		To translate all the source code of a program from a high-level language into object code before the execution of the program.
Bulk Copy Program	BCP	A command-line tool used to import or export data against a Microsoft SQL Server or Sybase database.
Business Requirements Document	BRD	A BRD is a formal document that outlines the goals and expectations an organization hopes to achieve by partnering with a vendor to complete a specific project. Remember, it is important to understand this is different from a

Appendix F – Programming Acronyms & Terms

Name	Acronym	Description
		functional requirement document (FRD)
Cascading Style Sheets	CSS	A style sheet language used for describing the presentation of a document written in a markup language like HTML. CSS is a cornerstone technology of the World Wide Web, alongside HTML and JavaScript.
Certificate	Cert	A digital document used for authentication and network security that binds a public key to an entity that holds the corresponding private key.
Certificate of Authenticity	COA	Computer COAs have a license number on them, which verifies that the program is a genuine, legal copy.
Certification Authority	CA!	In cryptography, a certificate authority or certification authority is an entity that issues digital certificates. A digital certificate certifies the ownership of a public key by the named subject of the certificate.
Character	Char	Is a display unit of information equal to one alphabetic letter or symbol. The value of a char variable could be any one-character value, such as 'a', '1', '$' and 'X'. This definition of character relies on the general definition of a character as a sole unit of written language. However, char as an abbreviation is a reserved keyword in languages such as C, C++, C#, and Java.
Child Class		In class-based programming, inheritance is done by defining new

Appendix F – Programming Acronyms & Terms

Name	Acronym	Description
		classes as extensions of existing classes: the existing class is the parent class, and the new class is the child class.
Class		In OOP, a class refers to a set of related objects with common properties. Classes and the ability to create new classes render OOP a powerful and flexible programming model. For example, there might be a class called shapes which contains objects which are triangles, pentagons, squares, and circles.
Client		A process, such as a program or a task, which requests a service provided by another program--for example, a word processor that calls on a sort routine built into another program. The client process uses the requested service without having to "know" any working details about the other program or the service itself.
Client		An entity, such as a device or program, which connects to another entity over a network.
Client		In object-oriented programming, a member of a class (group) uses the services of another class to which it is not related.
Client Access License (associated with a server product e.g., SQL Server)	CALS	A client access license is a commercial software license that allows clients to use server software services. Most commercial desktop apps are licensed so that payment is required for each installation.

Appendix F – Programming Acronyms & Terms

Name	Acronym	Description
Cloud		Generic /marketing term for providers like Microsoft Azure, Amazon Web Services, and more.
Code Access Security	CAS	Code Access Security, in the Microsoft .NET framework, is Microsoft's solution to prevent untrusted code from performing privileged actions. When the CLR loads an assembly, it will obtain evidence for the assembly and use this to identify the code group that the assembly belongs to.
Collaboration Data Objects	CDO	Previously known as OLE Messaging or Active Messaging, is an application programming interface included with Microsoft Windows and Microsoft Exchange Server products. The library allows developers to access the Global Address List and other server objects, in addition to the contents of mailboxes and public folders.
Collaboration Data Objects for Windows NT Server	CDONTS	Primarily used by Web developers as a thin client for mailing Web forms. The DLL for CDONTS, also known as Cdonts.dll, is installed with Microsoft Windows NT Option Pack 4. The SMTP service must also be installed. Windows NT Option Pack 4 installs with backward compatibility for Microsoft Windows 2000. However, we recommend CDO for Windows 2000 (CDOSYS) for the Windows 2000 operating system.
Collaborative Application Markup Language	CAML	An XML based markup language used with Microsoft SharePoint technologies (Windows Sharepoint Services and Office SharePoint Server). Unlike plain XML, CAML

Appendix F – Programming Acronyms & Terms

Name	Acronym	Description
		contains specific groups of tags to both define and display (render) data.
COM Callable Wrapper	CCW	When a COM client calls a .NET object, the common language runtime creates the managed object and a COM callable wrapper (CCW) for the object. Unable to reference a .NET object directly, COM clients use the CCW as a proxy for the managed object.
COM Class Identifier	CLSID	The CLSID or Class Identifier is a string of alphanumeric (both numbers and alphabet characters) symbols that are used to represent a specific instance of a Component Object Model or COM-based program.
Command-line Interface	CLI	A user interface based on the text. The UI is used to view and manage computer files. Command-line interfaces are also called command-line user interfaces, console user interfaces and character user interfaces.
Comma-separated Values	CSV	A comma-separated values (CSV) file is a delimited text file that uses a comma to separate values. Each line of the file is a data record. Each record consists of one or more fields, separated by commas. A delimiter such as a tab that is not present in the field data allows simpler format parsing.
Common Data Service	CDS	Let us you securely store and manage data that are used by business applications. Data within Common Data Service is stored

Appendix F – Programming Acronyms & Terms

Name	Acronym	Description
		within a set of entities. An entity is a set of records used to store data, similar to how a table stores data within a database.
Common Intermediate Language	CIL	Formerly called Microsoft Intermediate Language or Intermediate Language, is the intermediate language binary instruction set defined within the Common Language Infrastructure specification.
Common Language Runtime	CLR	Is the virtual machine component of the Microsoft .NET framework, manages the execution of .NET programs. Just-in-time compilation converts the managed code (compiled intermediate language code), into machine instructions which are then executed on the CPU of the computer.[1] The CLR provides additional services including memory management, type safety, exception handling, garbage collection, security, and thread management.
Common Type System	CTS	Is a standard that specifies how type definitions and specific values of types are represented in computer memory. It is intended to allow programs written in different programming languages to easily share information.
Community Technology Preview	CTP	A Community Technology Preview (CTP) is a version of a Microsoft product that is released to early users and software developers for testing before the start of general availability.

Appendix F – Programming Acronyms & Terms

Name	Acronym	Description
Compilation		The process of creating an executable program through code written in a compiled programming language is called compilation. Through compiling, the computer can understand and run the program without using the programming software used to create it. A compiler is a program that translates computer programs written using letters, numbers, and characters into a machine language program.
Component Object Model	COM	A binary-interface standard for software components introduced by Microsoft in 1993. It is used to enable inter-process communication object creation in a large range of programming languages.
Component Object Model Hosting Services	COM+	Provides developers with support for distributed transactions, resource pooling, disconnected applications, event publication and subscription, better memory, and processor (thread) management, as well as to position Windows as an alternative to other enterprise-level operating systems, Microsoft introduced a technology called Microsoft Transaction Server (MTS) on Windows NT 4.
Conceptual Schema Definition Language	CSDL	A conceptual schema is a high-level description of informational needs underlying the design of a database. It typically includes only the main concepts and the main relationships among them. Typically, this is a first-cut model, with insufficient detail to build an actual

Appendix F – Programming Acronyms & Terms

Name	Acronym	Description
		database. This level describes the structure of the whole database for a group of users. The conceptual model is also known as the data model that can be used to describe the conceptual schema when a database system is implemented. It hides the internal details of physical storage and targets describing entities, data types, relationships, and constraints.
Conditionals		Conditionals, conditional statements, and conditional expressions are features of programming language, which help the code make a choice and result in either TRUE or FALSE. These perform different actions depending on the need of the programmer, and multiple conditions can be combined into a single condition, as long as the final value of the condition is either TRUE or FALSE.
Configuration		About a single microcomputer, the sum of a system's internal and external components, including memory, disk drives, keyboard, video, and generally less critical add-on hardware, such as a mouse, modem, or printer. Software (the operating system and various device drivers), the user's choices established through configuration files such as the AUTOEXEC.BAT and CONFIG.SYS files on IBM PCs and compatibles and sometimes hardware (switches and jumpers) are needed to "configure the configuration" to work correctly. Although system configuration can

Appendix F – Programming Acronyms & Terms

Name	Acronym	Description
		be changed, as by adding more memory or disk capacity, the basic structure of the system--its architecture--remains the same.
Constants	CONST	A constant (also known as Const) is a term used to describe a value that does not change throughout the execution of the program, unlike a variable. Constant cannot be altered and will remain fixed, and a constant can be a number, character, and string.
Continues Integration and Continues Delivery	CI/CD	Continuous delivery is an extension of continuous integration to make sure that you can release new changes to your customers quickly in a sustainable way. This means that on top of having automated your testing, you also have automated your release process and you can deploy your application at any point in time by clicking on a button.
Controller		A device that other devices rely on for access to a computer subsystem. A disk controller, for example, controls access to one or more disk drives, managing physical and logical access to the drive or drives.
Coordinated Universal Time	UTC	UTC is the primary time standard by which the world regulates clocks and time. It is within about 1 second of mean solar time at 0° longitude and is not adjusted for daylight saving time. It is effectively a successor to Greenwich Mean Time (GMT).

Appendix F – Programming Acronyms & Terms

Name	Acronym	Description
Cosmos DB		Azure Cosmos DB is Microsoft's globally distributed, multi-model database service. With a click of a button, Cosmos DB enables you to scale throughput and storage elastically and independently across any number of Azure regions worldwide. You can elastically scale throughput and storage, and take advantage of fast, single-digit-millisecond data access using your favorite API including SQL, MongoDB, Cassandra, Tables, or Gremlin. Cosmos DB provides comprehensive service level agreements (SLAs) for throughput, latency, availability, and consistency guarantees, something no other database service offers.
Create, Read, Update, Delete	CRUD	Usually refers to data in a database.
Cross-Site Scripting	XSS	Cross-site scripting is a type of security vulnerability typically found in web applications. XSS attacks enable attackers to inject client-side scripts into web pages viewed by other users. A cross-site scripting vulnerability may be used by attackers to bypass access controls such as the same-origin policy.
Cryptography	Crypto	The study or analysis of codes and encoding methods used to secure information. Cryptography is used to provide confidentiality, data integrity, authentication (entity and data origin), and nonrepudiation.
Cyclomatic Complexity	CC	A software metric is used to indicate the complexity of a program. It is a quantitative measure of the number

Appendix F – Programming Acronyms & Terms

Name	Acronym	Description
		of linearly independent paths through a program's source code. It was developed by Thomas J. McCabe, Sr. in 1976. Cyclomatic complexity is computed using the control flow graph of the program: the nodes of the graph correspond to indivisible groups of commands of a program, and a directed edge connects two nodes if the second command might be executed immediately after the first command. Cyclomatic complexity may also be applied to individual functions, modules, methods, or classes within a program. *For me, this number means the minimum number of unit tests needed to be written for the method, just to properly test encapsulation.*
Data Access Object	DAO	In computer software, a data access object is a pattern that provides an abstract interface to some type of database or other persistence mechanisms. By mapping application calls to the persistence layer, the DAO provides some specific data operations without exposing details of the database.
Data Definition Language	DDL	In the context of SQL, data definition or data description language (DDL) is a syntax like a computer programming language for defining data structures,

Appendix F – Programming Acronyms & Terms

Name	Acronym	Description
		especially database schemas. DDL statements create and modify database objects such as tables, indexes, and users. Common DDL statements are CREATE, ALTER, and DROP.
Data Encryption Standard	DES	The Data Encryption Standard is a symmetric-key algorithm for the encryption of digital data. Although its short key length of 56 bits makes it too insecure for applications, it has been highly influential in the advancement of cryptography.
Data Manipulation Language	DML	A computer programming language used for adding (inserting), deleting, and modifying (updating) data in a database. A DML is often a sublanguage of a broader database language such as SQL, with the DML comprising some of the operators in the language.[1] Read-only selecting of data is sometimes distinguished as being part of a separate data query language (DQL), but it is closely related and sometimes also considered a component of a DML; some operators may perform both selecting (reading) and writing.
Data Source	DS	In communications, the portion of a Data Terminal Equipment (DTE) device that sends data.
Data Transformation Services - SQL Server	DTS	A set of objects and utilities to allow the automation of extract, transform, and load operations to or from a database. The objects are DTS packages and their components, and the utilities are called DTS tools. DTS was included

Appendix F – Programming Acronyms & Terms

Name	Acronym	Description
		with earlier versions of Microsoft SQL Server and was almost always used with SQL Server databases, although it could be used independently with other databases.
Data Types	DT	Is the classification of a particular type of data. We as humans can understand the difference between a name and a number, but the computer cannot. The computer uses special internal codes to distinguish between different types of data it receives and processes.
Database	DB	An organized collection of data generally stored and accessed electronically from a computer system. Where databases are more complex, they are often developed using formal design and modeling techniques.
Database Console Commands for SQL Server	DBCC	There are many DBCC commands in SQL Server. We generally use these commands to check the consistency of the databases, i.e., maintenance, validation task, and status checks. They are grouped as Maintenance: Maintenance tasks on Db, filegroup, index, etc.
Database Management System	DBMS	The software that interacts with end-users, applications, and the database itself to capture and analyze the data. The DBMS software additionally encompasses the core facilities provided to administer the database. The total of the database, the DBMS, and the associated applications can be referred to as a "database system".

Appendix F – Programming Acronyms & Terms

Name	Acronym	Description
		Often the term "database" is also used to loosely refer to any of the DBMS, the database system, or an application associated with the database.
Declaration		A statement that describes a variable, function, or any other identifier is called a declaration. A declaration helps the compiler or interpreter identify the word and understand its meaning, and how the process should be continued.
Denial of Service	DoS	In computing, a denial-of-service attack is a cyber-attack in which the perpetrator seeks to make a machine or network resource unavailable to its intended users by temporarily or indefinitely disrupting services of a host connected to the Internet.
Dependency Injection	DI	In software engineering, dependency injection is a technique in which an object receives other objects that it depends on. These other objects are called dependencies. In the typical "using" relationship the receiving object is called a client and the passed object is called a service.
Digital Twins		Gain insights that help you drive better products, optimize operations and costs, and create breakthrough customer experiences. Apply your domain expertise on top of Azure Digital Twins to build connected solutions. Model any environment and bring digital twins to life in a scalable and highly secure manner.

Appendix F – Programming Acronyms & Terms

Name	Acronym	Description
Directory	DIR	An object in a filesystem that contains files and other directories.
Disk	DSK	A round, flat piece of nonmagnetic, shiny metal encased in a plastic coating, designed to be read from and written to by optical (laser) technology.
Disk Operating System	DOS/MS-DOS	DOS is a platform-independent acronym for Disk Operating System which later became a common shorthand for disk-based operating systems on IBM PC compatibles. DOS primarily consists of Microsoft's MS-DOS and a rebranded IBM version under the name PC DOS, both of which were introduced in 1981. Later compatible systems from other manufacturers include DR DOS, ROM-DOS, PTS-DOS, and FreeDOS. MS-DOS dominated the IBM PC compatible market between 1981 and 1995.
Distributed Component Object Model	DCOM	Distributed Component Object Model (DCOM) is a proprietary Microsoft technology for communication between software components on networked computers. DCOM, which originally was called "Network OLE", extends Microsoft's COM, and provides the communication substrate under Microsoft's COM+ application server infrastructure.
Distributed Internet Applications Architecture	DNA	An application development model from Microsoft for highly adaptable business solutions that use Microsoft's digital nervous system paradigm. Windows DNA The Windows DNA framework includes

Appendix F – Programming Acronyms & Terms

Name	Acronym	Description
		support for client/server PC-based computing and Web services for building a new class of distributed computing solutions for the Windows platform.
Distributed Transaction Coordinator	MSDTC	The Microsoft Distributed Transaction Coordinator (MSDTC) service is a component of modern versions of Microsoft Windows that is responsible for coordinating transactions that span multiple resource managers, such as databases, message queues, and file systems. MSDTC is included in Windows 2000 and later operating systems and is also available for Windows NT 4.0.
Docker		Docker is an open platform for developing, shipping, and running applications. Docker enables you to separate your applications from your infrastructure so you can deliver software quickly. With Docker, you can manage your infrastructure in the same ways you manage your applications.
Document Object Model	DOM	The Document Object Model (DOM) is a cross-platform and language-independent interface that treats an XML or HTML document as a tree structure wherein each node is an object representing a part of the document. The DOM represents a document with a logical tree. Each branch of the tree ends in a node, and each node contains objects. DOM methods allow programmatic access to the tree; with them, one can change the structure, style, or

Appendix F – Programming Acronyms & Terms

Name	Acronym	Description
		content of a document. Nodes can have event handlers attached to them. Once an event is triggered, the event handlers get executed.
Document Type Definition	DTD	
Domain Controller	DC	In an Active Directory forest, a server that contains a writable copy of the Active Directory database participates in Active Directory replication and controls access to network resources.
Domain Name Service	DNS	A hierarchical, distributed database that contains mappings of DNS domain names to various types of data, such as IP addresses. DNS enables the location of computers and services by user-friendly names, and it also enables the discovery of other information stored in the database.
Domain Specific Languages	DSL	A computer language specialized to a particular application domain. This is in contrast to a general-purpose language (GPL), which is broadly applicable across domains. There is a wide variety of DSLs, ranging from widely used languages for common domains, such as HTML for web pages, down to languages used by only one or a few pieces of software, such as MUSH soft code.
Domain-Driven Design	DDD	Domain-driven design (DDD) is the concept that the structure and language of your code (class names, class methods, class variables) should match the business domain. For example, if your software processes loan

Appendix F – Programming Acronyms & Terms

Name	Acronym	Description
		applications, it might have classes such as LoanApplication and Customer, and methods such as AcceptOffer and Withdraw.
DOS Copy Command	XCOPY	A command used on IBM PC DOS, MS-DOS, IBM OS/2, Microsoft Windows, FreeDOS, ReactOS, and related operating systems for copying multiple files or entire directory trees from one directory to another and for copying files across a network.
Driver		Software that enables hardware (e.g., peripherals) to work with your computer or mobile device.
Driver Development Kit	DDK	A software product offered by a software vendor or third-party development firm. It allows hardware vendors to develop software drivers for their hardware products. A DDK is intended to make the development process easy and typically includes detailed documentation and sample projects.
Dynamic Data Exchange	DDE	A technology for interprocess communication used in early versions of Microsoft Windows or OS/2. DDE allows programs to manipulate objects provided by other programs and respond to user actions affecting those objects.
Dynamic HTML	DHTML	A collection of technologies used together to create interactive and animated websites by using a combination of a static markup language, a client-side scripting language, a presentation definition

Appendix F – Programming Acronyms & Terms

Name	Acronym	Description
		language, and the Document Object Model.
Dynamic Link Library	DLL	An operating system feature that allows executable routines (generally serving a specific function or set of functions) to be stored separately as files with .dll extensions. These routines are loaded only when needed by the program that calls them.
Element		A unit of information within a markup language that is defined by a tag, or a pair of tags surrounding some content, and includes any attributes defined within the initial tag.
Encrypting File System	EFS	On Microsoft Windows is a feature introduced in version 3.0 of NTFS that provides filesystem-level encryption. The technology enables files to be transparently encrypted to protect confidential data from attackers with physical access to the computer.
Endless Loop		An endless loop or infinite loop is a continuous repetition of a program snippet, which is everlasting. This occurs majorly due to conditional operators and functions which redirect the code back to the snippet, making it endless.
Enterprise Services	ES	Are reusable business services that can be combined with other services to meet new requirements. Enterprise services can be assembled to compose new applications or enable new business processes.

Appendix F – Programming Acronyms & Terms

Name	Acronym	Description
Entity Data Model	EDM	A set of concepts that describe the structure of data, regardless of its stored form. The EDM borrows from the Entity-Relationship Model described by Peter Chen in 1976, but it also builds on the Entity-Relationship Model and extends its traditional uses.
Entity Framework	EF	An open-source object-relational mapping framework for ADO.NET. It was a part of the .NET Framework, but since Entity Framework version 6 it is separated from the .NET framework.
Event Tracing for Windows	ETW	Is a facility to analyze the sequence and timing of application and operating system events for problem diagnosis and performance analysis. This chapter describes using Tcl to control, read, and write traces.
Exception	EX	A special, unexpected, and anomalous condition encountered during the execution of a program is known as an exception. It can also be termed as an error or a condition that alters the way of the program or the microprocessor to a different path. An example of an exception can be the case when a program tries to load a file from the disk, but the file does not exist. The exceptions must be handled and eradicated in the program code to avoid any fatal error.
Executable File	EXE	In computing, executable code, executable file, or executable program, sometimes simply referred to as an executable or binary,

Appendix F – Programming Acronyms & Terms

Name	Acronym	Description
		causes a computer "to perform indicated tasks according to encoded instructions", as opposed to a data file that must be parsed by a program to be meaningful.
Expression		Is a legal grouping of letters, symbols, and numbers being used to represent the value of one or more variables. Expressions are highly used in several programming languages and many other programs, with each having its own set of legal and illegal expressions. Every expression contains one or more operands (objects being manipulated) and operators (symbols representing actions).
Extensible Application Markup Language	XAML	A declarative XML-based language developed by Microsoft that is used for initializing structured values and objects. It is available under Microsoft's Open Specification Promise. The acronym originally stood for Extensible Avalon Markup Language, Avalon being the code-name for Windows Presentation Foundation (WPF).
Extensible Hypertext Markup Language	XHTML	Extensible Hypertext Markup Language is the markup language used to create webpages. It is similar to HTML but uses a stricter XML-based syntax. The first version of XHTML (1.0) was standardized in 2000. For several years, XHTML was the most common language used to create websites.
Extensible Markup Language	XML	Is a metalanguage that allows users to define their customized markup

Appendix F – Programming Acronyms & Terms

Name	Acronym	Description
		languages, especially to display documents on the internet.
Extensible Stylesheet Language Transformations	XSLT	An XML -based language used, in conjunction with specialized processing software, for the transformation of XML documents. Although the process is referred to as "transformation," the original document is not changed; rather, a new XML document is created based on the content of an existing document.
File created by the Entity Data Model Wizard	EDMX	Visual Studio provides the Entity Designer for visual creation of the EDM and the mapping specification. The output of the tool is the XML file (*.edmx) specifying the schema and the mapping. EDMX file contains EF metadata artifacts (CSDL/MSL/SSDL content). These three files (csdl, msl, ssdl) can also be created or edited by hand.
FileSystemObject	FSO	Provides access to a computer's file system.
First in First Out	FIFO	Represents first in, first out – in computing and systems theory, is a method for organizing the manipulation of a data structure – often, specifically a data buffer – where the oldest entry, or 'head' of the queue, is processed first.
Framework		Framework in programming is a foundation with a specified level of complexity that may be altered by the programmer, making use of their code. A framework might include different software libraries, APIs, compilers, and much more. In

Appendix F – Programming Acronyms & Terms

Name	Acronym	Description
		simpler terms, a framework provides a favorable environment for a certain type and level of programming for a project. A framework allows the developers to bypass the general necessities and focus on more project-related specifics.
Framework Class Library	FCL	A component of Microsoft's .NET Framework, the first implementation of the Common Language Infrastructure. In much the same way as Common Language Runtime implements the CLI Virtual Execution System, the FCL implements the CLI foundational Standard Libraries. As a CLI foundational class library implementation, it is a collection of reusable classes, interfaces, and value types, and includes an implementation of the CLI Base Class Library.
Front-end		Is the user interface of a computer or device. For example, any operating system provides users with ease of navigation. A program or OS is considered good if the UI or Front-end is easy to use and seamless to navigate. Front-end developers are the programmers who design and develop the user interface of a device.
Functional Requirements Document	FRD	The functional requirements document is a formal statement of an application's functional requirements. It serves the same purpose as a contract. The developers agree to provide the capabilities specified. The client

Appendix F – Programming Acronyms & Terms

Name	Acronym	Description
		agrees to find the product satisfactory if it provides the capabilities specified in the FRD.
Garbage Collector	GC	A form of automatic memory management. The garbage collector, or just collector, attempts to reclaim garbage or memory occupied by objects that are no longer in use by the program. Garbage collection was invented by American computer scientist John McCarthy around 1959 to simplify manual memory management in Lisp.
Garbage In, Garbage Out	GIGO	In computer science, garbage in, garbage out (GIGO) is the concept that flawed, or nonsense input data produces nonsense output or "garbage". Sometimes the term rubbish in, rubbish out (RIRO) is used.
Global Assembly Cache	GAC	A machine wide CLI assembly cache for the Common Language Infrastructure (CLI) in Microsoft's .NET Framework. The approach of having a specially controlled central repository addresses the flaws in the shared library concept and helps to avoid pitfalls of other solutions that led to drawbacks like DLL hell. **The GAC has been depreciated for .NET Core and .NET 5.**
Globally Unique Identifier	GUID	Is a unique reference number used as an identifier in computer software. The term GUID typically refers to various implementations of the universally unique identifier standard. GUIDs are usually stored as 128-bit values and are commonly displayed as 32 hexadecimal digits

Appendix F – Programming Acronyms & Terms

Name	Acronym	Description
		with groups separated by hyphens, such as {21EC2020-3AEA-4069-A2DD-08002B30309D}. They may or may not be generated from random numbers. GUIDs generated from random numbers normally contain 6 fixed bits and 122 random bits; the total number of unique such GUIDs is 2^{122}. This number is so large that the probability of the same number being generated randomly twice is negligible; however other GUID versions have different uniqueness properties and probabilities, ranging from guaranteed uniqueness to likely duplicates. Assuming uniform probability for simplicity, the probability of one duplicate would be about 50% if every person on earth as of 2014 owned 600 million GUIDs.
Hardcode /Hardcoded		In computer programming, the term hard code or hardcode is used to describe code that is not likely to change. Hardcoded features are built into hardware or software in such a way so that they cannot be modified later.
Hardware Compatibility List	HCL	A list of computer hardware (typically including many types of peripheral devices) that is compatible with a particular operating system or device management software. In today's world, there is a vast amount of computer hardware in circulation, and many operating systems too. A hardware compatibility list is a database of hardware models and

Appendix F – Programming Acronyms & Terms

Name	Acronym	Description
		their compatibility with a certain operating system.
Hardware Compatibility Test	HCT	A type of Software testing to check whether your software can run on different hardware, operating systems, applications, network environments or Mobile devices.
Host Integration Server	HIS	A gateway application providing connectivity between Microsoft Windows networks and IBM mainframe and AS/400 systems. Support is provided for SNA, 3270, 5250, CICS, APPC, and other IBM protocols. Support is also provided for advanced integration with Windows networks and software, such as linking Microsoft Message Queuing applications to IBM WebSphere MQ, binding Microsoft DTC transactions with CICS, and cross-protocol access to DB2 databases on IBM platforms.
HTTP Secure	HTTPS	Hypertext Transfer Protocol Secure is an extension of the Hypertext Transfer Protocol (HTTP). It is used for secure communication over a computer network and is widely used on the Internet. In HTTPS, the communication protocol is encrypted using Transport Layer Security (TLS) or, formerly, Secure Sockets Layer (SSL). The protocol is therefore also referred to as HTTP over TLS, or HTTP over SSL.
HyperText Markup Language	HTML	HyperText Markup Language is the set of markup symbols or codes inserted into a file intended for display on the Internet. The markup

Appendix F – Programming Acronyms & Terms

Name	Acronym	Description
		tells web browsers how to display a web page's words and images.
Hypertext Preprocessor	PHP	Hypertext Preprocessor is an HTML-embedded Web scripting language. This means PHP code can be inserted into the HTML of a Web page. When a PHP page is accessed, the PHP code is read or "parsed" by the server the page resides on.
Hypertext Transfer Protocol	HTTP	The Hypertext Transfer Protocol is an application layer protocol for distributed, collaborative, hypermedia information systems. HTTP is the foundation of data communication for the World Wide Web, where hypertext documents include hyperlinks to other resources that the user can easily access, for example by a mouse click or by tapping the screen in a web browser.
Identification	ID	A unique number to identify an object, such as a Person object.
IDL		In object-oriented programming, a language that lets a program or object written in one language communicate with another program written in an unknown language. An IDL is used to define interfaces between client and server programs. For example, an IDL can provide interfaces to remote CORBA objects.
Information Systems	IS	Information system, an integrated set of components for collecting, storing, and processing data and for

Appendix F – Programming Acronyms & Terms

Name	Acronym	Description
		providing information, knowledge, and digital products.
Infrastructure as a Service	IaaS	Infrastructure as a service is online services that provide high-level APIs used to dereference various low-level details of underlying network infrastructure like physical computing resources, location, data partitioning, scaling, security, backup, etc.
Input/ Output	IO	In computing, input/output or I/O is the communication between an information processing system, such as a computer, and the outside world, possibly a human or another information processing system. Inputs are the signals or data received by the system and outputs are the signals or data sent from it.
Integrated Development Environment	IDE	An integrated development environment is a software application that provides comprehensive facilities to computer programmers for software development. An IDE normally consists of at least a source code editor, build automation tools, and a debugger.
Intellectual Property	IP	Intellectual property is a category of property that includes intangible creations of the human intellect. There are many types of intellectual property, and some countries recognize more than others. The most well-known types are copyrights, patents, trademarks, and trade secrets.

Appendix F – Programming Acronyms & Terms

Name	Acronym	Description
Interface		Software that enables a program to work with the user (the user interface, which can be a command-line interface, menu-driven, or a graphical user interface), with another program such as the operating system, or with the computer's hardware.
Internet Authentication Service	IAS	Is a component of Windows Server operating systems that provides centralized user authentication, authorization, and accounting.
Internet Cache Protocol	ICP	The Internet Cache Protocol is a UDP-based protocol used for coordinating web caches. Its purpose is to find out the most appropriate location to retrieve a requested object in the situation where multiple caches are in use at a single site.
Internet Explorer	IE	Internet Explorer (formerly Microsoft Internet Explorer[b] and Windows Internet Explorer, commonly abbreviated IE or MSIE) is a series of graphical web browsers developed by Microsoft and included in the Microsoft Windows line of operating systems, starting in 1995. Has since been replaced by Microsoft Edge.
Internet Information Services	IIS	Internet Information Services (IIS, formerly Internet Information Server) is an extensible web server software created by Microsoft for use with the Windows NT family. IIS supports HTTP, HTTP/2, HTTPS, FTP, FTPS, SMTP and NNTP. It has been an integral part of the Windows NT family since Windows NT 4.0, though it may be absent from some editions (e.g.,

Appendix F – Programming Acronyms & Terms

Name	Acronym	Description
		Windows XP Home edition), and is not active by default.
Internet Information Services Express	IISE	Express is a free, simple, and self-contained version of IIS that is optimized for developers
Internet of Things	IoT	The Internet of things is a system of interrelated computing devices, mechanical and digital machines provided with unique identifiers and the ability to transfer data over a network without requiring human-to-human or human-to-computer interaction.
Internet Protocol	IP	A set of rules governing the format of data sent over the internet or other network.
Internet Protocol Suite	TCP/IP	The Internet protocol suite is the conceptual model and set of communications protocols used on the Internet and similar computer networks. It is commonly known as TCP/IP because the foundational protocols in the suite are the Transmission Control Protocol and the Internet Protocol.
Internet Protocol version 4	IPv4	Internet Protocol version 4 is the fourth version of the Internet Protocol. It is one of the core protocols of standards-based internetworking methods on the Internet and other packet-switched networks. IPv4 was the first version deployed for production on SATNET in 1982 and on the ARPANET in January 1983.
Internet Protocol version 6	IPv6	Internet Protocol version 6 is the most recent version of the Internet Protocol, the communications

Appendix F – Programming Acronyms & Terms

Name	Acronym	Description
		protocol that provides an identification and location system for computers on networks and routes traffic across the Internet.
Internet Security and Acceleration Server	ISA	Is a network router, firewall, antivirus program, VPN server, and web cache from Microsoft. It runs on Windows Server and works by inspecting all network traffic that passes through it. It has been renamed Microsoft Forefront Threat Management Gateway.
IP Address	IP	A binary number that uniquely identifies a host (computer) connected to the Internet to other Internet hosts, for communication through the transfer of packets.
IT Operations	DevOps	Aims to shorten the systems development life cycle and provide continuous delivery with high software quality.
Iteration		Iteration is a single pass through a set of operations that deal with code. One form of iteration in computer programming is via loops. A loop will repeat a certain segment of code until a condition is met and it can proceed further. Each time the computer runs a loop, it is known as an iteration. In simple terms, iteration is the process to repeat a particular snippet of code repeatedly to perform a certain action.
Java Script Object Notation	JSON	Is an open standard file format, and data interchange format, which uses human-readable text to store and transmit data objects consisting

Appendix F – Programming Acronyms & Terms

Name	Acronym	Description
		of attribute-value pairs and array data types (or any other serializable value).
Just in Time	JIT	In computing, the just-in-time compilation is a way of executing computer code that involves compilation during the execution of a program – at run time – rather than before execution. Most often, this consists of source code or more commonly bytecode translation to machine code, which is then executed directly.
Key		In IP security (IPSec), a value is used in combination with an algorithm to encrypt or decrypt data. Key settings for IPSec are configurable to provide greater security.
Key Combination		Any combination of keys that must be pressed simultaneously.
Key Performance Indicators	KPI	A type of performance measurement.[1] KPIs evaluate the success of an organization or of a particular activity (such as projects, programs, products, and other initiatives) in which it engages.
Keyword		A designation used to conduct sorting or searching operations.
Keywords		Words that are reserved by a programming language or a program as they have special meaning are known as keywords. These keywords are reserved to perform certain tasks, and they can be either commands or parameters. Each programming language has a set of reserved keywords (also

Appendix F – Programming Acronyms & Terms

Name	Acronym	Description
		known as reserved names) which cannot be used as variable names.
Label	LBL	A graphical control is used to display text.
Language-Integrated Query	LINQ	Language-Integrated Query (LINQ) is the name for a set of technologies based on the integration of query capabilities directly into the C# language. Traditionally, queries against data are expressed as simple strings without type checking at compile time or IntelliSense support.
Last in First Out	LIFO	An abbreviation for last in, first out. It is a method for handling data structures where the first element is processed last and the last element is processed first.
Layout		In programming, the order and sequence of input and output.
Library		A location on a SharePoint site where a collection of files and their associated metadata are stored.
License	LIC	The right of a person or entity to use the software in a particular way, as described in the terms of the license agreement. Copyright law also limits how a person may use the software. A person needs a license agreement for each software program they use.
Life Cycle Management	LCM	In program lifecycle management, a phase is defined as the stipulated period within which a series of events and activities take place as part of the development of the program. Five dominant phases

Appendix F – Programming Acronyms & Terms

Name	Acronym	Description
		determine the successful tenure of a program.
Lightweight Directory Access Protocol	LDAP	The Lightweight Directory Access Protocol is an open, vendor-neutral, industry-standard application protocol for accessing and maintaining distributed directory information services over an Internet Protocol network
Lightweight Transaction Manager	LTM	If only a single resource manager is enlisted in the transaction, the Lightweight Transaction Manager allows that resource manager to manage the transaction and the Lightweight Transaction Manager merely monitors it.
Line of Business	LOB	Line of business is a general term that refers to a product or a set of related products that serve a customer transaction or business need. In some industry sectors, like insurance, "line of business" also has a regulatory and accounting definition to meet a statutory set of insurance policies.
Load Balancer		Refers to the process of distributing a set of tasks over a set of resources (computing units), intending to make their overall processing more efficient. Load balancing techniques can optimize the response time for each task, avoiding unevenly overloading compute nodes while other compute nodes are left idle.
Local Area Network	LAN	A local area network is a computer network that interconnects computers within a limited area

Appendix F – Programming Acronyms & Terms

Name	Acronym	Description
		such as a residence, school, laboratory, university campus, or office building. By contrast, a wide area network not only covers a larger geographic distance but also generally involves leased telecommunication circuits.
Location		Any disk drive, folder, or other places in which you can store files and folders. Programs will commonly ask you to choose a location to save a file.
Log Analytics		Log analytics is the assessment of a recorded set of information from one or more events, captured from a computer, network, application operating system (OS) or another IT ecosystem component.
Logic App		Is a cloud service that helps you schedule, automate, and orchestrate tasks, business processes, and workflows when you need to integrate apps, data, systems, and services across enterprises or organizations. ... Process and route orders across on-premises systems and cloud services.
Long Term Support	LTS	Long-term support (LTS) is a product lifecycle management policy in which a stable release of computer software is maintained for a longer period than the standard edition.
Loop		A loop is a sequence of instructions that repeat the same process over and over until a condition is met and it receives the order to stop. In a loop, the program asks a

Appendix F – Programming Acronyms & Terms

Name	Acronym	Description
		question, and if the answer directs the program to act, the action is performed, and the loop runs again, performing the same task. It runs until the answer is such that no action is required, and the code can proceed further. Loops are considered one of the most basic and powerful concepts in programming.
Machine Language	ML	Also known as machine code, machine language is a lowest-level programming language consisting of binary digits or bits that are read by computers. Machine language is the only language understood by computers. As it consists of only numbers, they cannot be comprehended by humans. Therefore, programmers write code in the high-level language, which is then translated into assembly language or machine language by a compiler, which is then converted to a machine language by an assembler.
Machine Learning	ML	Is the study of computer algorithms that improve automatically through experience. It is seen as a subset of artificial intelligence.
Managed Extensibility Framework	MEF	Is a component of .NET Framework 4.0 aiming to create lightweight, extensible applications. It aims to allow .NET application developers to discover and use extensions with no configuration required.
Markup Language		Is a relatively simple language that consists of easily understood keywords and tags, used to format

Appendix F – Programming Acronyms & Terms

Name	Acronym	Description
		the overall view of the page and its contents. The language specifies codes for formatting the layout and style of a page, within a text file only. The most common markup languages are Hypertext Markup Language (HTML), Extensible Markup Language (XML), and Standard Generalized Markup Language (SGML).
Memory		Any temporary storage space used within or in conjunction with a computer, such as RAM or a USB flash drive.
Messaging Application Programming Interface	MAPI	Is an API for Microsoft Windows which allows programs to become email aware. While MAPI is designed to be independent of the protocol, it is usually used to communicate with Microsoft Exchange Server.
Microservices		A variant of the service-oriented architecture (SOA) structural style – arranges an application as a collection of loosely coupled services.[1] In a microservices architecture, services are fine-grained, and the protocols are lightweight.
Microsoft Active Accessibility	MSAA	Is an Application Programming Interface (API) for user interface accessibility. MSAA was introduced as a platform add-on to Microsoft Windows 95 in 1997. MSAA is designed to help Assistive Technology (AT) products interact with standard and custom user interface (UI) elements of an application (or the operating

Appendix F – Programming Acronyms & Terms

Name	Acronym	Description
		system), as well as to access, find, and manipulate an application's UI elements.
Microsoft Baseline Security Analyzer	MBSA	Is a discontinued software tool that is no longer available from Microsoft that figures out security state by assessing missing security updates and less-secure security settings within Microsoft Windows, Windows components such as Internet Explorer, IIS web server, and products Microsoft SQL Server, and Microsoft Office macro settings.
Microsoft Consulting Services	MCS	Helps organizations adopt tech solutions across digital strategy, data insight, sales, and more.
Microsoft Corporation	MS	An American multinational technology company, founded in 1975, with headquarters in Redmond, Washington. It develops, manufactures, licenses support, and sells computer software, consumer electronics, personal computers, and related services. Its best-known software products are the Microsoft Windows line of operating systems, the Microsoft Office suite, and the Internet Explorer and Edge web browsers. Its flagship hardware products are the Xbox video game consoles and the Microsoft Surface lineup of touchscreen personal computers. In 2016, it was the world's largest software maker by revenue. The word "Microsoft" is a portmanteau of "microcomputer" and "software". It is considered one of the Big Five technology companies alongside Amazon, Apple, Google, and Facebook.

Appendix F – Programming Acronyms & Terms

Name	Acronym	Description
Microsoft Data Access Components	MDAC	Also known as Windows DAC, is a framework of interrelated Microsoft technologies that allows programmers a uniform and comprehensive way of developing applications that can access almost any data store. Its components include ActiveX Data Objects (ADO), OLE DB, and Open Database Connectivity (ODBC).
Microsoft Data Engine	MSDE	Is a relational database management system developed by Microsoft. It is a scaled-down version of Microsoft SQL Server 7.0 or 2000 which is free for non-commercial use as well as certain limited commercial use
Microsoft Developer Network	MSDN	Microsoft Developer Network was the division of Microsoft responsible for managing the firm's relationship with developers and testers, such as hardware developers interested in the operating system (OS), and software developers developing on the various OS platforms or using the API or scripting languages of Microsoft's applications. The relationship management is situated in assorted media: websites, newsletters, developer conferences, trade media, blogs, and DVD distribution. From January 2020, the website has been fully integrated with Microsoft Docs.
Microsoft Edge		A web browser developed by Microsoft. It was first released for Windows 10 and Xbox One in 2015, then for Android and iOS in 2017, and macOS in 2019.

Appendix F – Programming Acronyms & Terms

Name	Acronym	Description
Microsoft Forefront Threat Management Gateway	Forefront TMG	Microsoft Forefront Threat Management Gateway, formerly known as Microsoft Internet Security and Acceleration Server, is a network router, firewall, antivirus program, VPN server and web cache from Microsoft. It runs on Windows Server and works by inspecting all network traffic that passes through it.
Microsoft Foundation Classes	MFC	Introduced in 1995, is a C++ object-oriented library for developing desktop applications for Windows.
Microsoft Healthcare Bot		Empowers healthcare organizations to build and deploy an AI-powered, compliant, conversational healthcare experience at scale. The service combines built-in medical intelligence with natural language capabilities, extensibility tools, and compliance constructs, allowing healthcare organizations such as Providers, Payers, Pharma, HMOs, Telehealth to give people access to trusted and relevant healthcare services and information.
Microsoft HTML Engine and Interfaces	MSHTML	Is a proprietary browser engine for the Microsoft Windows version of Internet Explorer.
Microsoft Identity Integration Server	MIIS	Is an identity management (IdM) product offered by Microsoft. It is a service that aggregates identity-related information from multiple data sources. The goal of MIIS is to provide organizations with a unified view of a user's/ resources identity across the heterogeneous enterprise and supply methods to automate routine tasks.

Appendix F – Programming Acronyms & Terms

Name	Acronym	Description
Microsoft Intermediary Language	MSIL	Is the intermediate language binary instruction set defined within the Common Language Infrastructure specification.
Microsoft Management Console	MMC	Microsoft Management Console is a part of Windows 2000 and its successors that provides system administrators and advanced users an interface for configuring and monitoring the system.
Microsoft Message Queue Server	MSMQ	Microsoft Message Queuing is a message queue implementation developed by Microsoft and deployed in its Windows Server operating systems since Windows NT 4 and Windows 95. Windows Server 2016 and Windows 10 also includes this component. In addition to its mainstream server platform support, MSMQ has been incorporated into Microsoft Embedded platforms since 1999 and the release of Windows CE 3.0.
Microsoft Most Valuable Professional	MVP	The Microsoft Most Valuable Professional award is given by Microsoft to "technology experts who passionately share their knowledge with the community." They are awarded to people who "actively share their ... technical expertise with the different technology communities related directly, or indirectly to Microsoft".
Microsoft Network	MSN	MSN is a web portal and related collection of Internet services and apps for Windows and mobile devices, provided by Microsoft and launched on August 24, 1995, the same release date as Windows 95.

Appendix F – Programming Acronyms & Terms

Name	Acronym	Description
Microsoft Office SharePoint Server	MOSS	Microsoft Office SharePoint Server (MOSS) is the full version of a portal-based platform for collaboratively creating, managing, and sharing documents and Web services. MOSS enables users to create "Sharepoint Portals" that include shared workspaces, applications, blogs, wikis, and other documents accessible through a Web browser. The free version, Windows SharePoint Server (WSS), usually referred to as simply "Sharepoint," is available as a free download included with every Windows Server license.
Microsoft Point of Service for .NET	POS	The new set of .NET class libraries enables software developers and original-equipment manufacturers to write .NET applications for retail and hospitality that work across a wide variety of retail peripherals.
Microsoft Regional Director	RD	Trusted advisors to the developer and IT professional audiences and Microsoft.
Microsoft Script Debugger	MSD	Microsoft Script Debugger is a relatively minimal debugger for Windows Script Host-supported scripting languages, such as VBScript and JScript. Its user interface allows the user to set breakpoints and/or step through the execution of script code line by line and examine values of variables and properties after any step.
Microsoft XML Core Services	MSXML	Microsoft XML Core Services are a set of services that allow applications written in JScript, VBScript, and Microsoft

Appendix F – Programming Acronyms & Terms

Name	Acronym	Description
		development tools to build Windows-native XML-based applications.
Million Instructions Per Second	MIPS	Instructions per second is a measure of a computer's processor speed. For CISC computers different instructions take different amounts of time, so the value measured depends on the instruction mix; even for comparing processors in the same family, the IPS measurement can be problematic.
Mode		The operational state of a computer or a program.
Model View Controller	MVC	Model–view–controller is a software design pattern commonly used for developing user interfaces that divide the related program logic into three interconnected elements. This is done to separate internal representations of information from the way's information is presented to and accepted from the user.
Model View View Controller	MVVC	Model–view–viewmodel is a software architectural pattern that helps the separation of the development of the graphical user interface (the view) – be it via a markup language or GUI code – from the development of the business logic or back-end logic (the model) so that the view is not dependent on any specific model platform. The view model of MVVM is a value converter, meaning the view model handles exposing (converting) the data objects from the model in such a way that objects are easily managed and

Appendix F – Programming Acronyms & Terms

Name	Acronym	Description
		presented. In this respect, the view model is more model than the view and handles most if not all of the view's display logic. The view model may implement a mediator pattern, organizing access to the back-end logic around the set of use cases supported by the view.
Multipurpose Internet Mail Extensions	MIME	Is an Internet standard that extends the format of email messages to support text in character sets other than ASCII, as well as attachments of audio, video, images, and application programs. Message bodies may consist of multiple parts, and header information may be specified in non-ASCII character sets.
N - Tier Architecture	N-Tier	In software engineering, multitier architecture or multilayered architecture is a client-server architecture in which presentation, application processing, and data management functions are physically separated. The most widespread use of multitier architecture is the three-tier architecture.
Network Basic Input/Output System	NetBIOS	NetBIOS is an acronym for Network Basic Input/Output System. It supplies services related to the session layer of the OSI model allowing applications on separate computers to communicate over a local area network. As strictly an API, NetBIOS is not a networking protocol.
Network File System	NFS	Network File System is a distributed file system protocol originally

Appendix F – Programming Acronyms & Terms

Name	Acronym	Description
		developed by Sun Microsystems in 1984, allowing a user on a client computer to access files over a computer network much like local storage is accessed.
Network Interface Card	NIC	A network interface controller is a computer hardware component that connects a computer to a computer network. Early network interface controllers were commonly implemented on expansion cards that plugged into a computer bus.
New Technology File System	NTFS	NTFS is a proprietary journaling file system developed by Microsoft. Starting with Windows NT 3.1, it is the default file system of the Windows NT family
NuGet		NuGet is a package manager designed to enable developers to share reusable code. It is a software-plus-service solution whose client app is free and open-source. The Outercurve Foundation initially created it under the name NuPack.
NULL		Defines the lack of any value whatsoever. A null character is a programming code, which stands for a character with no value, missing value, or the end of a character string.
Object	OBJ	An object is a combination of related variables, constants, and other data structures that can be selected and manipulated together. An object can include shapes that appear on a screen or the age of students in a school.

Appendix F – Programming Acronyms & Terms

Name	Acronym	Description
Object Linking and Embedding	OLE	Object Linking & Embedding is a proprietary technology developed by Microsoft that allows embedding and linking to documents and other objects. For developers, it brought OLE Control Extension, a way to develop and use custom user interface elements.
Object Linking and Embedding Database	OLE DB	OLE DB, an API designed by Microsoft, allows accessing data from a variety of sources in a uniform manner. The API supplies a set of interfaces implemented using the Component Object Model; it is otherwise unrelated to OLE.
Object Relational Mapper	ORM	Object-relational mapping (ORM, O/RM, and O/R mapping tool) in computer science is a programming technique for converting data between incompatible type systems using object-oriented programming languages. This creates, in effect, a "virtual object database" that can be used from within the programming language. Entity Framework is the ORM that is part of Microsoft .NET.
Object-Oriented Programming	OOP/ OO	Is a model defined by programmers that revolve around objects and data rather than 'actions' and 'logic'. In OOP, not only the data type of a data structure is defined, but also the types of functions that can be applied to it. Through this, the data structure becomes an object that consists of both data and functions. Languages that use OOP concepts are Java, Python, C++, and Ruby.

Appendix F – Programming Acronyms & Terms

Name	Acronym	Description
Off-Topic	OT	Usually used at the beginning of the subject line to show the message or email is off topic for the group.
Online Analytical Processing	OLAP	Online analytical processing, or OLAP, is an approach to answer multi-dimensional analytical queries swiftly in computing. OLAP is part of the broader category of business intelligence, which also encompasses relational databases, report writing, and data mining.
Online Transaction Processing	OLTP	In Online transaction processing, information systems typically facilitate and manage transaction-oriented applications
Open Data Protocol	OData	In computing, Open Data Protocol is an open protocol that allows the creation and consumption of queryable and interoperable REST APIs in a simple and standard way. Microsoft started OData in 2007. Versions 1.0, 2.0, and 3.0 are released under the Microsoft Open Specification Promise.
Open Database Connectivity	ODBC	In computing, Open Database Connectivity is a standard application programming interface for accessing database management systems. The designers of ODBC aimed to make it independent of database systems and operating systems.
Open-Source Software	OSS	Open-source software is a type of computer software in which source code is released under a license in which the copyright holder grants users the rights to use, study, change, and distribute the software

Appendix F – Programming Acronyms & Terms

Name	Acronym	Description
		to anyone and for any purpose. Open-source software may be developed in a collaborative public manner.
Operand		Is a term used to denote the objects which can be manipulated using different operators.
Operating System	OS	A software system that enables applications to interact with hardware and that manages software resources on a computer.
Operator		An operator is a term used to denote the object which can manipulate different operands.
Pacific NorthWest	PNW	Is the home of Microsoft!
Package		Is an organized module of related interfaces and classes. Packages are used to organize classes that belong to the same category or supply related functionality.
Parallel LINQ	PLINQ	Parallel LINQ (PLINQ) is a parallel implementation of the Language-Integrated Query (LINQ) pattern. PLINQ implements the full set of LINQ standard query operators as extension methods for the System.Linq namespace and has more operators for parallel operations. PLINQ combines the simplicity and readability of LINQ syntax with the power of parallel programming.
Parameter	param	Refers to method parameters.
Parent Class		That class is called a superclass, or parent class. The derived class is called subclass, or child class. You

Appendix F – Programming Acronyms & Terms

Name	Acronym	Description
		use the keyword extends to identify the class that your subclass extends. If you do not declare a superclass, your class implicitly extends the class Object.
Path		A sequence of folders (directories) that leads to a specific file or folder. A backslash is used to separate each folder in the path. For example, the path to a file called invoice.txt might be C:\Documents\July\invoice.txt.
Plain Old CLR Objects	POCO	In software engineering, a plain old CLR object, or plain old class object is a simple object created in the .NET Common Language Runtime that is unencumbered by inheritance or attributes. This is often used in opposition to the complex or specialized objects that object-relational mapping frameworks often require.
Plain Old XML	POX	Plain Old XML (POX) is the basic XML, sometimes mixed in with other, blendable specifications like XML Namespaces, Dublin Core, XInclude, and XLink. This contrasts with complicated, multilayered XML specifications like those for web services or RDF. The term may have been derived from or inspired by the expression plain old telephone service (POTS) and, similarly Plain Old Java Object (POJO).
Platform as a Service	PaaS	Platform as a service (PaaS) or application platform as a service (aPaaS) or platform-based service is a category of cloud computing services that provides a platform

Appendix F – Programming Acronyms & Terms

Name	Acronym	Description
		allowing customers to develop, run, and manage applications without the complexity of building and supporting the infrastructure typically associated with developing and launching an app.
Pointer		A pointer is a variable that contains the address of a location in the memory. The location is the commencing point of an object, such as an element of the array or an integer.
POP3		The POP protocol is used to retrieve email and that supports download-and-delete from a remote mailbox.
Port		Hardware- or software-based interface used to transfer information between a computer and other devices. Hardware ports are physical connections that are visible on the outside of the computer. Software ports are the numbered gateways in programs that software programs use to exchange information.
Portable Document Format	PDF	PDF (Portable Document Format) is a file format that has captured all the elements of a printed document as an electronic image that you can view, navigate, print, or forward to someone else. PDF files are created using Adobe Acrobat, Acrobat Capture, or similar products.
Portable Network Graphics	PNG	Portable Network Graphics is a raster graphics file format that supports lossless data compression. PNG was developed as an

Appendix F – Programming Acronyms & Terms

Name	Acronym	Description
		improved, non-patented replacement for Graphics Interchange Format. PNG supports palette-based images, grayscale images, and full-color non-palette-based RGB or RGBA images.
Post		A set of routines stored in read-only memory (ROM) that tests various system components such as RAM, disk drives, and the keyboard, to see if they are properly connected and operating. If problems are found, these routines alert the user with a series of beeps or a message, often accompanied by a diagnostic numeric value. If the POST is successful, it passes control to the bootstrap loader.
Post Office Protocol	POP	In computing, the Post Office Protocol is an application-layer Internet standard protocol used by e-mail clients to retrieve e-mail from a mail server. POP version 3 is the version in common use.
Power BI		Power BI is a business analytics service by Microsoft. It aims to provide interactive visualizations and business intelligence capabilities with an interface simple enough for end-users to create their reports and dashboards.
Pretty Good Privacy	PGP	Pretty Good Privacy is a cryptographic method that supplies privacy and authentication for data communication. PGP is used for signing, encrypting, and decrypting texts, e-mails, files, directories, and whole disk partitions and to increase the security of e-mail

Appendix F – Programming Acronyms & Terms

Name	Acronym	Description
		communications. Phil Zimmermann developed PGP in 1991.
Privilege		A user's right to perform a specific task, usually, one that affects an entire computer system rather than a particular object. Privileges are assigned by administrators to individual users or groups of users as part of the security settings for the computer.
Product Group	PG	A collection of products used for presentation, sales campaigns, or e-business.
Project Manager, Product Manager, Program Manager	PM	
Property		An attribute of an object that is used to define its state, appearance, or value.
Proxy Server	PS	A server located on a network between client software, such as a Web browser, and another server. It intercepts all requests to the server to decide whether it can fulfill them itself. If not, it sends the request to another server.
Quality Assurance	QA	Quality assurance is a way of preventing mistakes and defects in manufactured products and avoiding problems when delivering products or services to customers, which ISO 9000 defines as "part of quality management focused on providing confidence that quality requirements will be fulfilled".
Queue		A multi-element data structure from which (by strict definition) elements

Appendix F – Programming Acronyms & Terms

Name	Acronym	Description
		can be removed only in the same order in which they were inserted; that is, it follows a first in, first-out (FIFO) constraint.
Random Access Memory	RAM	Random-access memory is a form of computer memory that can be read and changed in any order, typically used to store working data and machine code. A random-access memory device allows data items to be read or written in almost the same amount of time irrespective of the physical location of data inside the memory.
Rapid Application Development	RAD	Rapid-application development, also called rapid-application building, is both a general term for adaptive software development approaches and the name for James Martin's approach to rapid development.
Read-Only Memory	ROM	Read-only memory is a type of non-volatile memory used in computers and other electronic devices. Data stored in ROM cannot be electronically changed after the manufacture of the memory device.
Really Simple Syndication	RSS	RSS is a web feed that allows users and applications to access updates to websites in a standardized, computer-readable format. These feeds can, for example, allow a user to keep track of many different websites in a single news aggregator.
Redundant Array of Independent Disks	RAID	RAID is a data storage virtualization technology that combines multiple

Appendix F – Programming Acronyms & Terms

Name	Acronym	Description
		physical disk drive components into one or more logical units for data redundancy, performance improvement, or both.
Relational Database Management System	RDBMS	A relational database is a type of database. It uses a structure that allows us to find and access data with another piece of data in the database. Often, data in a relational database is organized into tables.
Remote		Not in the immediate vicinity, as a computer or other device located in another place (room, building, or city) and accessible through some type of cable or communications link.
Remote Procedure Call	RPC	In distributed computing, a remote procedure call is when a computer program causes a procedure to execute in a different address space, which is coded as if it were a normal procedure call, without the programmer explicitly coding the details for the remote interaction.
Representational State Transfer	REST	Representational state transfer is a software architectural style that defines a set of constraints to be used for creating Web services. Web services that conform to the REST architectural style, called RESTful Web services, provide interoperability between computer systems on the internet.
Resource		Generally, any part of a computer system or networks, such as a disk drive, printer, or memory, can be

Appendix F – Programming Acronyms & Terms

Name	Acronym	Description
		allotted to a running program or a process.
Rich Internet Applications	RIA	A rich web application is a web application that has many of the characteristics of desktop application software. The concept is closely related to a single-page application, and may allow the user interactive features such as drag and drop, background menu, WYSIWYG editing, etc.
Rich Text Format	RTF	The Rich Text Format is a proprietary document file format with published specification developed by Microsoft Corporation from 1987 until 2008 for cross-platform document interchange with Microsoft products.
Robot, Internet Bot, Web Robot	BOT	A software application that runs automated tasks (scripts) over the Internet. Typically, bots perform tasks that are simple and repetitive, much faster than a person could. The most extensive use of bots is for web crawling, in which an automated script fetches, analyzes, and files information from web servers. More than half of all web traffic is generated by bots.
Routing Information Protocol	RIP	The distance vector routing protocol used in small- to medium-sized Internet Protocol (IP) and Internetwork Packet Exchange (IPX) internetworks.
Rubbish in, Rubbish Out	RIRO	**Read Garbage In, Garbage Out* for description*
Runtime		Is the period during which a program is running on a computer.

Appendix F – Programming Acronyms & Terms

Name	Acronym	Description
		If an operation occurs at 'runtime', it occurred when a program is running or the moment at which the program begins to run.
Runtime Callable Wrapper	RCW	A Runtime Callable Wrapper is a proxy object generated by the .NET Common Language Runtime to allow a Component Object Model object to be accessed from managed code.
Scalable Vector Graphics	SVG	Scalable Vector Graphics is an Extensible Markup Language-based vector image format for two-dimensional graphics with support for interactivity and animation. The SVG specification is an open standard developed by the World Wide Web Consortium since 1999. SVG images and their behaviors are defined in XML text files.
Schema		A definition of the structure of a particular type of data, which includes a definition of the allowed attributes and allowed relationships with other objects.
Secure Sockets Layer	SSL	Transport Layer Security, and its now-deprecated predecessor, Secure Sockets Layer, are cryptographic protocols designed to provide communications security over a computer network. Several versions of the protocols find widespread use in applications such as web browsing, email, instant messaging, and voice over IP.
Security Certificate		A digital document used for authentication and network security that binds a public key to an entity

Appendix F – Programming Acronyms & Terms

Name	Acronym	Description
		that holds the corresponding private key.
Serverless		Serverless computing is a cloud computing execution model in which the cloud provider runs the server, and dynamically manages the allocation of machine resources. Pricing is based on the actual number of resources consumed by an application, rather than on pre-purchased units of capacity.
Server-side		When procedures and processes are performed on the server, they are considered server-side. On the other hand, the client-side is at the end of the user. Many programming languages are designed for server-side programming such as PHP, Perl, and ASP.NET.
Service Bus		An enterprise service bus implements a communication system between mutually interacting software applications in a service-oriented architecture.
Service Order Line	SOL	The part of a service order that specifies detailed information about the requested service.
Service Pack	SP	In computing, a service pack forms a collection of updates, fixes, or enhancements to a software program delivered in the form of a single installable package.
Service-Oriented Architecture	SOA	A service-oriented architecture is a style of software design where services are provided to the other components by application components, through a

Appendix F – Programming Acronyms & Terms

Name	Acronym	Description
		communication protocol over a network.
SharePoint Portal Server	SPS	SharePoint is a web-based collaborative platform that integrates with Microsoft Office. Launched in 2001, SharePoint is primarily sold as a document management and storage system, but the product is highly configurable, and usage varies substantially among organizations.
SharePoint Portal Service	SPS	A portal is a Microsoft SharePoint site on your intranet that has a large number of site viewers who consume content on the site. ... Typically, portals have relatively few people who create and author the site and its content. Most visitors to the portal only read and consume the content.
SharePoint Team Services	STS	The new Office XP includes SharePoint Team Services, which allows end-users to create and add content to team, departmental, or project-based Web sites.
Shortcut Key		Any combination of keys that must be pressed simultaneously.
Simple Object Access Protocol	SOAP	SOAP is a messaging protocol specification for exchanging structured information in the implementation of web services in computer networks. Its purpose is to provide extensibility, neutrality, verbosity, and independence.
Single Sign-On	SSO	An authentication process that allows a user to log on to a system once with a single set of credentials

Appendix F – Programming Acronyms & Terms

Name	Acronym	Description
		to access multiple applications or services.
Snippet		A small piece of programming code that is part of a larger program. Usually, the code snippet performs a specific function or task.
Software as a Service	SaaS	Software as a service is a software licensing and delivery model in which software is licensed on a subscription basis and is centrally hosted. It is sometimes referred to as "on-demand software" and was formerly referred to as "software plus services" by Microsoft.
Software Developers Kit	SDK	A software development kit is a collection of software development tools in one installable package. They help the creation of applications by having a compiler, debugger, and perhaps a software framework. They are normally specific to a hardware platform and operating system combination.
Software Development Live Cycle	SDLC	In systems engineering, information systems, and software engineering, the systems development life cycle, also referred to as the application development life cycle, is a process for planning, creating, testing, and deploying an information system.
SOLID	SOLID	In object-oriented computer programming, SOLID is a mnemonic acronym for five design principles intended to make software designs more understandable, flexible, and maintainable. It is not related to the GRASP software design principles. The principles are a subset of many

Appendix F – Programming Acronyms & Terms

Name	Acronym	Description
		principles promoted by American software engineer and instructor Robert C. Martin. Though they apply to any object-oriented design, the SOLID principles can also form a core philosophy for methodologies such as agile development or adaptive software development.
Solid State Drive	SSD	A solid-state drive is a solid-state storage device that uses integrated circuit assemblies to store data persistently, typically using flash memory, and functioning as secondary storage in the hierarchy of computer storage.
Source data or Source		Is the key location from which data is used in the program. The source data can come from a database, spreadsheet, or even a hard-coded data location. When a program is executed to display data in a table, the program retrieves the data from its source and then presents it in the arrangement as defined in the code.
SQL Server		Microsoft SQL Server is a relational database management system developed by Microsoft. As a database server, it is a software product with the primary function of storing and retrieving data as requested by other software applications—which may run either on the same computer or on another computer across a network.
SQL Server Integration Services	SSIS	SQL Server Integration Services is a component of the Microsoft SQL Server database software that can

Appendix F – Programming Acronyms & Terms

Name	Acronym	Description
		be used to perform a broad range of data migration tasks. SSIS is a platform for data integration and workflow applications. It features a data warehousing tool used for data extraction, transformation, and loading.
SQL Server Stored Procedure	SP	A stored procedure is a subroutine available to applications that access a relational database management system. Such procedures are stored in the database data dictionary. Uses for stored procedures include data-validation or access-control mechanisms.
Startup		The process of starting or resetting a computer or a device. When first turned on (cold boot) or reset (warm boot), the computer runs the software that loads and starts the computer's operating system, which prepares it for use.
Statement		Is a single line of code written legally in a programming language that expresses an action to be carried out. A statement might have internal components of its own, including expressions, operators, and functions.
Static Random-Access Memory	SRAM	Static random-access memory is a type of random-access memory that uses latching circuitry to store each bit. SRAM is volatile memory; data is lost when power is removed. The term static differentiates SRAM from DRAM which must be periodically refreshed.

Appendix F – Programming Acronyms & Terms

Name	Acronym	Description
Storage		A device that can retain data for subsequent retrieval.
Storage Area Network	SAN	A storage area network or storage network is a computer network that provides access to consolidated, block-level data storage. SANs are primarily used to access storage devices, such as disk arrays and tape libraries from servers so that the devices appear to the operating system as direct-attached storage.
Stream		To transfer digital data in a continuous flow across a network.
Structured Query Language	SQL	SQL is a domain-specific language used in programming and designed for managing data held in a relational database management system, or for stream processing in a relational data stream management system.
Swagger		By reading your API's structure, Swagger can automatically build beautiful and interactive API documentation.
Synchronize	Sync	To reconcile the differences between the two sets of stored data, where once the differences are determined, both sets are updated to be the same.
Synchronous Dynamic Random-Access Memory	SDRAM	Synchronous dynamic random-access memory (synchronous dynamic RAM or SDRAM) is any DRAM where the operation of its external pin interface is coordinated by an externally supplied clock signal.

Appendix F – Programming Acronyms & Terms

Name	Acronym	Description
Syntax		Like human languages, programming languages have their own set of rules on how statements can be conveyed. The set of these rules is known as syntax. While many programming languages share many features, functions, and capabilities, they differ in syntax. Without the proper use of the syntax, one cannot write an executable program, and a wrong syntax will lead to a plethora of errors.
Table Per Type	TPT	Table-per-type inheritance uses a separate table in the database to maintain data for non-inherited properties and key properties for each type in the inheritance hierarchy.
Tagged Image File Format	TIFF	Tag Image File Format, abbreviated TIFF or TIF, is a computer file format for storing raster graphics images, popular among graphic artists, the publishing industry, and photographers. TIFF is widely supported by scanning, faxing, word processing, optical character recognition, image manipulation, desktop publishing, and page-layout applications.
Target Framework Moniker	TFM	Is a textual representation of a moniker that uniquely identifies a Target Framework.
Task Parallel Library	TPL	Is a set of public types and APIs in the System.Threading and System.Threading.Tasks namespaces. The purpose of the TPL is to make developers more productive by simplifying the

Appendix F – Programming Acronyms & Terms

Name	Acronym	Description
		process of adding parallelism and concurrency to applications.
Test-Driven Development	TDD	Test-driven development is a software development process that relies on the repetition of a very short development cycle: requirements are turned into very specific test cases, then the code is improved so that the tests pass.
Text Template Transformation Toolkit	T4	Text Template Transformation Toolkit is a free and open-source template-based text generation framework included with Visual Studio. T4 source files are usually denoted by the file extension ".tt".
Third-Party Installer	3PI (1)	Using Microsoft Installer Package (MSI) to install third party programs onto computers on the network.
Third-Party Integrator	3PI (2)	A company other than the OEM Customer that creates an image on the OEM Customer's behalf. An Integrator can only distribute the product back to the OEM Customer
Third-Party Logistics Provider	3PL	A first that provided service to its customers of outsourced (or "third-party") logistics services for part, or all their supply chain management.
Thread		A type of object within a process that runs program instructions. Using multiple threads allows concurrent operations within a process and enables one process to run different parts of its program on different processors simultaneously. A thread has its own set of registers, its kernel stack, a thread environment block,

Appendix F – Programming Acronyms & Terms

Name	Acronym	Description
		and a user stack in the address space of its process.
Token		Is the smallest individual unit in a program, often referring to a portion of a much larger data piece.
Transact-SQL	T-SQL	Transact-SQL is Microsoft's and Sybase's proprietary extension to the SQL used to interact with relational databases.
Transfer	Xfer	The movement of information from one location to another, either within a computer (as from a disk drive to memory), between a computer and an external device (as between a file server and a computer on a network), or between separate computers.
Transmission Control Protocol	TCP	The Transmission Control Protocol is one of the main protocols of the Internet protocol suite. It originated in the initial network implementation in which it complemented the Internet Protocol. Therefore, the entire suite is commonly referred to as TCP/IP.
Transport Layer Security	TLS	Transport Layer Security, and its now-deprecated predecessor, Secure Sockets Layer, are cryptographic protocols designed to provide communications security over a computer network. Several versions of the protocols find widespread use in applications such as web browsing, email, instant messaging, and voice over IP.
TypeScript	TS	An open-source programming language developed and maintained by Microsoft. It is a strict

Appendix F – Programming Acronyms & Terms

Name	Acronym	Description
		syntactical superset of JavaScript and adds optional static typing to the language. TypeScript is designed for the development of large applications and transcompiles to JavaScript.[4] As TypeScript is a superset of JavaScript, existing JavaScript programs are also valid TypeScript programs.
Unicode Transformation Format	UTF	Unicode Transformation Format refers to several types of Unicode character encodings, including UTF-7, UTF-8, UTF-16, and UTF-32.
Unified Modeling Language	UML	The Unified Modeling Language is a general-purpose, developmental, modeling language in the field of software engineering that is intended to provide a standard way to visualize the design of a system.
Uniform Resource Identifier	URI	Is a string of characters that unambiguously identifies a particular resource. To guarantee uniformity, all URIs follow a predefined set of syntax rules, but also maintain extensibility through a separately defined hierarchical naming scheme (e.g., http://).
Uniform Resource Locator	URL	Colloquially termed a web address, is a reference to a web resource that specifies its location on a computer network and a mechanism for retrieving it. A URL is a specific type of Uniform Resource Identifier (URI), although many people use the two terms interchangeably.

Appendix F – Programming Acronyms & Terms

Name	Acronym	Description
Uniform Resource Name	URN	A Uniform Resource Name is a Uniform Resource Identifier that uses the urn scheme. URNs are globally unique persistent identifiers assigned within defined namespaces so they will be available for a long period, even after the resource which they identify ceases to exist or becomes unavailable.
Unit Testable	UT	This is a phrase I use to warn people that if their code is hard to unit test, they are doing it wrong.
Universal Data Access	UDA	Microsoft's strategic interoperability architecture for supplying access to information across the enterprise. From the desktop to departmental servers, to mainframes, Universal Data Access supplies the means for high-performance client/server and Web-based applications to interoperate across the enterprise on private networks or across the world via the Internet.
Universal Runtime	URT	The ancient name for what ended up being .NET
Universal Serial Bus	USB	Universal Serial Bus is an industry-standard that establishes specifications for cables and connectors and protocols for connection, communication and power supply between computers, peripherals, and other computers.
Universal Windows Platform	UWP	Universal Windows Platform is a computing platform created by Microsoft and first introduced in Windows 10. The purpose of this platform is to help develop universal apps that run on Windows 10,

Appendix F – Programming Acronyms & Terms

Name	Acronym	Description
		Windows 10 Mobile, Xbox One, and HoloLens without the need to be re-written for each.
User Acceptance Testing	UAT	In engineering and its various subdisciplines, acceptance testing is a test conducted to determine if the requirements of a specification or contract are met. It may involve chemical tests, physical tests, or performance tests.
User Datagram Protocol	UDP	In computer networking, the User Datagram Protocol is one of the core members of the Internet protocol suite. The protocol was designed by David P. Reed in 1980 and formally defined in RFC 768
User Experience	UX	User experience is a person's emotions and attitudes about using a product, system, or service. It includes the practical, experiential, affective, meaningful, and valuable aspects of human-computer interaction and product ownership.
User Interface	UI	The user interface, in the industrial design field of human-computer interaction, is the space where interactions between humans and machines occur.
Validation		The process of comparing files on local volumes with their associated data in secondary storage by Remote Storage. Volumes that are validated ensure that the correct data is recalled from remote storage when a user attempts to open the file from a local volume.
Variable	Var	Is a location that stores temporary data within a program which can

Appendix F – Programming Acronyms & Terms

Name	Acronym	Description
		be modified, store, and display whenever need.
Video Random Access Memory	VRAM	Video RAM, or VRAM, is a dual-ported variant of dynamic RAM, which was once commonly used to store the framebuffer in graphics adapters. Note that most computers and game consoles do not use this form of memory, and dual-ported VRAM should not be confused with other forms of video memory.
Virtual Local Area Network	VLAN	A virtual LAN is any broadcast domain that is partitioned and isolated in a computer network at the data link layer (OSI layer). LAN is the abbreviation for local area network and in this context, virtual refers to a physical object recreated and altered by additional logic. VLANs work by applying tags to network frames and handling these tags in networking systems – creating the appearance and functionality of network traffic that is physically on a single network but acts as if it is split between separate networks.
Virtual Machine	VM	In computing, a virtual machine is an emulation of a computer system. Virtual machines are based on computer architectures and provide the functionality of a physical computer. Their implementations may involve specialized hardware, software, or a combination.
Virtual Method Table	MT	Is a mechanism used in a programming language to support

Appendix F – Programming Acronyms & Terms

Name	Acronym	Description
		dynamic dispatch (or run-time method binding)
Virtual Private Network	VPN	A virtual private network extends a private network across a public network and enables users to send and receive data across shared or public networks as if their computing devices were directly connected to the private network.
Visual Basic	VB	Visual Basic is a third-generation event-driven programming language from Microsoft known for its Component Object Model programming model first released in 1991 and declared legacy during 2008. Microsoft intended Visual Basic to be relatively easy to learn and use.
Visual Basic for Applications	VBA	Visual Basic for Applications is an implementation of Microsoft's event-driven programming language Visual Basic 6, which was declared legacy in 2008, and is an associated integrated development environment.
Visual Basic Script/ VBScript	VBS	VBScript is an Active Scripting language developed by Microsoft that is modeled on Visual Basic. It allows Microsoft Windows system administrators to generate powerful tools for managing computers with error handling, subroutines, and other advanced programming constructs.
Visual Display Unit	VDU	An electronic visual display, informally a screen, is a display device for the presentation of images, text, or video transmitted

Appendix F – Programming Acronyms & Terms

Name	Acronym	Description
		electronically, without producing a permanent record. Electronic visual displays include television sets, computer monitors, and digital signage.
Visual Studio	VS	Microsoft Visual Studio is _the best-_integrated development environment from Microsoft. It is used to develop computer programs, as well as websites, web apps, web services, and mobile apps.
Visual Studio for Applications	VSA	Let us you enable end-users to customize your existing applications using Visual Basic and Visual C#. ... In standalone mode, VSTA provides your application with the means to load, compile, and run end-user customizations.
Visual Studio Industry Partner	VSIP	Allows third-party developers and software vendors to develop tools, components, and languages for use in the Microsoft Visual Studio.
Visual Studio Team Services	VSTS	VSTS includes more benefits than what you could get from the Team Foundation Server, such as an integrated Build Service, which gives you an easy way to access build agents that have been pre-configured and have several tools already installed. These tools are from Microsoft, as well as third-party sources.
Visual Studio Tools for Office	VSTO	Visual Studio Tools for Office is a set of development tools available in the form of a Visual Studio add-in and a runtime that allows Microsoft Office 2003 and later versions of

Appendix F – Programming Acronyms & Terms

Name	Acronym	Description
		Office applications to host the .NET Framework Common Language Runtime to expose their functionality via .NET.
Web Service Security	WS*	Web Services Security is an extension to SOAP to apply security to Web services. It is a member of the Web service specifications and was published by OASIS.
Web Services Description Language	WSDL	The Web Services Description Language (WSDL) is an XML-based interface description language that is used for describing the functionality offered by a web service.
Web Services Enhancements	WSE	Web Services Enhancements is an obsolete add-on to the Microsoft .NET Framework, which includes a set of classes that implement additional WS-* web service specifications chiefly in areas such as security, reliable messaging, and sending attachments.
WebAssembly	WASM	An open standard that defines a portable binary-code format for executable programs, and a corresponding textual assembly language, as well as interfaces for facilitating interactions between such programs and their host environment. The main goal of WebAssembly is to enable high-performance applications on web pages, but the format is designed to be executed and integrated with other environments as well, including standalone ones.

Appendix F – Programming Acronyms & Terms

Name	Acronym	Description
WEP		An encryption algorithm system included as part of the 802.11 standards, developed by the Institute of Electrical and Electronics Engineers as a security measure to protect wireless LANs from casual eavesdropping. WEP uses a shared secret key to encrypt packets before transmission between wireless LAN devices and monitors packets in transit to detect attempts at modification. WEP offers both 40-bit and 128-bit hardware-based encryption options.
What You See Is What You Get	WYSIWYG	What You See Is What You Get, or WYSIWYG is where computer editing software allows content to be edited in a form that resembles its final appearance.
Windows Activation Service	WAS	Windows Process Activation Service is the process activation mechanism introduced within Internet Information Services v7.0.
Windows Based Terminal	WBT	A Windows client machine that functions as an input/output terminal. It can be a full-blown PC with terminal software or a dedicated "thin client" terminal running an embedded version of Windows.
Windows Communication Foundation	WCF	The Windows Communication Foundation, previously known as Indigo, is a free and open-source runtime and a set of APIs in the .NET Framework for building connected, service-oriented applications.
Windows Identity Foundation	WIF	Windows Identity Foundation (WIF) is a new extension to the Microsoft

Appendix F – Programming Acronyms & Terms

Name	Acronym	Description
		.NET Framework that makes it easy for developers to enable advanced identity capabilities in the .NET Framework applications. Based on interoperable, standard protocols, Windows Identity Foundation and the claims-based identity model can be used to enable single sign-on (SSO), personalization, federation, strong authentication, identity delegation, and other identity capabilities in ASP.NET and Windows Communication Foundation (WCF) applications that run on-premises or in the cloud.
Windows Installer	MSI	Windows Installer (previously known as Microsoft Installer,[3] codename Darwin)[4][5] is a software component and application programming interface (API) of Microsoft Windows used for the installation, maintenance, and removal of software. The installation information, and optionally the files themselves, are packaged in installation packages, loosely relational databases structured as COM Structured Storages and known as "MSI files", from their default filename extensions.
Windows Internet Name Service	WINS	Windows Internet Name Service is Microsoft's implementation of NetBIOS Name Service, a name server and service for NetBIOS computer names. Effectively, WINS is to NetBIOS names what DNS is to domain names — a central mapping of hostnames to network addresses.

Appendix F – Programming Acronyms & Terms

Name	Acronym	Description
Windows Management Instrumentation	WMI	Windows Management Instrumentation consists of a set of extensions to the Windows Driver Model that provides an operating system interface through which instrumented components provide information and notification.
Windows NT (New Technology)	NT	Windows NT is a family of operating systems produced by Microsoft, the first version of which was released on July 27, 1993. It is a processor-independent, multiprocessing, and multi-user operating system. The first version of Windows NT was Windows NT 3.1 and was produced for workstations and server computers.
Windows PowerShell cmdlets	APPX	Designed to streamline the administration of MSIX or AppX package management.
Windows Presentation Foundation	WPF	Windows Presentation Foundation is a free and open-source graphical subsystem originally developed by Microsoft for rendering user interfaces in Windows-based applications. WPF, previously known as "Avalon", was initially released as part of .NET Framework 3.0 in 2006.
Windows Script Host	WSH	The Microsoft Windows Script Host is an automation technology for Microsoft Windows operating systems that provides scripting abilities comparable to batch files, but with a wider range of supported features.
Windows SharePoint Services	WSS	A portal-based platform for creating, managing, and sharing documents and customized Web services. WSS is available as a free

Appendix F – Programming Acronyms & Terms

Name	Acronym	Description
		download included with every Windows Server license and is part of the Office 2003 productivity suite.
Windows Workflow Foundation	WF	Windows Workflow Foundation is a Microsoft technology that provides an API, an in-process workflow engine, and a rehostable designer to implement long-running processes as workflows within .NET applications.
Windows Workflow Markup Language	XOML	XOML is the acronym for Extensible Object Markup Language and is a serialization format for Windows Workflow Foundation's workflow objects. Based on XAML, it is mostly used for creating user interfaces in plain XML.
WMI Query Language	WQL	Windows Management Instrumentation Query Language is Microsoft's implementation of the CIM Query Language, a query language for the Common Information Model standard from the Distributed Management Task Force. It is a subset of ANSI standard SQL with minor semantic changes.
World Wide Web	WWW	The World Wide Web, commonly known as the Web, is an information system where documents and other web resources are identified by Uniform Resource Locators, which may be interlinked by hypertext, and are accessible over the Internet.
World Wide Web Consortium	W3C	The World Wide Web Consortium is the main international standards organization for the World Wide Web. Founded in 1994 and currently

Appendix F – Programming Acronyms & Terms

Name	Acronym	Description
		led by Tim Berners-Lee, the consortium is made up of member organizations that maintain full-time staff working together in the development of standards for the World Wide Web. https://www.w3.org/
Write		To transfer information either to a storage device, such as a disk or to an output device, such as the monitor or a printer. Writing is how a computer provides the results of processing. A computer can also be said to write to the screen when it displays information on the monitor.
XAML Browser Application	XBAP	Windows technology used for creating Rich Internet Applications. While windows applications are normally compiled to a .exe file, browser applications are compiled to an extension. XBAP and can be run inside Internet Explorer.
XML Path Language	XPath	XPath is a query language for selecting nodes from an XML document. Also, XPath may be used to compute values from the content of an XML document. XPath was defined by the World Wide Web Consortium.
XML Query	XQuery	XQuery is a query and functional programming language that queries and transforms collections of structured and unstructured data, usually in the form of XML, text, and with vendor-specific extensions for other data formats. The language is developed by the XML Query working group of the W3C.

Appendix F – Programming Acronyms & Terms

Name	Acronym	Description
XML Schema Document	XSD	Is a World Wide Web Consortium (W3C) recommendation that specifies how to formally describe the elements in an Extensible Markup Language (XML) document.
Zero Administration for Windows	ZAW	The Zero Administration initiative for Windows builds on the existing investment companies have in the Microsoft Windows operating system, while allowing them to automate PC management and deploy the widest choice of applications in a controlled way.

Index

#

#define	21
#endregion	23

.

.NET Core	6, 14, 133, 140, 177, 197, 199, 200, 214
.NET Framework	5, 66, 71, 90, 131, 140
.NET Memory Profiler	214
.NET Portable	200
.NET Standard	110, 177, 199, 200
.snk	21

A

Abbreviations	146
abstract	143
Abstract	
Method	100
Method	101
Property	100
Property	101
Acronyms	25
Active Directory	136
ADO.NET	135, 235
Agile	127
All Data is Bad	112
API	93, 132, 237
App	
AppInfo()	189
CurrentCulture()	190
CurrentUICulture	190
ExecutingFolder	189
FrameworkDescripion	192
GetEnviromentVariables()	191
IsProcessRunning()	181
IsRunning()	181
IsUserAdministrator()	180
Kill()	181
app.config	21
AppDomain	
FirstChanceException	125
AppendFormat()	51
AppendLine()	51
Application	
Architecture	127
ThreadException	121
Application Information	9
Application Processing	128
appsettings.json	21
Architecture	128, 138, 157, 165
Application Layer	67, 72, 120, 122
Business Entities	130
Business Layer	130, 131, 140
Client–Server	128
Communications Layer	130, 131, 140
Data Entity	130, 140
Data Layer	129, 130, 140
Data Model	130
Data Storage Tier	128
Domain Logic Tier	128
Identity Layer	131, 133, 136
Model Class	137
Multilayered	128
Multitier	128, 139
Multitier	128
N-Tier	136
N-Tier	128
N-Tier	139
Presentation Layer	133
Presentation Tier	128
Three-Tier	128
User Experience Layer	132, 133
argument validation	57
Array	55, 112
ForEach()	55
as 49, 114	
ASP.NET	72, 93, 133, 140, 142, 214, 234
Caching	135
UseExceptionHandler	121
Assembly Name	9
AssemblyCompany	21
AssemblyCopyright	21
AssemblyDescription	21
Attribute	27, 79, 89, 92, 94, 95, 97, 98, 99
authentication keys	135
authorized users	136
await	
foreach()	199
AWS	236
Azure	72, 74, 139
API Management	236
App Service	131
Application Gateway	236
Application Insights	72, 74, 122, 236
Cosmos DB	82, 83, 93, 129, 140, 252
Data Explorer	238
DevOps	150
DevTest Labs	239
Durable Function	131
Event Hubs	239
Front Door	239
Function	72, 73, 74, 130, 131, 140, 239

321

Index

Queue	74
Relay	240
Security Center	240
ServiceBus Queue	139, 140
Stream Analytics	240
Stream Analytics Job	240
Synapse Analytics	241
WebJob	72, 130, 131

B

Backend Services	131
backingup source	150
base class	26, 30, 37, 38, 114
base.	36, 46
batching	132
Benchmark Tests	202
blank lines	59
Blazor	140
books	159
bool	117
bracket placement	56
brackets	56, 57
Bug	243
Bugs	
Cost	109
build events	17
build process	17
Business Components	131
Business Logic	88
Business Rule	84, 85
ByRef	59

C

Caching	131, 133, 134, 135, 136
Callback	27
calls per second	132
Camel casing	25, 94, 145, 167
capitalization	25
capitalization summary	145
case sensitivity	26
Case Sensitivity	45
Child Class	244
Chunky Not Chatty	132
CIL 248	
class	26, 34, 35, 36, 42, 46, 55, 78, 82, 89, 92, 94, 97, 101, 104, 143
Class	21, 26, 27, 28, 37, 46, 61, 80, 81, 88, 93, 245
Abstract	28, 30, 79, 99, 100, 101, 102, 233
Abstract Base Class	99
Base	27
Base Class	30, 46
Concrete Type	99
Constructor	35, 36, 40, 88, 112, 219
Design	79, 81
Destructors	21
Element Order	21, 22
Elements	22
Empty Constructor	88
Entities	130
Fields	21, 33
Helper Method	29
Immutable	102, 103
Inheritance	27, 30
Interface	21, 26, 28, 30, 31, 49, 99, 143
internal	80
Magic Constructor	88
Member Variables	21
Method	22, 80, 177
Methods	112
Parent	80
Partial	29
Private Field	88
Properties	22, 84, 112
Property	29, 33, 39, 40, 41, 64, 168
Property Setter	85
Public Instance Fields	34
Read-Only Fields	33
Read-Only Property	40
Static	29
Types	99
Variable	34
CLI 247	
ClickOnce	138
Client-Side Caching	134
CLR	248
Code	
Analysis	13, 171, 214
Coverage	111
Maintenance	105
Performance	6
Quality	157, 158, 160, 161, 163, 166, 173
Refactoring	213
Reuse	137, 138, 141
Review	132, 162, 171
Spaghetti Code	158
Code Access Security	13, 246
Code Analysis	
.NET Memory Profiler	214
Memory Profiling	214, 216
Code First	130
CodeAccessPermission	28
CodeRush	5, 33, 212, 213, 214
Coding Standards	169, 171, 173, 174
Collection	28, 40, 89, 90, 91, 103, 104, 105
Command-line Interface	247
Committing Code	148
Common Intermediate Language	248
Common Language Runtime	248
communications layer	65
Compare()	54
CompareTo()	89, 90
Comparing Strings	52, 53
Composition	133
ComputerInfo()	190
Concrete Type	99
Config	21

322

Index

Config.cs	183
Config<T>	185
const	32, 33, 34, 46, 143
Constants	32, 33, 46, 251
constructor	89
ControlChars	192
Controls	139
CRUD	252
CSS	133
Cyclomatic Complexity	252

D

DAO	253
Data Access	140
Data Context	130
Data Hiding	80, 81, 82
Data Management	128
Data Related Processing	131
Data Storage	93
Data Validation	40, 81, 82, 83, 84, 88, 130, 219
Database	83, 129, 130, 140, 158, 255
Naming Standards	153
Server	117
DataContract	94, 203
DataMember	94, 95
DataSet	110, 112, 130
DateTime	117, 186
GetLast()	186
GetNext()	186
Intersects()	186
IsInRange()	187
LocalTimeFromUtc()	187
Max()	187
NextDayOfWeek()	187
ToFriendlyDateString()	188
DateTimeOffset	81, 97, 186
DayOfWeek	186, 187
DDD	259
DebuggerDisplay	92, 203
Debugging	91, 92
decompiler	25
Defensive Programming	74, 107, 110
Delegate	28
Delegates	21, 37, 75
Dependency Injection	122, 256
derived class	42
deserialization	88
Design Patterns	159
designing classes	79, 85
destructor	37
destructors	36
DevExpress	140
Dictionary	28
Directory	257
DirectoryHelper	
EnumerateFiles()	199
LoadFiles()	197
LoadFilesAsync()	199
DirectoryInfo	180
GetSize()	180
LoadFiles()	198
LoadFilesAsync()	198
Dispose()	11, 36, 37, 47, 178, 179, 180
DisposeCollection()	180
DisposeFields()	179, 180
DLL	261
Docker	258
Documentation	104, 147
dotNetDave Says	127, 137, 142, 148
dotNetTips.Utility	177, 209
dotNetTips.Utility.Logger	123
Duplicate Code	142

E

EditorBrowsable	89, 97
Encapsulatating Logic	103
Encapsulation	33, 34, 39, 80, 81, 82, 84, 85, 88, 103, 104, 105, 111, 112, 119
data hiding	112
TryValidateParam	200, 201
Entity Framework	130, 203, 262
enum	23, 114, 117
Enum	38, 39, 70, 143, 145
Enumerations	21, 23, 38, 58
Environment	180
Equals()	53
event	27, 30, 37, 38, 75, 83, 100, 104, 143, 194
Event	21, 40, 41, 72
event handler	27, 37, 65
EventArgs	27, 38
EventHandler	27, 37, 38, 100, 194
Exception	27, 65, 67, 69, 70, 71, 72, 73, 74, 111, 114, 120, 122, 123, 124, 200, 262
Inner Exception	67
Logging	121, 124
Message	69, 120
when()	66
Exceptions	36, 64, 65, 66, 68, 69, 70, 71, 72, 74, 110, 111, 120, 121, 122, 133
ActivationException	67, 122
ApplicationException	68, 70, 71, 122
ArgumentException	66, 72, 113, 200, 201
ArgumentInvalidException	201
ArgumentNullException	58, 66, 71, 83, 104, 113, 200
ArgumentOutOfRangeException	58, 66, 83, 114, 201
ArgumentReadOnlyException	201
DataException	70
DispatcherUnhandledException	121
Documentation	71
FileNotFoundException	64, 112
Global Exception Handling	133
ILogger	122
IndexOutOfRangeException	66
Inner	122
InnerException	65
InvalidOperationException	40, 65, 66

Index

Logging		72, 122, 133
NotSupportedException		66
NullReferenceException		49
Reserved Types		71
SecurityException		67
SqlException		67, 122
Stack Trace		67, 70, 122
SystemException		68, 71, 122
Throwing		69
WriteException		69
EXE		262
Existential Types		99

F

Facebook	136
File	
Exists	64, 112
FileHelper	
CopyFileAysnc()	181
DownloadFileFromWebAsysc()	188
FileProcessor	194
DeleteFiles	195
FileProgressEventArgs	194
FileStream	181
Finagle's Law	108
Finalizers	36
finally	143
FlagsAttribute	38
Fluid Validation	105
Folder Structure	18
for 56, 60	
foreach	55, 56, 62, 73, 104, 143, 198, 199
ForEach	50
Forms	139
Future Proofing	180

G

GAC	266
Garbage Collector	36, 37, 266
GC 36, 266	
GC.SuppressFinalize	36
Generics	26
GetHashCode()	91, 219
GetValueOrDefault()	35
GhostDoc	72, 75, 147, 211
git ignore	150
GitHub	150, 163
Global Exception Handling	74
Globalization	44, 52, 53, 54, 86
CultureInfo	190
CurrentCulture	53
CurrentCultureIgnoreCase	53, 54
IvariantCultureIgnoreCase	54
Localization	52
Google	136
gRPC	131

GUID	266

H

Hash Code	91
Helper Methods	177
HTTP	269
HTTP trigger	131
HttpResponse	
IsClientConnected	117
HTTPS	268
Hungarian Notation	25, 57, 78, 167, 168

I

IAsyncEnumerable	197, 199
IAsyncEnumerable<T>	198, 199
ICloneable<T>	30
ICollection	28
ICollection<T>	28
IComparable	89, 204, 219
IComparable<>	204
IComparable<T>	89, 203, 219
ICoordinate	204
IDE	270
Identity	136
IDictionary<TKey, TValue>	180
IDisposable	36, 37, 47, 179, 180
IEnumerable	28, 180, 202
IEnumerable<T>	27, 28, 105, 180, 195, 197
IEquatable	29
IEquatable<>	204
IEquatable<T>	203
IgnoreDataMember	97
IIS 271	
IList	28
IList<T>	28
ILogger	68, 73, 114
Indentation	60
Information Hiding	80
Inheritance	80, 99, 101
init102, 103	
Input	133
Integer	114
IntelliSense	32, 75, 78, 89, 147
IntelliTests	141
Interface	30, 271
Interface vs. Abstract Class	99
internal	22, 23, 28, 32, 41, 112
Internationalization	52
Internet	134
Interpolation	52
InvariantCulture	53
InvariantCultureIgnoreCase	53
IoT136, 272	
IPerson	203
IsNullOrEmpty()	12

Index

J

JIT	274
JSON	62, 85, 93, 94, 95, 97, 99, 219, 273

K

Keywords	143
Contextual	144

L

Lambda	55, 63, 64
Expressions	63
Language-Integrated Query	62
Layout	133
Lazy<T>	135
Learning	159
LINQ	45, 62, 63, 64, 275
List	40
Local Variables	46
Localization	52, 133
Log	122
Log4Net	72
Logging	68, 70, 72
Events	122
Messages	52
Loop	277
Loop Variable	60

M

m_	34
Management	158
MCV	141
Memory Caching	135
Memory Profiling	180
.NET Memory Profiler	180
Method	21, 29, 30, 36, 40, 41, 42, 43, 66, 71, 75, 110, 168
Overloading	42
Method Overloading	43
Microservices	279
Microsoft	161
Microsoft Framework Design Guidelines	171
Microsoft Outlook	135
Microsoft Sync Framework	135
Mobile Apps	134
Model Class	82, 93, 99
Model-View-Presenter	133
MSI	316
MSIL	283
MVC	285
MVP	133
MVVC	285

N

Name Case	45
Named Parameter	43
Namespace	9, 18, 23, 24, 45, 143, 219
Elements	22
Navigation	133
Network	117
NetworkHelper	
IsHostAvaialble()	188
IsHostAvailable()	188
NonSerialized	99
Nothing	65
N-Tier	286
N-Tier Architecture	128, 140
NuGet	17, 113, 125, 142, 150, 151, 155, 177, 186, 203, 207, 210, 287
null	38, 49, 59, 62, 65, 71, 83, 89, 104, 143, 179
Null Coalesce	35
Nullable Value Type	35
Null-Conditional Operator	111

O

Object	287
Initialization	64, 88
Initializers	36
Object Relational Mapping	130
Object-Oriented Programming	34, 39, 79, 80, 81, 82, 85, 93, 94, 95, 99, 105, 141, 161, 172, 199, 288
Encapsulation	161, 199
Object-Oriented Programming	159
ObjectPool	51
Occasionally Connected	134
Office 365	136
OKTA	136
OneDrive	139
OOP	288
Optional Parameters	43
Ordinal	54
OrdinalIgnoreCase	54
ORM	130, 288
out	59
Out Parameter	43
override	37, 42, 91, 92, 101, 144

P

Page	
IsValid	119
Validate	119
Parameters	57, 58, 88, 112
Arguments	113
Array	59
Name	57
Named	58
Passing	59

Index

params	43, 59, 144
Parenthesis Placement	45, 55, 56
Partial Class	28
Pascal case	18, 23, 25, 26, 44, 94, 145, 154, 167
Perceived speed	134
Performance	47, 50, 52, 53, 54, 85, 89, 90, 91, 103, 111, 112, 132, 134, 135, 141
Perceived Speed	135
Permission	28
PersonProper	90, 219
Plain Old CLR Objects	130
POCO	130, 291
Polymorphism	80
PowerShell	151, 155
Predefined Types	45
Presentation Layer	133
Preserve Stack Details	70
private	22, 23, 25, 32, 33, 58, 168
ProgressiveRetry()	196, 197
Project Managers	53
Project Settings	11, 12
Properties	39
protected	22, 23, 28, 32, 36, 38, 42, 57, 75, 113, 144, 147, 179, 194
Protected	39
protected constructor	101
protected internal	22
Protocols	99
public	22, 28, 32, 33, 39, 42, 57, 74, 75, 113, 114, 168

Q

QA 294	
Quality Assurance	110, 141

R

Random Data	203, 204
RandomData	207
GenerateCharacter()	204
GenerateCoordinate<T>()	204
GenerateCoordinateCollection<T>	204
GenerateDecimal()	204
GenerateDomainExtension()	204
GenerateEmailAddress()	204
GenerateFile()	205
GenerateFiles()	205
GenerateInteger()	205, 207
GenerateKey()	205, 207
GenerateNumber()	205
GeneratePerson<T>()	205
GeneratePersonCollection()	207
GeneratePersonCollection<T>()	205
GeneratePhoneNumberUSA	206
GenerateRandomFileName()	206
GenerateRelativeUrl()	206
GenerateTempFile()	206
GenerateUrl()	206
GenerateUrlHostName()	206
GenerateUrlHostnameNoProtocol()	206
GenerateUrlHostnameNoSubdomain()	206
GenerateUrlPart()	206
GenerateWord()	206
Readability	21, 25, 26, 32, 46, 56, 58, 59, 290
readonly	34, 144
record	102, 103
ref 59	
Reference Type	111
Reflection	89
Reflector	25
region	23
Reporting	133
Requirements	127
ReSharper	33
Resources	44, 117, 133
REST	296
<u>Reusable</u>	157
Reusable Applications	128
Reusable Assemblies	66, 84, 137, 142

S

Salesforce	95
sealed	26, 42, 101, 104, 144
Security	130
Admin Rights	180
Security Permissions	131
Self-Documenting	162
Serializable	97, 203, 204
Serialization	79, 88, 93, 96, 97, 98, 219
Services	
StartService()	73
Set Optimize Code	17
Settings	182, 185
Shared	34
Sign the assembly	13
Signing	12
SOLID	301
Solution Explorer	24
Sort()	91
Sorting	90
Source Control	147, 148, 149, 209, 210
Backup Source	210
Committing Code	149
Source Files	18
Spoofing	13
SQL	304
SQL Azure	129
SQL Server	67, 129, 139, 140, 142, 153, 186, 204, 209
Stored Procedures	153, 154
SQL Server Reporting Services	133
static	29, 34, 36, 41, 104, 144, 197, 198, 200, 201
Stream	28
string	49, 50, 74, 83, 144
Compare()	53, 54
String Extensions	

Index

ComputeHash()	189
Extract()	189
FromBase64()	189
Parse<T>()	189
ToBase64()	189
ToTitleCase()	189
String.Format	50, 52
StringBuilder	49, 50, 51, 201, 202
AppendBytes()	201
AppendValues()	202
StringReader	96
Strings	82, 83
Interpolation	52
struct	144
Structures	23, 26, 29, 61, 112
StyleCop	1, 5, 13, 25, 75, 147, 157, 163, 219
SA1201	22
switch case	60
Syncing Data	135

T

T4 Template	130
Tab	
Indentation	60
Task	
Run()	199
TCP/IP	272
Team Size	169
Techno Stress	164
TempFileManager	193, 194
CreateFile()	193
CreateFiles()	193
DeleteAllFiles()	194
DeleteFile()	194
FileList()	194
this.	46
Thread	306
ThreadExceptionEventHandler	121
throw	65
Tight Coupling	72
Time Zone Offset	187
ToString()	92, 219
TraceListeners	125
Training	
Channel 9	172
Pluralsight	159, 172
Videos	159
Treat warnings as errors	11
try/ catch	69, 120, 121
TryDispose()	179
TryValidateParam	118, 119
TryValidateParam()	119
Tuple	45, 61, 62
Twitter	136
typeof	96, 144, 200

U

UAT	310
UI	30
Underscores	34
Unit Testable	309
Unit testing	
Code Coverage	161
Unit Testing	161
IntelliTests	161
Unit Tests	107, 111, 141, 148, 149, 210
Code Coverage	141
Unit-Testable	157
Unity	133
URI	308
User	118
User Acceptance Testing	110
User Experience layer	118
User Interface	30, 133, 153, 194
User Messages	44
using	47, 96, 144, 179
UTC	187, 251
UWP	309
UX	132, 310

V

Validating	
Data	85, 118
Validation	58, 64, 82, 113, 117, 119, 130, 310
Variable Names	45
VB.NET	18, 26, 45, 133
Version Number	10
View Models	93
virtual	37, 38, 42, 100, 144, 179, 194
Virtual Memory	178
Visual Basic	1
Visual Studio	1, 2, 9, 12, 13, 16, 35, 63, 64, 65, 75, 78, 85, 91, 99, 110, 139, 142, 143, 147, 150, 155, 160, 161, 171, 173, 204, 207, 209, 210, 212
.editorConfig file	13, 14, 15, 16, 17
Analyze	1, 13, 14, 16, 17, 111, 147, 160, 163, 171, 173
EditorConfig	13, 14, 16
Extensions	160
FXCop	13
Live Unit Testing	111
Visual Studio Tools for Office	133
Visual Testing	141
void	35, 38, 42, 43, 46, 47, 58, 60, 73, 100, 101, 102, 104, 144, 179, 194, 200
VSTS	133

W

WCF	131, 315
Web API	131
Web Service	131

Index

WebApi	140
while	56, 144
Windows Communications Foundation	131
Windows Forms	121, 133, 138
Windows Presentation Foundation	133
Windows Service	131
Windows Store App	214
WinForm	121
with	103
Workflow	130, 131
WPF	121, 133, 317

X

Xamarin	133
XML	62, 95, 96, 97, 98, 99, 219, 263
XML Commenting	12, 45, 71, 74, 75, 219
<b>	77
<c>	77
<code>	77
<code>	77
<completionlist>	75
<example>	75
<exception>	71, 75
<i> 77	
<include>	76
<inheritdoc>	76
<list>	76, 77
<overloads>	76
<para>	76, 77
<param>	76
<paramref>	77
<permission>	76
<remarks>	76, 77
<returns>	76
<see>	77, 78
<seealso>	30, 31, 71, 76, 77, 78, 196
<typeparam>	76
<typeparamref>	77
<value>	77
XML Document File	12
XML Documentation	74
XmlElement	98
XmlIgnore	98
XmlRoot	97, 203
XmlSerializer	96
XmlWriter	96

Y

yield	199

www.ingramcontent.com/pod-product-compliance
Lightning Source LLC
Chambersburg PA
CBHW081424220526
45466CB00008B/2257